GW01019035

THE PSYCHOANALYTIC THERAPY
OF SEVERE DISTURBANCE

The Psychoanalytic Therapy of Severe Disturbance is one of a series of books under the title PSYCHOANALYTIC ideas which brings together the best of Public Lectures and other writings given by analysts of the British Psycho-Analytical Society on important psychoanalytic subjects.

Other titles in the Psychoanalytic ideas Series:

THE PSYCHOANALYTIC THERAPY OF SEVERE DISTURBANCE

Edited by Paul Williams

Series Editors

Inge Wise and Paul Williams

KARNAC

First published in 2010 by
Karnac Books Ltd
118 Finchley Road
London NW3 5HT

British Library Cataloguing in Publication Data

A C.I.P. for this book is available from the British Library

ISBN-13: 978-1-85575-640-3

Typeset by Vikatan Publishing Solutions (P) Ltd., Chennai, India

Printed in Great Britain

www.karnacbooks.com

CONTENTS

FOREWORD

In early 2007 colleagues at the Belfast Centre for Psychotherapy, Professor Paul Williams and Lord Alderdice conveyed their vision to me of running an international conference on the application of Psychoanalysis in Psychiatric Practice and Mental Health Services. This was at a time in Northern Ireland when the Royal College of Psychiatrists (RCPsych) were actively engaged in developing strategy for specialist services and training in Psychotherapy. We were also engaged in an initiative to reach out to other organisations and professionals in Mental Health care. Indeed, the then President of the RCPsych, Professor Sheila Hollins, had designated one of her special initiatives as "Increasing the Influence of Psychoanalysis on Psychiatry". For all these reasons their vision coincided closely with College strategy. The College enthusiastically committed to the opportunity to make this conference idea a reality. The subject matter of "The Psychoanalytic Therapy of Severe Disturbance" i.e., Psychosis and Personality Disorder was settled on as most pertinent to Psychiatric Services.

Under the very able leadership of Paul and John, a programme was drawn up and the most eminent international speakers on the subject engaged to speak. When we announced the Conference internationally there was an overwhelming response, such that the Conference venue had to limit numbers to 440 delegates. This was not entirely a surprise as throughout 25 years of Psychiatric practice in General Psychiatry and Addiction Services, I have found the application of Psychoanalytic understanding at it's most useful when clinical decisions are at their most challenging and demanding. I have also regularly observed that Mental Health staff and Psychiatrist trainees are at their most receptive and hungry for psychoanalytic concepts after they have acquired the basic phenomenological training and clinical experience. The meaning and understanding that Psychoanalytic concepts bring to the management of severe psychosis and personality disorder is particularly beneficial in this demanding work.

The success of the Conference I think is most concisely illustrated by a comment made to me on day 2 of the Conference by one of the American delegates; "I've never been at a Conference where **all** the seats are occupied for **all** of the sessions".

Much thanks is due to all the Psychoanalysts who gave so generously of their time for the Conference. Thanks also to the other collaborating organisations, the British Psychoanalytical Society, The Northern Ireland Institute of Human Relations (NIIHR), the Northern Ireland Institute for the Study of Psychoanalysis (NIASP) and the Department of Health, Social Services and Public Safety NI for their contributions and support. Finally, we are greatly indebted to Mrs Nora McNairney, Division Manager of the RCPsych NI Office whose organisational skills made this Conference such a success.

Cathal e Cassidy M.B. FRCPsych.
Chairman of the Royal College of
Psychiatrists (NI Division),
Chairman of the All Ireland
Institute of Psychiatry AIIP (2008)

ACKNOWLEDGEMENTS

A great deal of work went into mounting the conference on the 'Psychoanalytic Therapy of Severe Disturbance' in Belfast in June 2008. In addition to the speakers, without whom the conference would not have been possible, it is important to acknowledge the contributions of the individuals and groups involved in its preparation. The first of these is the organising committee: Maria O'Kane, Cathal Cassidy, John Alderdice, Brian Martindale and Richard Ingram. The support of other organizations was valuable. Thanks are due to Graham Johnston of the Northern Ireland Institute of Human Relations, and to Roselene Hayes, Sharon Elliott and Mary Simpson for the preparation of this manuscript. Finally, thanks go to the hundreds of people who came from all over the world to attend the conference and who contributed in such an enthusiastic way.

Paul Williams
Belfast 2009

WELCOME

Lord Alderdice

My name is John Alderdice. I'm a Psychiatrist and Psychotherapist here in Belfast and it is my very great pleasure to bid you a warm welcome to our home City here. It is great to see so many of you and some of you have come from a very long distance and we appreciate that enormously. Of course, I know that part of the reason you have come is because of the veritable galaxy of psychoanalytic stars who are also here. We appreciate them coming. It has been a tremendously encouraging and supportive thing to us and we appreciate that very much. Can I say that, as you have looked through the programme you will have noticed some tremendous speakers and extremely interesting topics but one of the things that we have really learned a lot of in this part of the World is that dialogue is critically important to progress and so although we are very pleased to be able to listen at the feet of some of these tremendous speakers, we also want to encourage you to get into dialogue with them after their presentations and indeed with each other because I think we are going to learn much more if we don't just listen and take in, but if we also engage with each other in conversation and in dialogue at the end of the presentations and in the coffee breaks and lunch and the evening social events as well. I think that will add very considerably to things. Of course you will appreciate that we have not just learned in this part of the World that dialogue is a good thing but also that co-operation is very important and we've had the encouragement and luxury of a lot of co-operation from various people. The Royal College of Psychiatrists has been tremendously supportive to us and we are going to hear a little bit later on from the President of the Royal College of Psychiatrists, Profession Sheila Hollins. I would like to thank her very much indeed for coming and also thank the representatives of the College; Dr Cathal Cassidy who runs the College here in Northern Ireland; Brian Martindale, who of course, has been extremely helpful to us on the organising committee and particularly Nora McNairney and Liz Main and our colleagues in the College office here in Belfast. They have been absolute gems. We appreciate very much the fact that we have got a Northern Ireland office of the College now and it has been doing such excellent work and I'd like you to just say thank you very much to them, even at this very early stage, for all the work and preparation that they have done. (Applause)

Let me maybe say a little word or two about why we are having this event. For the last 25 years or so we have been working to try to build up an understanding of psychoanalytic ideas and how to apply them, particularly in the clinical area, but not only there and 25 years seems like a long time but it has taken us that length of time to develop a cohort of people who have some interest and understanding and training and experience of working in this kind of way. We felt that it would be good to try to draw some of these resources together into a Centre and we have acquired a building, paid for by the National Health Service, where we have been able to put together, not just individual offices and spaces for group therapy, but also a music therapy suite, an art therapy suite, a training and teaching suite with video conference facilities and this has enabled us to get a range of analytically informed therapies under way and also a couple of Masters courses, one in Psychoanalytic Psychotherapy and one in Art Psychotherapy. We wanted to try to give a bit of momentum to this work for those who are involved in it. Paul Williams, who was invited to come over to work with us and give us encouragement and guidance just a few years ago, came up with the idea that if we could have a conference that would bring together some of the best in the World, this would be a tremendous encouragement to those who were working here and growing and developing in their clinical and professional experience, but it would also send a message to people in this community, and not least of all, people in the health care community and in the Ministry or Department of Health and Social Services—namely, that Psychoanalytic Psychotherapy had an important contribution to make in some of the very difficult pieces of work that we have to address. We have a tradition in this part of the World of applying psychoanalytic understandings to difficult things. The father of psychoanalysis in this part of the World was Dr Tom Freeman, and he worked as a General Psychiatrist and Psychoanalyst all his working life with patients with serious psychotic disorders, particularly schizophrenic illnesses but also manic depressive psychosis, and so all of us grew up with a sense that psychoanalysis had something to say to some of the very difficult problems and so this conference is going to focus on psychosis, on disturbances of personality and also on the application of our ideas to socio-cultural problems because that is one of the other things we have tried to do in this part of the World—to understand why this community gets so disturbed with violence; violence within itself, against each other and against people themselves.

In the 1970s we began to observe that as the homicide rate went up, the suicide rate came down and since the end of the overt terrorism, one of the things we have notices has been an increase in the rate of suicides, particularly amongst young men. So these socio-cultural developments are not something outside of and divorced from our clinical work; they impact very much on it. Our psychoanalytic understandings have really something valuable and important to say to all of that and so we are grateful that so many people have come to assist us in understanding these things. I say, "us" because this has been a collaborative venture; I mentioned the Royal College of Psychiatrists and the Centre for Psychotherapy but we have also had support from our Health and Social Services Trust here in Belfast and Dr Maria O'Kane who is the Director of the Primary Care Services in Mental Health, has been part of our Planning and Programme Team and has been very helpful to us. The Northern Ireland Association for the Study of Psychoanalysis has been intimately involved in the work of preparation and the Northern Ireland Institute of Human Relations has also been part of the network of people that have been working together. Finally, The British Psychoanalytical Society in London has also been a joint sponsor of this conference. I am really very grateful to all the colleagues who have co-operated so well in putting all of this together.

Now I don't want to scare you that this is Belfast and therefore I need to give you some emergency precautions. This is a health and safety issues of which you will all be very much aware so we have got fire exits on the right hand side and on the left hand side—we generally don't use them but just so you know they are there. The second thing is more a precaution for the speakers and that is to ask that all of you who have mobile phones, put them off or put them on to vibrate mode at this point. Those that put them off we will know pay attention, those that smile from time to time, we know you have got it on vibrate mode.

Well, I think we are going to have a good time. I think we are going to have a good time in this Hall and listening to those who make the presentations. I hope very much that you are going to enjoy Belfast. It's a fun City and people in this part of the World do know how to have a good time, so if you don't, just ask any of them and they will show you one. We will have the reception this evening and then if the weather stays any way good, you will get out and enjoy the City and I hope a number of you will be coming up to Parliament Buildings tomorrow evening and you will enjoy that—that is an interesting place to be.

But I want now to introduce to you and to thank very much indeed the President of the Royal College of Psychiatrists, Professor Shelia Hollins. Those of you who are not members of the College will not quite appreciate what a significant thing it is that she has given such support to this event going ahead at this time and on top of all of that, that she is actually here herself. Let me explain to you why. First of all next week is the Annual General Meeting of the Royal College of Psychiatrists. This is not a one-hour meeting to approve minutes. This is a full week of meetings, with a whole series of parallel sessions, of research papers and presentations. It is a very big event at the Imperial College, London, and usually, in fact it is the rule, that the College does not approve or support any other conference within six weeks of that event. Well, you will recognise there is no six week gap between Friday and next Tuesday and Professor Hollins will be more aware of this than some of the rest of us. That is an expression of the support that there has been for Psychoanalytic Psychotherapy, for our approach and for those of us in Northern Ireland who have been trying to build it up. During her time as President she has overseen a number of very important reports; one on Acute Mental Health Care, one of Assessment of Risk and one on Psychological Therapies in Primary Care and in Psychiatry. These are very important pieces of work and particularly for the third one, I want, on behalf of myself and behalf of all of you, to thank Professor Hollins for that level of support from the President of The Royal College of Psychiatrists—it is very important indeed. On top of all of that she actually finishes up her three-year tenure as President of the College at the beginning of next week. So she has cleared a space to come over here, to be with us, to show her support for this work, for what we are trying to do and I think for all of us to know that and appreciate that, it is something we value very greatly indeed Professor Hollins, and I would like to invite you to come to the podium and open the conference.

Professor Sheila Hollins

Thank you, Lord Alderdice. It is a real pleasure to be here. Clearing my office hasn't quite been as easy as I thought it might be as my PA went on maternity leave a week ago. So, any of you lucky enough to have a PA will understand what that means. Part of my mission as President of the College has been to try to increase and promote the influence of psychoanalytic thinking on psychological therapies on the training of psychiatrists but also on psychiatric services. There isn't a lot that a President can do, but the Report on Psychological Therapies, which Lord Alderdice just mentioned, was an attempt to try to raise our awareness and thinking about psychological therapies, as they are now called in the NHS, across all specialties of psychiatry and when I set up that working group, I set it up with the intention that it would not be led by our Psychotherapy Faculty, but it would be a cross-College initiative in order that it would be owned by the whole College. It ended up as a report published jointly with the Royal College of General Practitioners.

In England there is a little bit of a worry that the improving access to psychological therapies initiative might lead to a dumbing down of psychotherapy. The idea is that a reasonably large injection of money into developing psychotherapy in Primary Care might lead to psychotherapy in specialist mental health services diminishing and there is some evidence in some places that that is happening and in particular that the psychiatric component to those services might also be lessened, which again was a good reason for us to look at it and write a report. Some of the main things that the report says are that GPs need to become much more psychologically minded and to know how to refer. But it also states that minority groups need to be served equally and I just want to say a little bit more about that.

I am a Psychiatrist working with adults with learning disabilities. For those of you who don't work in the United Kingdom, the term "learning disabilities" is equivalent to "intellectual disability" or "mental retardation" or "mental handicap". Different words have been used and the problem about providing psychological therapies to this client group: the evidence and the guidelines that are produced for psychological therapies do not mention this group of people. Yet they are a group who are probably more traumatised than other members of our society and if we are talking about severe disturbance, probably more severely disturbed in some instances than others too. So should we assume that treatment guidelines are transferable? Does it mean that the added complexity of treating trauma and relationship difficulties in someone with a learning disability means that such patients need to be immediately referred to a specialist service, if it exists?

My clinical work for the last 15 years has been with severely traumatised disabled people and I want to just introduce this conference with a short extract from a piece of work that I've been involved with over those years in a group for men with moderate and severe learning disabilities, a weekly psychoanalytic group which I run with Valerie Sinason, a psychoanalyst.

This short extract is from a session three years after treatment began and three weeks before the last Christmas break. The men had all suffered sexual abuse. They were all now abusing others. Two of the men in this extract were living in a locked ward and were brought weekly to therapy, some 25 miles distance from their hospital. One of the men had been imprisoned for 6 months accused of abusing children.

Mr A: "I'm upset, very upset. It happened last night. I wet myself. I couldn't help it. She rubbed my nose in the urine. She hit me. She did".

He became very agitated. Valerie and I were both aware that this had been a regular occurrence in his past where that kind of behaviour by nurse but it didn't take place in his current environment.

Valerie: "I wonder if because Mr A is so miserable with Christmas coming, he is remembering something from the past that used to happen but he feels it is happening now".

Mr A: sat still listening.

Sheila: "Did you understand that, Mr A? Valerie says that when you think about what your Mum used to do, it feels as if it is happening now"

Mr A: "I know. Yes".

Mr B: "I phoned my Mum at 1 o'clock in the morning. She was very cross. I rang because I was paranoid."

Sheila: "What does paranoid mean?"

Mr B: "I thought people knew more about me than they did— like the police might come and ask about something and I hadn't done it."

Valerie: "You and Mr A have got something in common that helps the whole group. In the past bad things have happened for both of you; things other people did to you and things you did. For example, Mr B, sometimes the police came and it was fair and sometimes you didn't think it was fair. But perhaps, frighteningly, there was evident but you couldn't remember doing it."

Mr B: (After a long pause). "That's right".

Valerie: "In those cases, the police did know more than you".

Mr B: "You mean, I'm not paranoid because sometimes the police do know more than me."

Mr A: "I'm going to miss my Mum at Christmas, really miss her".

Sheila: "The magic has really gone out of Christmas, hasn't it?"

Mr D: "Yep, no champagne, or rides in a Rolls Royce to Group Therapy anymore!"

Mr E: "My Mum won't have any beer at Christmas because of fighting".

Valerie: "And Mr C hasn't got a Mum to see. He hasn't seen her since he was really little and he has no idea where she is. And Mr A doesn't see his Mum and Mr B's Mum doesn't want to be woken up at 1.00 am when he is anxious and Sheila and I are bad mothers not looking after you all at Christmas and perhaps Mr B you're worried that if you move near your Mum, she won't manage to help you."

Mr A: "I'm not going to my mother's. I used to run away to get to her. I used to run away to find her".

Sheila: "I think you're frightened Mr A that when your hospital closes down, you might have to be with your Mum, who didn't look after you. But that won't happen. You will be in another safe place".
A sigh of relief passed round the group.

Mr B: "We don't have magic about Christmas anymore".

Valerie: "You're pleased there will be ward parties but you're sad and when you're sad or sad and angry, all the bad memories come back".

I wanted to share this short extract to show you how we find earlier trauma being expressed through flash backs for example with one man or through an incomplete memory for another and the importance of trauma in the lives of people with learning disabilities who may have been abused or traumatised in such a way.

I'm very pleased to introduce the conference. And I believe that the complexity of the people whose stories we are going to hear today and of the work that is being done to help them, is part of what we need to do as mental health professionals, to understand, I think, the importance of multi-disciplinary approaches to working, and of the different contributions that different professions can bring, including psychiatry, to the Psychoanalytic Treatment of Severe Disturbance and I wish the conference well.

CHAPTER ONE

The therapeutic action in psychoanalytic psychotherapy of borderline personality disorder

Glen O. Gabbard

How does psychoanalytic psychotherapy work? Let me state at the outset that the answer is clear—we don't know. Therapeutic action has been much discussed in the psychoanalytic literature, but many of the discussions are inextricably bound to particular psychoanalytic theories. Times have changed; we no longer practice in an era in which interpretation is regarded as the exclusive therapeutic arrow in the analyst's quiver (Gabbard and Westen, 2003). Abend (2001) observed that "no analyst today would suggest that the acquisition of insight is all that transpires in a successful analysis, or even that it identifies the sole therapeutic influence of the analytic experience" (p. 5). As Abend implies in his distinction between psychoanalysis and "therapeutic influence," there has been an unfortunate divide between what is analytically pure and what helps the patient. In recent contributions (Gabbard, 2007; Gabbard and Westen, 2003), I have argued that we need to identify what strategies help patients change, rather than worrying about adherence to a particular analytic ideal. In any case, Wallerstein (2000) stressed that after reviewing the data from the monumental 30-year follow-up of the Menninger Foundation Psychotherapy Research Project patients, differentiating therapeutic change from analytic change is virtually impossible anyway.

There is no single path to therapeutic change. Single mechanism theories of therapeutic action, no matter how complex, are unlikely to prove therapeutically useful simply because there are a variety of targets of change and a variety of strategies for effecting change in those targets.

While there once was a debate regarding whether insight or the therapeutic relationship was the key vehicle for change, that either/ or polarization of interpretation vs. the relationship with the therapist has given way to a broad consensus that both aspects of treatment contribute to change in the patient (Cooper, 1989; Jacobs, 1990; Pulver, 1992; Pine, 1998; Gabbard, 2000; Gabbard and Westen, 2003).

Another shift over time has been away from an archaeological approach to psychoanalytic treatment. Rather than focusing on the excavation of buried relics in the patient's past, most contemporary analytic therapists, especially those who work with borderline personality disorder, focus more on the here-and-now interaction between the therapist and the patient. The therapist's participation in enactments and projective identification allow her to identify a characteristic "dance" that the patient recreates in a variety of settings based on that patient's internal object relations. Hence by studying what transpires between therapist and patient, one has a sense of what has come before and what is going on every day outside the treatment relationship.

Attempting to study the therapeutic action of psychotherapy is complex. If one asks patients what was helpful some time after their treatment, what one hears is often disappointing to the psychoanalytic therapist. One of my patients came back to see me several years after she had terminated a multi-year analytic process. I asked her what she had found most helpful, and she replied, "Each day when I came to your office, you were there." She evidently failed to recall any of my carefully formulated interpretations or any of the insights she'd gathered in the course of her treatment with me. I realized, however, that my "being present" meant a lot to her because she had a father who was perennially absent. Hence what was important to her and what was important to me may have been entirely different. Patients may not really know what helped them.

If one investigates the issue of how therapy works by interviewing therapists, one immediately has to deal with the stark reality that they are a biased group. They are narcissistically invested in the outcomes of their patients, and they may view the patient's improvement in terms that shed favourable light on how they conceptualized and formulated the treatment. Moreover, those who are adherents to a particular theoretical school will emphasize strategies deriving from that school regardless of whether or not they were helpful to the patient.

Researchers, on the other hand, have the advantage of objectivity when studying therapeutic action. However, they also are viewing the process from a disadvantaged point of view in some respects. Psychoanalytic psychotherapy is largely about the interior spaces of the patient and the subtle interactions that occur unconsciously between two people. The therapist who is immersed in the transference-countertransference vicissitudes has an immediate sense of who the patient is and what the patient needs in the way of specific therapeutic strategies. Moreover, there are moments of meeting (Stern et al, 1998) that may be extraordinarily meaningful to both patient and therapist but are not part of a therapeutic plan. They occur spontaneously when the two parties share a joke or a deeply moving experience where tears come to the eyes of both. A psychotherapy researcher studying a transcript may entirely miss such moments.

Because all the methodologies to study therapeutic action have a set of problems associated with them, we must acknowledge that we may continue to be in the dark for some time in solving this puzzle. Greenberg (2005) has suggested that the therapeutic action of psychoanalytic treatment may ultimately be unknowable for any specific patient.

Empirical research on transference interpretation

Despite the fact that the therapeutic action of psychoanalytic psychotherapy may be unknowable, we nevertheless will embark on an overview of what is known about effective treatment for borderline personality disorder, with the assumption that the research seeking to find an efficacious treatment will shed some light on therapeutic action. We know that at least five different types of therapy have now been empirically validated in randomized controlled trials: mentalization-based therapy (Bateman and Fonagy, 1999), dialectical behaviour therapy (Linehan et al, 2006), transference-focused therapy (Clarkin et al, 2007), schema-focused therapy (Giesen-Bloo et al, 2006), and supportive psychotherapy (Clarkin et al, 2007).

Two of these empirically validated treatments are psychodynamic forms of therapy: mentalization-based therapy (MBT) and transference-focused therapy (TFP). One of the central controversies in the discussion of these two treatments is the role played by transference interpretation. While there is no head-to-head comparison in the literature between MBT and TFP, there is a small body of literature that has investigated the relative role of psychoanalytic treatments that focus on transference interpretation vs. those that do not.

In a landmark Norwegian study, Høglend (2006) conducted a randomized controlled trial of dynamic psychotherapy designed to determine the impact of a moderate level of transference interpretations (1–3 per session) in a once-weekly psychotherapy for the duration of one year. One hundred patients were randomly assigned to a group using either interpretation of the transference or a group that did not use such interventions. The authors included brief vignettes from the therapy so the reader could gain some understanding of the types of interventions considered to be transference interpretations. They attempted to avoid the "allegiance effect" so common in psychotherapy research, where researchers pit their favoured treatment against one that they don't really think will work. The investigators cross-trained therapists in each of the therapies used and arranged for the same therapists to conduct both treatments. The results came as something of a surprise: there were no overall differences in outcome between the two treatment cells, but the subgroup of patients with impaired object relations benefited more from the therapy using transference interpretation than from the alternative treatment.

The conventional wisdom in predicting psychotherapy outcome has long been that "the rich get richer" (Gabbard, 2006). In other words, patients who have greater psychological resources and more mutually gratifying relationships tend to form a solid therapeutic alliance with the therapist and gain greater benefit from the therapy. Such patients would, according to conventional thinking, be more capable of tolerating transference interpretation than those who are more disturbed with a shakier therapeutic alliance with the therapist. Moreover, studies of transference interpretation in brief dynamic therapy indicate that there is not a positive correlation between that particular intervention and outcome (Piper et al, 1991).

When the patients who had lower scores on the quality of object relations in the Høglend study were examined, it was discovered that

61% of those subjects were diagnosable with personality disorders on the SCID-II (Spitzer et al, 1990). By contrast, only 20% of those measured as having had high quality object relations had personality disorders. Hence there appeared to be a correlation between personality disorders and improvement with transference interpretation.

The study design had shortcomings that must be taken into account. Axis I disorders were not rigorously diagnosed using standard research interviews. For example, the effects of depression on outcome could not be evaluated with precision. It is also possible that some experienced therapists secretly felt that the patients deprived of transference work were getting less than optimal treatment. Similarly, while investigators attempted to "blind" the raters who were listening to the audiotapes, the content of these tapes might well indicate to which group the patient belonged (Gabbard, 2006). Nevertheless, a subsequent report from Høglend et al (2008) showed that the beneficial effect of transference interpretation for this subgroup of patients was sustained at three years' follow-up.

Therapeutic action and borderline personality disorder

While the findings of the Norwegian study are of heuristic value, they are not specific for any particular personality disorder. When we focus on borderline personality disorder in particular, we have at least one randomized controlled trial that emphasizes transference interpretation. In a head-to-head comparison of transference-focused therapy (TFP), dialectical behaviour therapy (DBT), and supportive therapy (SP) at Cornell-Westchester, 90 patients were randomly assigned to one of these three treatment groups. Over a 12-month period, six domains of outcome measures were assessed at 4-month intervals by raters blind to the treatment group. When results were analyzed using individual growth-curve analysis, all three treatments appeared to have brought about positive change in multiple domains to a roughly equivalent extent. However, in some areas, TFP seemed to do better than the alternative treatments. In fact, TFP was associated with significant improvements in 10 out of the 12 variables across the six symptom domains, compared with improvement of six variables with SP, and five with DBT. Only transference-focused psychotherapy brought about significant changes in impulsivity, irritability, verbal assault, and direct

assault. Both TFP and DBT—therapies that specifically target suicidal behaviours—did better than supportive therapy in reducing
suicidality.

In a report from the same study on a different dimension of these
findings, Levy et al (2006) demonstrated that TFP produced additional improvements that were not found with either DBT or SP. The
study subjects who received TFP were more likely to move from
an insecure attachment classification to a secure one. In addition,
they showed significantly greater changes in mentalizing capacity
(measured by reflective functioning) and in narrative coherence,
compared with those in other groups. Problems in mentalization
(a capacity to attribute independent mental states to the self and
others in order to explain and predict behaviour) have been identified as a specific area of psychopathology in borderline personality disorder, and another empirically validated treatment, MBT, has
been designed to address it. This randomized controlled trial of the
three studies at Cornell-Westchester provided suggestive evidence
that other therapeutic approaches may also have beneficial effects
on the capacity to mentalize.

While this particular study suggests that TFP is superior to either
treatment, it is also important to note that supportive psychotherapy
did almost as well as TFP but was provided once weekly instead of
twice weekly like the TFP. To be sure, SP in this study was a psychoanalytically sophisticated treatment that shared much in common with TFP, but proscribed transference interpretations. It was
not simply a control condition involving giving praise and advice.
The study also raises a provocative question that goes unanswered
with the data—would reflective functioning and the other symptom
domains have improved to the same degree as TFP if the supportive
therapy had been offered twice weekly?

Giesen-Bloo et al (2006) did a direct comparison between TFP and
schema-focused therapy (SFT) that lasted three years. In this randomized controlled trial, SFT seemed to produce better outcomes than
transference-focused therapy. However, Yeomans (2007), a consultant to the project, clarified that the therapists doing TFP in the study
were actually not well trained in that approach so that the comparison was not valid. In his view, they were using a more generic form
of dynamic therapy rather than the specific transference-focused

psychotherapy developed by Kernberg, Clarkin, and the other members of the research team.

MBT vs. TFP

As noted earlier, two different psychodynamic psychotherapies, mentalization-based therapy (MBT) and transference-based therapy (TFP), have both been shown to be efficacious for BPD patients in randomized controlled trials. Moreover, TFP, a treatment not specifically designed to improve mentalizing, nevertheless showed greater gains in that area than either of the control treatments.

When one takes into account the differences between MBT and TFP, one has difficulty attributing the therapeutic action to the transference interpretation component. The two modalities approach transference interpretation quite differently. MBT explicitly de-emphasizes the provision of insight through transference interpretation. The rationale is that transference interpretation, especially of anger, is likely to destabilize borderline patients (Gunderson et al, 2007).

Instead, MBT focuses on the current mental state and mental functioning of the patient. This strategy is designed to help patients become introspective and develop more of a sense of self-agency. In other words, the patient begins to find a sense of interiority and subjectivity through interaction with a therapist who is curious about the mental functioning of both patient and therapist and through their alternative perspectives on shared experiences. An MBT therapist would not be likely to interpret that a particular feeling the patient is having has its origins in childhood experiences with a parent.

By contrast, TFP sees unintegrated anger as a core problem. Therapists trained in this modality address the splitting off of anger and its associated self and object representations. Through the use of interpreting transference developments, they attempt to integrate anger and the object and self-representations associated with it into whole object rather than split off part-object relations (Gunderson et al, 2007). Given these differences, how do we understand that both MBT and TFP are effective in promoting mentalizing and improving the symptoms of BPD?

There are several possible answers: 1) all therapeutic approaches provide a systematic conceptual framework that organizes the internal chaos of the borderline patient. Patients with BPD characteristically are in a healthcare system that is chaotic. Because of the splitting mechanism typical of borderline patients, they often receive highly disparate advice from different treaters and diverse treatment agencies. They may feel pulled from all angles by their healthcare system or even thrown out of the system because they are thought to be "manipulators" or "splitters." Any therapeutic strategy based on an overarching theoretical premise makes them feel there is a coherent treatment plan that offers hope.

2) Different borderline patients may respond to different elements of the therapeutic action. BPD has a diverse etiology that involves such things as childhood abuse, childhood neglect, highly confusing and problematic family interactions that do not involve overt abuse, genetic vulnerability, neuropsychological difficulties, and the influence of Axis I disorders that are more than often present (Gabbard, 2005). While we lack sufficient data to determine which patients with BPD are likely to respond to which components of therapeutic action, the work of Blatt and Ford (1994) suggests that this form of research is possible. They have delineated two broad subgroups of character pathology that require different therapeutic strategies. The anaclitic type is mainly concerned about relationships with others, and these individuals have longings to be nurtured, protected, and loved. They appear to respond more to the relational aspect of psychotherapy than to insight delivered through interpretation. On the other hand, the introjective subtype is primarily focused on self-development, and these individuals struggle with feelings of unworthiness, failure, and inferiority. They are highly self-critical, perfectionistic, and competitive, and they appear to do better with a predominately interpretative approach.

3) The therapeutic action may largely be attributed to secondary strategies that are not emphasized by the therapist. Gabbard and Westen (2003) have identified a number of these that may receive less attention than transference interpretation and the therapeutic relationship. Various forms of confrontation carry implicit or explicit suggestions for change. For example, therapists frequently confront dysfunctional beliefs in the same way they confront problematic behaviours in the borderline patient. While cognitive therapy emphasizes this approach, dynamic therapy does not, but few therapists would deny that it is involved in the psychoanalytic psychotherapy of BPD. Therapists also engage

in directive interventions that are designed to address the patient's conscious problem solving or decision-making processes. This effort to help the patient solve problems may assist the patient in making more adaptive life choices or also help them master strong affect states by using more explicit reasoning. Exposure, one of the central mechanisms of change in behavioural treatments, is almost always present in dynamic psychotherapy of BPD, even though few dynamic therapists write about it. In brief, exposure involves presenting the patient with a situation that provokes anxiety and assisting the patient in confronting the situation until it no longer creates anxiety because the patient has habituated to it. The diminution of transference anxieties over time is in part related to exposure, as the patient recognizes that the original fears of being criticized or attacked by the therapist are unrealistic. At the same time, the therapist encourages the patient to confront feared situations outside the therapy. Judicious self-disclosure is yet another mode of action. The therapist may share a particular feeling with the patient to promote mentalizing. The careful use of self-disclosure may help the patient see that her own perception of the therapist is simply a representation rather than an absolute truth. Finally, affirmation may be critically important for patients who have experienced severe trauma (Killingmo, 1989). Such patients may have experienced parents who invalidated their experiences, and the therapist's affirmative validation of the patient's experience can be highly beneficial.

4) The other possibility is that the nature of the therapeutic alliance is responsible for improvement in the patient. Norcross (2000) notes that psychotherapy research indicates that the therapeutic relationship accounts for most of the outcome variance—technique generally accounts for only 12–15% of the variance across different kinds of therapy. The therapeutic alliance, often defined as the degree to which the patient feels helped by the therapist and is able to collaborate with the therapist in pursuit of common therapeutic goals (Gabbard, 2004), has been shown in research to be the most potent predictor of outcome in psychotherapy (Horvath and Symonds, 1991; Martin et al, 2000).

The role of the therapeutic alliance

Considerations of the therapeutic alliance provide a context for considering the role that transference interpretation plays. It is possible that the emphasis on the frequency or centrality of transference interpretation may be misplaced. Timing may be of much greater importance. Gabbard et al (1994) studied psychotherapy process involving audiotapes of long-term dynamic psychotherapy with three BPD patients. One group of investigators in the project looked at the impact of the therapist's interventions on the therapeutic alliance. A second group collaborated on identifying the interventions used to effect the therapeutic alliance. These investigators found that transference interpretation had greater impact on the therapeutic alliance—both positive and negative—than other interventions. They concluded that transference interpretation is a high-risk, high-gain intervention in the psychotherapy of BPD patients.

When the researchers looked at the interventions made by the therapist leading up to the transference interpretation, they found that the most effective interpretations of transference, i.e., those that had a positive impact on the therapeutic alliance, had something in common. The way had been paved for the interpretation by a series of empathic, validating, and even supportive interventions that created a holding environment in Winnicott's sense. The patient felt understood and validated. A surgeon needs anaesthesia to operate, and the psychotherapist of a borderline patient needs a solid therapeutic alliance to interpret transference. Hence the therapeutic alliance and transference interpretation may work synergistically. In this regard, Høglend et al's study (2006) could be understood as demonstrating that interpretive work in the therapeutic relationship strengthens the therapeutic alliance. Patients with poor object relations may be able to see the therapist as a trusting, helpful figure, when the distortions in the relationship are clarified and understood (Gabbard, 2006).

The therapeutic alliance, though, can work independently of transference interpretation, and the therapeutic action doesn't necessarily depend on their linkage. The relationship between therapist and patient can be strengthened through experiential means without resorting to interpretation or clarification within the transference. The therapist's role as a *witness* of the patient's internal experience may itself be therapeutic (Poland, 2000). By listening non-judgmentally to the patient's narrative, the patient is provided with an experience of someone who is "present" with them and able to bear the affect states that the patient finds unbearable. Wallerstein (1986) studied the original Menninger Foundation psychotherapy research project patients in a 30-year follow-up. Although these patients were not rigorously diagnosed at the time, most would now be diagnosed as BPD. Wallerstein found that supportive treatments appear to be as effective and as durable as expressive treatments in patients with poor object relations.

Among the mechanisms of therapeutic action he identified in these patients who had successful supportive treatments, he noted that many "transferred their transference" to someone else. In other words, these patients may have found a supportive romantic partner who could contain their affect states and love them non-judgmentally in such a way that the relationship itself was healing independent of the transference to the therapist. He also noted that some patients improved through transference cure—i.e., they improved to gain the therapist's approval and unconditional positive regard. Others became "therapeutic lifers," patients who never really terminated but continued to see their therapist at intervals varying from months to years. As long as these patients knew that no definitive termination was planned, they functioned well, but faced with the possibility of terminating, they would experience a recurrence of symptoms.

Neurobiological factors

In looking at the research in recent years on the neurobiological correlates of BPD, we may discover some clues as to the types of psychotherapeutic interventions that are helpful. Examining neurobiological correlates is not an exercise in reductionism. Rather, it is an attempt to expand or understand psychodynamic therapy interventions by investigating how they work on the brain. For example, patients with BPD who have histories of childhood trauma have been shown to have hyperreactive amygdala responses (Herpertz et al, 2001). The amygdala is part of the limbic system and serves to increase vigilance and to evaluate the potential for a novel or dangerous situation. This hyperreactivity extends to faces. Two different studies (Donegan et al, 2003; Wagner and Linehan, 1999) found that patients with BPD, compared with control subjects, show significantly greater left amygdalar activation to varied facial expressions. Of even greater importance, however, was the tendency for patients with BPD to attribute negative qualities to neutral faces. Standardized pictures of neutral faces were regarded as threatening, untrustworthy, and possibly nefarious by BPD subjects but not by controls. Hence a hyperreactive amygdala may be involved in the predisposition to be hypervigilant and overreactive to relatively benign emotional expressions. This misreading of neutral facial expressions is probably related to the transference misreadings that occur in psychotherapy of patients with borderline personality disorder. They tend to develop "bad object" transferences even when the therapist is behaving professionally and empathically.

Another factor that influences the development of the negative transference in BPD is a hyperreactive hypothalamic-pituitary-adrenal (HPA) axis. Rinne et al (2002) studied 39 female BPD patients who were given combined dexamethasone/corticoptropin-releasing hormone (CRH) tests, using 11 healthy subjects as controls. Twenty-four of these women had histories of sustained childhood abuse. Fifteen of them had no histories of childhood abuse. When the authors examined the results, the chronically abused BPD patients had significantly enhanced adrenocorticotropic hormone (ACTH) and cortisol responses to the dexamethasone/CRH challenge compared with nonabused subjects. They concluded that a history of sustained childhood abuse is associated with hyperresponsiveness of ACTH release.

Along with the misinterpretation of faces associated with a hyperreactive amygdale, we can infer that this hypervigilance related to the overly active HPA axis contributes to a specific form of object relatedness. This paradigm is illustrated in Figure 1 below.

An affect state of hypervigilant anxiety links a perception of others as persecuting to perception of the self as victimized.

One of the implications for psychotherapy is that the patient's quasi-delusional conviction that the therapist is up to something malevolent must tactfully be challenged. Consider the following vignette:

Ms. A, a 27-year-old patient with BPD, was ending a session with me after doing some good work on understanding her affective storms. As she took her coat off the coat hanger on the back of

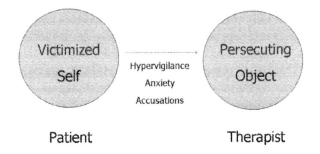

my office door, she got her left arm stuck trying to slip it into the sleeve. I moved over to assist her by holding up the collar of her coat so she could more easily get her arm through the sleeve. She erupted in rage and shouted, "I can do it myself!" I backed off and told her it was fine if she preferred to do it on her own. She then left the session without making further comment.

When she returned the following week, she made no mention of the incident. I brought up what had happened, and she said that it no longer applied to her since she didn't feel that way today; hence there was no reason to discuss it. She said, "Besides, that's not me. I'm not like that." I explained to her that in fact, there was a part of her that was like that. She reluctantly reflected on the last session. She said that her perception was that I was treating her like a small child who didn't know how to put on her coat. I asked, "Is there any other possible perspective on this situation besides that one?" She said that she was sure that was how I had viewed her. I persisted in exploring other options with her. Ultimately, she conceded, now that she was no longer affectively distressed, that it was possible that the therapist had other intentions. She went on to say that she hated the way her mother had infantilized her and didn't want that to be repeated with me. I also offered an interpretive understanding after several minutes of exploring it with her: "It could be that if you acknowledge that the "not me" part of you is here now, you're concerned that that's all I'll see. That would worry you that all the loving, positive parts of you would be destroyed by that rage, and I would be driven away." The patient contemplated the possibility and said she would have to think about it.

In this vignette, I challenged the patient's emotional certainty— namely, that she was viewing me in the only way possible—i.e., as an infantilizing mother. I helped her explore other possibilities to enhance her mentalizing capacity about her own subjective state and that of others. After paving the way, I also offered an interpretive understanding of her fears in the transference—namely, that if she integrated the "bad" part of her with the more positive, loving part of her, the hate would destroy the love and I would be driven away. Hence a major effort was made to help the patient reflect on what had transpired and see other possible perspectives.

Both TFP and MBT encourage reflection by the patient on the perceptions and conclusions that the therapist draws from interactions. Ochsner et al (2002) have shown that actively rethinking or reappraising feelings activates the prefrontal area of the brain that modulates amygdalar-based negative feelings such as fear. Hence one possibility in terms of therapeutic action is that the reflection and contemplation of affective states and their meaning may increase the prefrontal control of the amygdalar hyperreactivity.

At least one study not involving borderline personality disorder suggests that conscious effort to think may increase the prefrontal volume. Peterson et al (1998) found that in Tourette's patients, some were able to consciously suppress the motor tics when they had a premonitory urge that they were coming. Others were not good at consciously suppressing them. Those who made a stronger effort to consciously suppress the tics actually increased the volume of the frontal cortex compared to those who were not able to consciously suppress the motor tics, according to functional MRI scans. Whether a similar change in prefrontal volume is part of the therapeutic action with borderline personality disorder remains to be studied.

Further research suggests there may actually be a frontolimbic network that is central to the emotional dysregulations in BPD (Schmahl and Bremner, 2006). This network consists of the anterior cingulated cortex (ACC), orbitofrontal cortex (OFC), dorsolateral prefrontal cortex (DPC), hippocampus, and amygdala. The ACC may be regarded as the brain area involved in mediating emotional control, and studies show that it is deactivated in response to stressful stimuli in BPD. Hence ACC dysfunction is probably a key component in the emotional dysregulation seen in BPD.

Silbersweig et al (2007) designed an ingenious study to examine the mechanisms involved in frontolimbic dysfunction. BPD patients were asked to push a button for words in standard font but not for those in italicized font. BPD patients, as expected, were more impulsive than controls, particularly when the italicized words were negative. In contrast to controls, BPD patients showed increased amygdalar reaction and decreased activity in the subgenual cingulated and the medial OFC. Also in response to negative words, the BPD subjects showed increased activity in the dorsal ACC. Hence even though there were not able to exercise impulse control, this finding suggested that they were aware that they needed to devote other resources to monitoring it.

We can conclude, then, that neuroimaging data implicates the prefrontal cortex and the ACC as target areas for psychotherapeutic intervention to help decrease emotional dysregulation in BPD patients.

Another contribution to understanding neurobiological correlates of the therapeutic action involves timetables for change in the neurobiology of learning. Wiltgen et al (2004) stressed that insight has separate and different effects than repeated experience has on changing what has been learned in the past. Insight based on hippocampal learning provides quick new ways of looking at new information and adapting to new situations. However, other neuronal connections are based on implicit, nonhippocampal learning and have never been conscious nor do they have the capacity to be easily retrieved by shifting one's attention. These types of neuronal associations develop through intense repeated experiences early in life are likely to remain strong, despite interpretation and insight. Hence explicit and declarative memory systems may change with insight, while implicit and procedural memories may require multiple exposures over an extended period of time for change to be achieved (Folensbee, 2007).

Structural change is often regarded as strengthening of the ego or modification of the superego. However, with our growing knowledge of neural networks, we also know that changes can be understood in terms of what happens in the brain. Through repeated experiences, certain representations of object and self, connected by an affect state, are embedded in neural networks. Those that occur on a regular basis, such as a father who repeatedly hits his son when angry, will become activated automatically when there is a threat. Over time, a psychotherapist offers a new model of relationship for internalization. In this way, the neural network associated with the old object and self-representation gradually weakens, while new associative linkages are occurring that are strengthened through repeated exposure to the psychotherapist, who is a benign and caring instead of an abusive one. The capacity for conscious self-reflection allows the patient to override unconscious dynamics once they are recognized and to begin resetting some of the relevant connections. Hence the old neural networks do not disappear but are relatively weakened while the new neural networks, containing the new object relationship of the therapy, is strengthened.

Conclusion

Summarizing what we know about therapeutic action, we can conclude that there is no single path to therapeutic change. Diverse models of psychotherapy appear to be effective with patients who have borderline personality disorder. Some principles of change and some techniques for eliciting change are likely to be useful for all patients, whereas others may be useful only for some (Gabbard and Westen, 2003). Moreover, the research suggests that patients with impaired object relations may respond well to interpretive techniques, so it is not accurate to assume that strictly supportive techniques are necessary for all patients with borderline psychopathology. Nor is it accurate to conclude that transference interpretation is essential for change.

In his classic 1912 paper on technique, Freud suggested that "For when all is said and done, it is impossible to destroy anyone in absentia or in effigy" (p. 108). The implication was that analytic cure involved eradicating the transference. However, our increasing knowledge from the neurosciences as well as follow-up data from studies of psychoanalysis and psychoanalytic psychotherapy, we know that transference is never destroyed and that such ambitious goals would be unreasonable. Rather, structural change involves weakening old networks while strengthening new ones formed in the therapy and other positive relationships.

References

Abend, S.M. (2001). Expanding psychological possibilities. *Psychoanal Q* 70:3–14.

Bateman, A. & Fonagy, P. (1999). Effectiveness of partial hospitalization in the treatment of borderline personality disorder: a randomized controlled trial. *Am J Psychiatry*; 156:1563–1569.

Blatt, S.J. & Ford, T.Q. (1994). *Therapeutic change: an object relations perspective*. New York: Springer.

Clarkin, J.R., Levy, K.N, Lenzenweger M.F. et al (2007). Evaluating three treatments for borderline personality disorder: a multiwave study. *Am J Psychiatry* 164:922–928.

Cooper, A.M. (1989). Concepts of therapeutic effectiveness in psychoanalysis: A historical review. *Psychoanal Inq* 9:4–25.

Donegan, N.H., Sanislow C.A., Blumberg H.P. et al (2003). Amygdalar hyperreactivity in borderline personality disorder: implications for emotional dysregulation. *Biol Psychiatry* 54:1284–1293.

Dutra, L., Eddy K, Westen D (2001). *A multidimensional meta-analysis of psychotherapy for obsessive-compulsive disorder.* Unpublished manuscript: Boston Univ.

Folensbee, R.W. (2007). *The neuroscience of psychological therapies.* Cambridge: Cambridge University Press.

Freud, S. (1912b). *The dynamics of transference.* Standard Edition 12. p. 108. London: Hogarth Press.

Gabbard, G.O. (2000). *Psychodynamic psychiatry in clinical practice,* Third Edition. Washington, DC: American Psychiatric Press.

Gabbard, G.O. (2004). *Long-Term Psychodynamic Psychotherapy: a Basic Text.* Arlington, VA: American Psychiatric Publishing.

Gabbard, G.O. (2005). *Psychodynamic Psychiatry in Clinical Practice: Fourth Edition.* Arlington, VA: American Psychiatric Publishing.

Gabbard, G.O. (2006). When is transference work useful in dynamic psychotherapy? *Am J Psychiatry* 163:1667–1669.

Gabbard, G.O. (2007). Do all roads lead to Rome? New findings on borderline personality disorder. *Am J Psychiatry* 164(6):853–855.

Gabbard, G.O., Horwitz, L., Allen, J.G. et al (1994). Transference interpretation in the psychotherapy of borderline patients: a high-risk, high-gain phenomenon. *Harv Rev Psychiatry* 2(1):59–69.

Gabbard, G.O. & Westen, D. (2003). Rethinking therapeutic action. *Int J Psychoanal* 84:823–841.

Giesen-Bloo, J., van Dyck, R., Spinhoven, P. et al (2006). Outpatient psychotherapy for borderline personality disorder: randomized trial of schema-focused therapy vs. transference-focused therapy. *Arch Gen Psychiatry* 63:649–658.

Greenberg, J. (2005). Theories of therapeutic action and their technical consequences. In: Person, E.S., Cooper, A.M. & Gabbard, G.O. *The American Psychiatric Publishing Textbook of Psychoanalysis.* Arlington, VA: APPI, pp. 217–228.

Gunderson, J.G. & Bateman, A., Kernberg, O (2007). Alternative perspectives in *Psychodynamic psychotherapy of borderline personality disorder: the case of "Ellen." Am J Psychiatry* 164:1333–1339.

Herpertz, S.C., Dietrich, T.M. & Wenning, B. et al (2001). Evidence of abnormal amygdala functioning in borderline personality disorder: a functional MRI study. *Biol Psychiatry* 50:292–298.

Høglend, P., Amlo, S. & Marble, A. et al (2006). Analysis of the patient-therapist relationship in dynamic psychotherapy: an experimental study of transference interpretations. *Am J Psychiatry* 163:1739–1746.

Høglend, P., Bøgwald, K.-P. & Amlo, S. et al (2008). Transference Interpretations in Dynamic Psychotherapy: Do They Really Yield Sustained Effects? *Am J Psychiatry* 165:763–771.

Horvath, A.D., & Symonds, B.D. (1991). Relation between working alliance and outcome in psychotherapy: a meta-analysis. *Journal of Counseling Psychology* 38:139–149.

Jacobs, T.J. (1990). The corrective emotional experience—its place in current technique. *Psychoanalytic Inquiry* 10:433–54.

Killingmo, B. (1989). Conflict and deficits: Implications for technique. *Int J Psychoanal* 70:65–79.

Levy, K.N., Meehan, K.B. & Clarkin, J.F. et al (2006). Change in attachment patterns and reflective function in a randomized controlled trial of transference-focused psychotherapy for borderline personality disorder. *J Consult Clin Psychol* 74:1027–1074.

Linehan, M.M., Contois, K.A & Murray A.M. et al (2006). Two-year randomized controlled trial on follow-up with dialectical behavior therapy vs. therapy by experts for suicidal behaviors and borderline personality disorder. *Arch Gen Psychiatry* 63:757–766.

Martin, D.J., Garske, J.P. & Davis, K.K. (2000). Relation of the therapeutic alliance without common other variables: a meta-analytic review. *J Consult Clin Psychol* 68:438–450.

Norcross, J.C. (2000). Toward the delineation of empirically-based principles in psychotherapy: commentary on Beutler. *Prevention and Treatment* 3:1–5.

Ochsner, K.N., Bunge, S.A. & Gross J.J. et al (2002). Rethinking Feelings: An fMRI Study of the Cognitive Regulation of Emotion. *J Cogn Neurosci* 14(8):1215–1229.

Peterson, B.S., Skudlarski, P., Anderson, A.W. et al (1998). A Functional Magnetic Resonance Imaging Study of Tic Suppression in Tourette Syndrome. *Arch Gen Psychiatry* 55:326–333.

Pine, F. (1998). *Diversity and direction in psychoanalytic technique*. New Haven, CT: Yale Univ Press.

Piper, W.E., Avin, H.F. & Joyce A.S. et al (1991). Transference interpretations, therapeutic alliance, and outcome in short-term individual psychotherapy. *Arch Gen Psych* 48:946–953.

Poland, W.D. (2000). The analyst's listening and otherness. *JAPA* 48:17–34.

Pulver, S.E. (1992). Psychic change: Insight or relationship? *Int J Psychoanal* 73:199–208.

Rinne, T., de Kloet, E.R., & Wouters, L. et al (2002). Hyperresponsiveness of hypothalamic-pituitary-adrenal axis to combined dexamethasone/corticotropin-releasing hormone challenge in female borderline personality disorder subjects with a history of sustained childhood abuse. *Biol Psychiatry* 52:1102–1112.

Schmahl, C., Bremner., J.D. (2006). Neuroimaging in borderline personality disorder. *J Psych Res* 40:419–427.

Silbersweig, D., Clarkin, J.F. & Goldstein, M. et al (2007). Failure of frontolimbic inhibitory function in the context of negative emotion in borderline personality disorder. *Am J Psychiatry* 164:1832–1841.

Spitzer, R.L., Williams, J.B.W., Gibbon, N. et al (1990). *Structured clinical interview for DSM-IIIR personality disorders (SCID-II)*. Washington, DC: American Psychiatric Press.

Stern, D.N., Sander, L.W., & Nahum, J.P. et al (1998). Non-interpretive mechanisms in psychoanalytic therapy: The 'something more' than interpretation. *Int J Psychoanal* 79:903–21.

Wagner, A.W. & Linehan, M.M. (1999). Facial expression recognition ability among women with borderline personality disorder: implications for emotion regulation? *J Personal Disord* 13:329–344.

Wallerstein, R. (1986). *Forty-two lives in treatment*. New York: Guilford.

Wiltgen, B.J., Brown, R.A. & Talton, L.E. et al (2004). New circuits for old memories: the role of the neocortex in consolidation. *Neuron* 44: 101–108.

Yeomans, F. (2007). Letter to the editor: Questions concerning the randomized trial of schema-focused therapy vs. transference-focused psychotherapy. *Archives of General Psychiatry* 64:609–610.

CHAPTER TWO

Transference Focused Psychotherapy (TFP)

Otto F. Kernberg

Transference Focused Psychotherapy (TFP) was based upon the Menninger Foundation's psychotherapy research project (Kernberg et al., 1972), that indicated that the optimal treatment of patients with severe personality disorders or "low ego strength" was a psychoanalytic psychotherapy, with systematic interpretation of the transference in the hours, and the provision of as much external support as the patient required outside the hours to permit the treatment to develop successfully. In contrast, neither the treatment with standard psychoanalysis nor with a purely supportive modality based on psychoanalytic principles was as effective. On this basis, at the Personality Disorders Institute of the Weill Cornell Medical College and The New York Hospital, we developed a psychoanalytic psychotherapy centered upon the principle of systematic interpretation of the transference, and the setting up of a treatment structure—including limit setting when needed, in order to protect the patient and the treatment from the severe acting out that is practically unavoidable in the treatment of these patients.

These efforts, over a period of approximately 15 years, culminated in the development of a manualized psychoanalytic psychotherapy, Transference Focused Psychotherapy, that fulfilled these general characteristics mentioned above. We tested the possibility of training psychotherapists in carrying out this manualized treatment, and, after sufficient adherence and competence in carrying out that treatment was confirmed, carried out a set of psychotherapy research projects that, at first, confirmed the efficacy of this treatment in comparison to treatment as usual for borderline patients, and then a randomized, controlled trial comparing TFP to Dialectic Behavior Therapy and to a supportive psychotherapy based on a psychoanalytic model. All three treatments were manualized, carried out by therapists who were convinced about the helpfulness of this model and proficient in carrying it out. The findings revealed the efficacy of all three forms of therapy, and showed significant differences regarding the treatment of suicidal and parasuicidal symptoms, more effective with TFP and DBT than with Supportive Psychotherapy. TFP was effective in reducing various aspects of aggressive affects and behaviour of these patients in comparison to the other modalities (Kernberg et al., 2008).

At various points of our developing work we studied the possibility of applying the principles of TFP to psychoanalytic group psychotherapy, and developed a tentative model that seemed clinically satisfactory. We have applied this mostly to a day-hospital setting, and in sporadic attempts to apply it to an in-patient setting as well. While clinicians involved in this effort have felt encouraged to pursue it further, we have not yet carried out empirical research on the efficacy of such a group psychotherapy, and the present paper is a first effort to spell out, the general model of this form of group psychotherapy and its relationship to other related models. I shall first present an outline of the basic principles of TFP as applied to individual patients, and then present an overview about how these principles apply to a corresponding TFP group psychotherapy.

Overview of TFP for individual patients

We evolved a differentiation of overall, long range treatment objectives and corresponding "treatment strategies," the systematization of interventions in each session that are conditions necessary for working with a borderline patient population or "treatment tactics", adopting specific instruments of psychoanalytic treatment throughout its course, or "treatment techniques". In what follows, I shall outline these treatment strategies, tactics and techniques.

Strategies

Our assumption was that patients with severe personality disorders or borderline personality organization suffer from the syndrome of identity diffusion, that is, a chronic, stable lack of integration of the concept of self and of the concept of significant others, and that the ultimate cause of that syndrome was the failure of psychological integration resulting from the predominance of aggressive internalized object relations over idealized ones. In an effort to protect the idealized segment of the self and object representations, these patients' ego was fixated at a level of primitive dissociative or splitting mechanisms and their reinforcement by a variety of other primitive defensive operations predating the dominance of repression, namely, projective identification, omnipotence and omnipotent control, devaluation, denial, and primitive idealization. Identity diffusion is reflected clinically in the incapacity to accurately assess self and others in depth, to commit in depth to work or a profession, to establish and maintain stable intimate relationships, and in a lack of the normal subtlety of understanding and tact in interpersonal situations. Primitive defensive operations, which correspond to patients' split psychological structure and identity diffusion, are manifest in patient's behavior and are an important feature of their maladaptive dealing with negative affect and conflictual interpersonal situations, contributing fundamentally to chaos and breakdown in intimacy, in work, in creativity, and in social life. In an earlier paper, I (Kernberg, 2006) have described in detail, the etiology, psychopathology, empirical research and clinical assessment of the syndrome of identity diffusion.

The main strategy in the transference focused psychotherapy (TFP) of borderline personality organization consists in the facilitation of the (re)activation in the treatment of split-off internalized object relations of contrasting persecutory and idealized natures that are then observed and interpreted in the transference. TFP is carried out in face to face sessions, a minimum of two and usually not more than three sessions a week. The patient is instructed to carry out free association (in a detailed, precise way), and the therapist restricts his role to careful observation of the activation of regressive, split-off relations in the transference, and to help identify them and interpret their segregation in the light of these patients' enormous difficulty in reflecting on their own behavior and on the interactions they get involved in. The interpretation of these split-off object relations is based upon the assumption that each of them reflects a dyadic unit of a self-representation, an object-representation and a dominant affect linking them, and that the activation of these dyadic relationships determines the patient's perception of the therapist and occurs with rapid role reversals in the transference, so that the patient may identify with a primitive self-representation while projecting a corresponding object representation onto the therapist, while, ten minutes later, for example, the patient identifies with the object representation while projecting the self-representation onto the therapist. Engaging the patient's observing ego in this phenomenon paves the way for interpreting the conflicts that keep these dyads, and corresponding views of self and other, separate and exaggerated. Until these representations are integrated into more nuanced and modulated ones, the patient will continue to perceive himself and others in exaggerated, distorted and rapidly shifting terms.

The oscillation or alternative distribution of the roles of the dyad has to be differentiated from the split between opposite dyads carrying opposite (idealizing and persecutory) affective charges. The final step of interpretation consists in linking of the dissociated positive and negative transferences, leading to an integration of the mutually split-off idealized and persecutory segments of experience with the corresponding resolution of identity diffusion. The interpretation of these split-off relationships occurs in a characteristic sequence of three steps. Step one is the formulation of the total relationship that seems to be activated at that point, using metaphorical statements to present the situation as completely as possible in a way that can be understood by the patient, and the clarification of who enacts what role in that interaction. The therapist's comments are based on his observations, his countertransference utilization, and on clarifications that have been sought of the patient's experience of the relationship at each moment.

Step two consists in the observation of the interchange of the corresponding roles between patient and therapist, an extremely important step that permits the patient, throughout time, to understand his unconscious identification with the object representation as well as the self representation, leading to a gradual awareness of the mutual complementarity of these two roles. Step two is carried out in the clarification and confrontation of both the oscillating poles of a given dyad. However, since the idealized and persecutory relationships that are activated remain typically split-off from each other in different dyads, the patient becomes more able to recognize the extreme dyadic nature of each of them while still maintaining the split or dissociated nature that separates all good from all bad relationships. Understanding the motivation for keeping these dyads separate is one of the main objectives of the interpretive work, the focus of the next step.

Step three, finally, consists in an interpretive linking of the mutually dissociated positive and negative transferences, the transferences reflecting the idealized and persecutory relationships, thus leading to an integration of the mutually split-off idealized and persecutory segments of experience, the corresponding resolution of identity diffusion, and the modulation of intense affect dispositions as primitive euphoric or hypomanic affects are integrated with their corresponding fearful, persecutory, aggressive opposites. This third step brings about a significant integration of the patient's ego identity, as an integrated view of self—more complex, rich and nuanced than the simplistic and extreme split-off representations—and a corresponding integrated view of significant others replace their split-off previous nature, and an experience of appropriate depressive affects, reflecting the capacity for acknowledging one's own aggression that had previously been projected or experienced as dysphoric affect, with concern, guilt, and the wish to repair good relationships damaged in fantasy or reality, becoming dominant.

Step one of this sequence begins in the first therapy session, and step two follows relatively quickly after the first few weeks and months of treatment. Step three characterizes the mid and advanced stages of the psychotherapy. At the same time, however, this three-step sequence is a highly repetitive process. Some step three interpretations may become possible relatively early, and step one, two and three may recycle again and again, it first taking weeks to develop the entire sequence, then the course of a few sessions, and, in the advanced stages of the treatment, all three steps eventually may be elaborated in the course of the same session.

The overall strategy mentioned, namely the resolution of identity diffusion and the integration of mutually split-off idealized and persecutory relationships, is facilitated by the fact that unconscious conflicts are activated in the transference mostly in the patient's behavior rather than in the emergence of preconscious subjective experiences reflecting unconscious fantasy. The intolerance of overwhelming emotional experiences is expressed in the tendency to replace such emotional experiences by acting out, in the case of most borderline patients, and somatization, in some other personality disorders (Green, A., 1993). The fact that primitive conflicts manifest themselves in dissociated behavior rather than in the content of free association is a fundamental feature of these cases that facilitates transference analysis with a relatively low frequency of sessions, while the very intensity of those conflicts facilitates the full analysis of these transference developments. What is important in these cases is establishing very clear boundaries and conditions of the treatment situation, so that a "normal" relationship is defined in the therapy that immediately enters into contrast with the distortions in the therapeutic relationship derived from the activation of primitive transferences. This leads to the discussion of a second major aspect of the treatment: the tactics used by the therapist in each session that create the conditions necessary for the use of interpretation and the other techniques of treatment.

Tactics

The tactics are rules of engagement that allow for the application of psychoanalytic technique in a modified way that corresponds to the nature of the transference developments in these cases. The tactics are: 1) setting the treatment contract, 2) choosing the priority theme to address in the material the patient is presenting, 3) maintaining an appropriate balance between, on the one hand, expanding the incompatible views of reality between the patient and therapist in preparation for interpretation and, on the other, establishing common elements of shared reality, and 4) regulating the intensity of affective involvement.

In the establishment of an initial treatment contract, in addition to the usual arrangements for psychoanalytic treatment, urgent difficulties in the borderline patient's life that may threaten the patient's physical integrity or survival, or other people's physical integrity or survival, or the very continuation of the treatment, all are taken up and structured, in the sense of setting up conditions under which the treatment can be carried out that involve certain responsibilities for the patient and certain responsibilities for the therapist. What is important in these structuring arrangements at the beginning of the treatment is first, that the therapeutic structure eliminate the secondary gain of treatment, and second that, in a situation where limits or restrictions need to be established in order to preserve the patient's life or the treatment, the transference implications of these restrictions or limit-settings need to be interpreted immediately. The combination of limit-setting and interpretation of the corresponding transference development is an essential, highly effective, and at times life saving tactic of the treatment. Yeomans, et al. (1992) have described in detail the techniques and vicissitudes of initial contract setting; and the manual of the technical aspects of Transference Focused Psychotherapy (Clarkin, Yeomans, and Kernberg, 2006) describes in detail the priorities to address in carrying out the therapy.

With regard to choosing which theme to address at any given moment in the material the patient brings to the session, the most important tactic is the general analytic rule that interpretation has to be carried out where the affect is most intense: affect dominance determines the focus of the interpretation. The most intense affect may be expressed in the patient's subjective experience, in the patient's non-verbal behavior, or, at times, in the countertransference—in the face of what on the surface seems a completely frozen or affectless situation (Kernberg, 2004). The simultaneous attention, by the therapist, to the patient's verbal communication, non-verbal behavior, and the countertransference permits diagnosing what the dominant affect is at the moment—and the corresponding object relation activated in the treatment situation. Every affect is considered to be the manifestation of an underlying object relation.

The second most important consideration in determining the selection of what is interpreted is the nature of the transference. When major affect development coincides with transference development that becomes easy to determine, but there are times where most affect occurs related to extra transferential conditions or the patient's external world. Such affective dominance in the patient's external world, of course, always has transference implications as well; the focus, however, has to start on the external affectively invested situation, only shifting into a transference interpretation when the corresponding transference development clearly occupies the centre of the patient's present interaction with the analyst. This is an important tactic derived from Fenichel's (1941) technical recommendations, and reflects a flexibility of this approach, that focuses simultaneously on the transference and on developments in these patients' external life at any time.

Still another tactical approach relates to certain general priorities that need to be taken up immediately, whether they reflect affective dominance or not in the session, although they usually do so anyway. These priorities include, by order of importance: 1) suicidal or homicidal behaviour, 2) threats to the disruption of the treatment, 3) severe acting out in the session or outside, that threaten the patient's life or the treatment, 4) dishonesty, 5) trivialization of the content of the hour and 6) pervasive narcissistic resistances, that must be resolved by consistent analysis of the transference implications of the pathological grandiose self (Kernberg, 1984, Clarkin, Yeomans and Kernberg, 2006). When none of these priorities seems dominant at the moment in the hour, the general tactic of affective dominance and transference analysis prevails.

An important tactical aspect of a treatment involves conditions of severe regression, including affects storms, micropsychotic episodes, negative therapeutic reactions, and "incompatible realities". We have developed specific technical approaches to these situations; the description of all of which would exceed the limits of this paper.

Techniques

While "strategies" refer to overall, long range goals and their implementation in transference analysis, and "tactics" to particular interventions in concrete hours of treatment, "techniques" refers to the general, consistent application of technical instruments derived from psychoanalytic technique. The main technical instruments of Transference Focused Psychotherapy (TFP) are those referred to by Gill (1954) as the essential techniques of psychoanalysis, namely, interpretation, transference analysis, and technical neutrality. If psychoanalysis consists in the facilitation of a regressive transference neurosis and the resolution of this transference neurosis by interpretation alone carried out by the psychoanalyst from a position of technical neutrality, TFP may be defined, in terms of its technical utilization, by these same three instruments, somewhat modified, however, as we shall mention below, and the important contribution of countertransference analysis as an additional major technical instrument.

The use of interpretation focuses particularly on the early phases of the interpretive process, namely, clarification of the subjective experience of the patient, (clarification of what is in the patient's mind rather than clarifying information to him), and confrontation, in the sense of a tactful drawing of attention to any inconsistencies or contradictions in the patient's communication—either between what the patient says at one point in contrast to another, between verbal and non-verbal communication, or between the patient's communication and what is evoked in the countertransference. Non-verbal aspects of behaviour become extremely important in the psychoanalytic psychotherapy of severe personality disorders. Interpretation per se, that is, the establishment of hypotheses regarding the unconscious functions of what has been brought forth by clarification and confrontation follows these two techniques. Interpretation as a hypothesis about unconscious meaning refers, first of all, to interpretation of unconscious meaning in the "here and now", the "present unconscious" (Sandler & Sandler, 1987), in contrast to genetic interpretations that link the unconscious meaning in the "here and now" with assumed unconscious meanings in the "there and then", that become important only in advanced stages of the treatment of severe personality disorders. Interpretation, in short, is applied systematically, but with heavy emphasis on its preliminary phases: clarification and confrontation, and the interpretation of the "present unconscious".

Transference analysis differs from the analysis of the transference in standard psychoanalysis in that, as mentioned before, it is always closely linked with the analysis of the patient's problems in external reality, in order to avoid the dissociation of the psychotherapy sessions from the patient's external life. Transference analysis also includes an implied concern for the long range treatment goals that, characteristically, are not focused upon in standard psychoanalysis, except if they emerge in the transference. In TFP, an ongoing concern regarding dominant problems in the patient's life is reflected in the occasional introduction of reference to major conflicts that brought the patient into treatment or that have been discovered in the course of the treatment, bringing such conflicts into the treatment situation even if they are not transference-dominant at that point. This introduction of "extra transference material" follows the therapist's assessment that a significant splitting operation is in process, shielding a certain important conflict in the patient's external life from exploration in the treatment. Here the therapist's overview of the total treatment situation and the total life situation of the patient may determine that he introduce a subject matter "arbitrarily", (at times, at least in the patient's mind), and then focus on the transference development that occurs as a consequence of introducing such a major life theme. While transference analysis starts from session one, and, in this regard the treatment has significant similarities with Kleinian technique, (both because of the dominant emphasis on transference analysis and on primitive defenses and object relations), this bringing in of external reality is a fundamental difference from Kleinian and, to some extent, also from ego psychological psychoanalysis.

Technical neutrality, as has probably become evident from what has been said before, is an ideal point of departure within the treatment at large and within each session, but at times needs to be disrupted because of the urgent requirement for limit-setting and even in connection with the introduction of a major life problem of the patient that, at such point, would seem a non-neutral intervention of the therapist. Such deviation from technical neutrality may be indispensable in order to protect the boundaries of the treatment situation, protect the patient from severe suicidal and other self-destructive behavior, and requires a particular approach in order to restore technical neutrality once it has been abandoned. What we do, following an intervention that clearly signifies a temporary deviation from technical neutrality, (for example, by taking measures to control a patient's accumulation of medication with suicidal intentions), is the analysis of the transferential consequences of our intervention, to a point where these transferential developments can be resolved and then be followed with the analysis of the transference implications of the reasons that forced the therapist to move away from technical neutrality. Technical neutrality, in short, fluctuates throughout the treatment, but is constantly worked on and reinstated as a major process goal.

The utilization of countertransference as a major therapeutic tool has already been referred to as an important source of information about affectively dominant issues in the hour. The intensity of the countertransferences evoked by patients with severe character pathology and consequent severely regressive behavior and acting out in the transference requires an ongoing alertness to countertransference developments that the therapist has to tolerate in himself/herself, even under conditions of significant regression in countertransference fantasies and impulses of an aggressive, dependent, or sexual kind. That internal tolerance of counter-transference permits its analysis in terms of the nature of the self representation or the object representation that is being projected onto the therapist at that point, facilitating full interpretation of the dyadic relationship in the transference, so that countertransference is utilized in the therapist's mind for transference clarification. It is important that countertransference not be communicated directly to the patient but worked into transference interpretations. In this regard TFP follows strictly analytic criteria typical for the ego psy-chological, Kleinian, British Independent, and French approaches. At times, partial acting out of the countertransference is unavoid-able, and the therapist has to be honest in acknowledging the real-ity of what his behavior shows to the patient, without exceeding this communication with guilt determined "confessions" or deny-ing the reality of a behavioural response on the therapist's part that has become obvious to the patient. This, in essence, is not different from what standard psychoanalytic technique would expect from the analyst, except that the very intensity and dominant nature of countertransference information is characteristic of the process of TFP with severe personality disorders.

These then are the essential elements of the techniques of TFP. It also needs to be said that the frequency of interpretive interventions, at whatever level of regression, is high in comparison with transfer-ence interpretation in psychoanalysis. As Green (2000) has pointed out, the avoidance of traumatogenic associations drives borderline patients to jump from one subject to the next, thus expressing their "central phobic position", and may seem bewildering to an analyst used to expect the gradual development of a specific theme in free association, thus leading to clarify the subject matter that is being explored. Here, waiting for such a gradual deepening of free asso-ciation is useless, because of this defensive jump from one subject to the next, also related to the splitting operations that affect the very language of the patient (Bion, 1968).

The corresponding technical approach in TFP consists of an effort to interpret rapidly the implication of each of the fragments that emerge in the hours, with the intention of establishing continuity by the very nature of the interpretive interventions that gradually establish a continuity of their own. This approach may be compared to the interpretive work with dreams, where the interpretation of apparently isolated fragments of the manifest dream content leads gradually to the latent dream content that establishes the continuity between the apparently disparate elements of the manifest content.

Indications and contraindications

The most general indication for Transference Focused Psychotherapy (TFP) is for patients with borderline personality organization, that is, presenting severe identity diffusion, severe breakdown in work and intimate relationships, in their social life, and with specific symptoms linked to their particular personality disorder. This indication includes most personality disorders functioning at a borderline level, such as, the borderline personality disorder per se, the more severe cases of histrionic personality disorder, paranoid personality disorders, schizoid personality disorders, narcissistic personality disorders functioning on an overt borderline level, (that is, having all the symptoms of borderline personality disorder and narcissistic personality disorder at the same time), and patients functioning at a borderline level with severe complications typical for these cases, if and when such complications can be treated first and controlled. These include alcoholism, drug dependency, severe eating disorders, particularly severe anorexia nervosa, patients with antisocial behavior but definitely not with an antisocial personality proper (that has no indication for psychotherapeutic treatment at all), schizotypal disorders, and severe hypochondriasis. In all individual cases, we evaluate first whether, even for such severe personality disorders, psychoanalysis may be the treatment of choice, which is the case for many histrionic personality disorders. The broad spectrum of severe personality disorders, who, in addition, usually suffer from severe, chronic anxiety, characterologically based depression, somatization, phobic symptoms, and dissociative reactions, are optimal candidates for TFP, which thus expands the total realm of patients that can be treated with a psychoanalytically based approach.

The main contraindications include, as mentioned before, the antisocial personality proper, and some narcissistic patients with severe antisocial features, as well as patients with chronic dishonesty that affects their capacity for verbal communication, such as pervasively dominant pseudologia fantastica: in short, severe degrees of chronic dishonesty that limit the capacity for honest communication and make the resolution of these psychopathic transferences very difficult. In contrast, patients with aggressive, provocative, irresponsible social behavior who, however, still are able to experience some degree of loyalty, investment in friendship and work, are optimal candidates for TFP.

Another major contraindication is overwhelming secondary gain of illness, provided by financial social support, supportive housing, financial means provided to many patients with severe personality disorders, who, unfortunately, are treated as if they were chronic schizophrenic patients, and whose capacity to lead a parasitic life depending on the State or on wealthy families becomes a major life sustaining goal. Patients without any social life at all, reduced for many years to staying in their room, watching television, and drifting in some way through life also have a reserved prognosis but in many cases can be treated if an adequate treatment contract is in place. Patients should optimally have a normal IQ in order to undergo TFP.

There are patients in whom an inordinate amount of self-directed aggression expresses self-destruction as a major life goal, and the wishes to destroy themselves may be more powerful than the wishes to live and be treated. Some of these patients can be recognized before the treatment starts, others only in the course of the treatment, although a long series of extremely severe suicidal attempts and a long history of what seems almost willful destruction of life opportunities may signal this condition. The same is true for patients with the most severe degree of negative therapeutic reaction reflecting a profound identification with a battering object, and patients with the syndrome of malignant narcissism, where self-destructiveness implies the only possible triumph over an otherwise envied external world not suffering from the same conditions that they do. Many of the patients with contraindications for TFP psychotherapy may have an indication for supportive psychotherapy, a subject that goes beyond the realm of this particular communication, but to which our Personality Disorders Institute has contributed significantly (Rockland, 1992, Appelbaum, 2006).

This completes the outline of Transference Focused Psychotherapy for individual patients.

References

Appelbaum, A.H. (2006). Supportive Psychoanalytic Psychotherapy for Borderline Patients: an Empirical Approach. In: *The American Journal of Psychoanalysis*, Vol. 66, No. 4.

Bion, W.R. (1961). *Experiences in Groups*. New York: Basic Books.

Clarkin, J.F., Yeomans F.E. & Kernberg O.F. (2006). *Psychotherapy for Borderline Personality: Focusing on Object Relations*. Washington, DC: American Psychiatric.

Fenichel, O. (1941). Problems of Psychoanalytic Technique. Albany: *Psychoanalytic Quarterly*.

Gill, M. (1954). Psychoanalysis and exploratory psychotherapy. *Journal of American Psychoanalytic Association* 2:771–797.

Green, A. (1993). *On Private Madness*. Madison, CT: International Universities Press.

Green, A. (2000). La position phobique centrale. In *La Pensée clinique*. Paris: Editions Odile Jacob.

Kernberg, O., Burnstein, E.D., Coyne, L. et al. (1972). Psychotherapy and Psychoanalysis. Final report of the Menninger Foundation's Psychotherapy research project. *In Bulletin of the Menninger Clinic* Vol. 36, Num. 1/2.

Kernberg, O.F. (1984). *Severe Personality Disorders: Psychotherapeutic Strategies*. New Haven: Yale University Press.

Kernberg, O.F. (2004). *Aggressivity, narcissism, and self-destructiveness in the psychotherapeutic relationship: New developments in the psychopathology and psychotherapy of severe personality disorders*. New Haven, CT: Yale University Press.

Kernberg, O.F. (2006). Identity: Recent findings and clinical implications. *Psychoanalytic Inquiry*, 75:969–1004.

Kernberg, O.F., Yeomans, F.E., Clarkin, J.F., & Levy, K.N. (2008). Transference Focused Psychotherapy: Overview and Update. In *International Journal of Psychoanalysis*, 89:601–620.

Rockland, L.H. (1992). *Supportive Therapy for Borderline Patients: A psychodynamic Approach*. New York: The Guilford Press.

Sandler, J., and A.M. Sandler. (1987). The past unconscious, the present unconscious, and the vicissitudes of guilt. *International Journal of Psychoanalysis* 8:331–341.

Yeomans, F.E., Selzer, M.A., & Clarkin, J.F. (1992). *Treating the Borderline Patient: A Contract-based Approach*. New York, NY: Basic Books.

CHAPTER THREE

The mentalization based approach to psychotherapy for borderline personality disorder

Peter Fonagy, Mary Target and Anthony Bateman

Introduction

Our approach to understanding self-pathology in personality disorder assumes that the capacity to mentalize, that is, the capacity to conceive of mental states as explanations of behaviour in oneself and in others, is a key determinant of self-organisation. Along with contributory capacities of affect regulation and attention control mechanisms, the capacity for mentalization is acquired in the context of early attachment relationships. Disturbances of attachment relationships will therefore disrupt the normal emergence of these key social-cognitive capacities and create profound vulnerabilities in the context of social relationships. Ours is fundamentally a psychoanalytic approach but we have elaborated our model of social development on the basis of empirical observations as well as clinical work.

We define mentalization as a form of mostly preconscious imaginative mental activity, namely, perceiving and interpreting human behaviour in terms of intentional mental states (e.g., needs, desires, feelings, beliefs, goals, purposes, and reasons). Mentalizing is imaginative because we have to imagine what other people might be thinking or feeling; an important indicator of high quality of mentalization is the awareness that we cannot know absolutely what is in someone else's mind. We suggest that a similar kind of imaginative leap is required to understand one's own mental experience, particularly in relation to emotionally charged issues. In order to conceive of others as having a mind, the individual needs a symbolic representational system for mental states and also must be able to selectively activate states of mind in line with particular intentions, which requires attentional control.

The ability to understand the self as a mental agent grows out of interpersonal experience, particularly primary object relationships (Fonagy, 2003). The baby's experience of himself as having a mind or self is not a genetic given; it evolves from infancy through childhood, and its development critically depends upon interaction with more mature minds, assuming these are benign, reflective, and sufficiently attuned. Mentalization involves both a self-reflective and an interpersonal component. It is underpinned by a large number of specific cognitive skills, including an understanding of emotional states, attention and effortful control, and the capacity to make judgments about subjective states as well as thinking explicitly about states of mind—what we might call mentalization proper. In combination, these functions enable the child to distinguish inner from outer reality and internal mental and emotional processes from interpersonal events.

This paper addresses the complex relation of attachment and mentalization. We discuss the role of mentalizing in the development of the agentive sense of self, and consider the contribution of attachment trauma to the development of psychopathology by virtue of undermining mentalizing capacity. We then give an overview of Mentalization Based Therapy (MBT), a fully manualised psychoanalytically oriented treatment for BPD based on this model, and finally summarise evidence for its effectiveness.

The interpersonal interpretive function

The capacity to interpret human behaviour (see Bogdan, 1997) requires the intentional stance: 'treating the object whose behaviour you want to predict as a rational agent with beliefs and desires' (Dennett, 1987 p. 15). We label the capacity to adopt this stance the *interpersonal interpretive function* (IIF), an evolutionary-developmental function of attachment. The IIF is a cluster of mental functions for processing and interpreting new interpersonal experiences that includes mentalization and the cluster of psychological processes on which effective mentalizing depends (Fonagy, 2003). Four emotional processing and control mechanisms contribute to the developmental unfolding of interpretive function: labelling and understanding affect, arousal regulation, effortful control, and specific mentalizing capacities (Fonagy and Target, 2002).

Since the mind needs to adapt to ever more challenging competitive conditions, the capacity for mentalization cannot be fixed by genetics or constitution. The social brain must continuously reach higher and higher levels of sophistication to stay on top. Evolution has charged attachment relationships with ensuring the full development of the social brain. The capacity for mentalization, along with many other social-cognitive capacities, evolves out of the experience of social interaction with caregivers. Increased sophistication in social cognition evolved hand in hand with apparently unrelated aspects of development, such as increased helplessness in infancy, a prolongation of childhood, and the emergence of intensive parenting.

We have proposed a mechanism for this process rooted in dialectic models of self-development (Cavell, 1991; Davidson, 1983). Our approach explicitly rejects the classical Cartesian assumption that mental states are apprehended by introspection; on the contrary, mental states are discovered through contingent mirroring interactions with the caregiver (Gergely and Watson, 1999). Therefore early disruption of affectional bonds will not only set up maladaptive attachment patterns (e.g. Waters et al., 2000) but will also undermine a range of capacities vital to normal social development. Understanding minds is difficult if one does not know what it is like to be understood as a person with a mind. Our argument may seem to place an excessive burden upon the caregiver-infant relationship, but we must remember that placing the social development of a human infant in the hands of one adult is a recent phenomenon compared to the previous average of four relatives who had a genetic stake in the child's survival (Hrdy, 2000). Recent neurobiological evidence discussed next buttresses the ecological view of attachment relationships as pivotally linked to mentalizing capacities.

The neurobiology of attachment

The neurobiology of attachment is now fairly well understood. It is linked to the mesocorticolimbic dopaminergic reward circuit, which also plays a key role in mediating the process of physical (as well as emotional) addiction. It is highly unlikely that nature created a brain system specifically to subserve cocaine and alcohol abuse. It is more likely that addictions are the accidental by-product of the activation of a biological system underpinning the crucial evolutionary function of attachment (Insel, 1997; MacLean, 1990; Panksepp, 1998). Attachment can be thought of as an 'addictive disorder' (Insel, 2003). Changes in attachment behaviour, such as falling in love, which are stimulated by social/sexual activity, entail the activation of an oxytocin and vasopressin sensitive circuit within the anterior hypothalamus (MPOA) linked to the VTA and the nucleus accumbens (Insel, 2003). fMRI studies indicate specific activation of the same pathways in the brain of somebody seeing their own baby or partner, compared to another familiar baby or other people's partners (Nitschke et al., 2004).

In two separate imaging studies, Bartels and Zeki (Bartels and Zeki, 2000, 2004), reported that the activation of areas mediating maternal and/or romantic attachments appeared simultaneously to suppress brain activity in several brain regions in two systems both responsible for different aspects of cognitive regulation and control but also including those associated with making social judgements and mentalizing. Bartels and Zeki (2004) suggest grouping these reciprocally active areas into two functional regions. The first (let us refer to it as system A) includes the middle prefrontal, inferior parietal and middle temporal cortices mainly in the right hemisphere, as well as the posterior cingulate cortex. These areas are specialised for attention and long-term memory (Cabeza and Nyberg, 2000), and have variable involvement in both positive (Maddock, 1999) and negative (Mayberg et al., 1999) emotions. Their role in both cognition and emotion suggests that these areas may be specifically responsible for integrating emotion and cognition (e.g. emotional encoding of episodic memories). Further, these areas may play a role in recalling emotion-related material and generating emotion-related imagery that may be relevant in relation to understanding the typology of attachment (Maddock, 1999).

The second set of areas deactivated by the activation of the attachment system includes the temporal poles, parietotemporal junction, amygdala, and mesial prefrontal cortex (let us call this system B). Activation of these areas is consistently linked to negative affect, judgements of social trustworthiness, moral judgements, 'theory of mind' tasks, attention to one's own emotions, and in particular, they constitute the primary neural network underlying our ability to identify mental states (both thoughts and feelings) in other people (Frith and Frith, 2003; Gallagher and Frith, 2003). Mentalization pertains not just to states of mind in others but also reflecting on one's own emotional and belief states and consequently such tasks appear to be associated with activation in the same neural system (Gusnard et al., 2001). Making judgements that involve mental states has been shown to be associated with activation of the same system. Thus intuitive judgements of moral appropriateness (rather than moral reasoning) are linked (Greene and Haidt, 2002) as is assessment of social trustworthiness based on facial expressions (Winston et al., 2002).

This suggests that being in an emotionally attached state inhibits aspects of social cognition, including mentalizing and the capacity accurately to see the attachment figure as a person. (Currently we are working to perform an independent replication of this study). The activation of the attachment system, mediated by dopaminergic structures of the reward system in the presence of oxytocin and vasopressin, inhibits neural systems that underpin the generation of negative affect. This is to be expected since a key function of the attachment system is to moderate negative emotions in the infant and presumably to continue to do so in later in development (Sroufe, 1996). Equally consistent with expectations, is the suppression of social and moral judgements (probably mediated by the second of the two regulatory systems) associated with the activation of the attachment system. Judgements of social trustworthiness and morality serve to distance us from others but become less relevant and may indeed interfere with our relationships with those to whom we are strongly attached (Belsky, 1999a; Simpson, 1999).

The configuration described by Bartels and Zeki has critical developmental implications. Attachment has been selected by evolution as the principal 'training ground' for the acquisition of mentalization because attachment is a marker for shared genetic material, reciprocal relationships and altruism. It is a non-competitive relationship in which the aim is not to outsmart and thus learning about minds can be safely practiced. Missing out on early attachment experience (as for the Romanian orphans) creates a long term vulnerability from which the child may never recover— the capacity for mentalization is never fully established, leaving the child vulnerable to later trauma and unable to cope fully with attachment relationships (e.g. Rutter and O'Connor, 2004). More importantly, trauma, by activating attachment will often decouple the capacity for mentalization. This of course is further exacerbated when the trauma is attachment trauma.

Implications of attachment-mentalization reciprocity

The apparently reciprocal relationship of mentalization and attachment may at first appear to contradict our earlier assumption that mentalization and secure attachment are positively correlated. Further scrutiny suggests greater complexity but no inconsistency. It is possible, taking an evolutionary perspective, that the parent's capacity to mentalize the infant or child serves to reduce the child's experienced need to monitor the parent for trustworthiness. This relaxation of the interpersonal barrier facilitates the emergence of a strong attachment bond. While at first sight the precocious emergence of theory of mind in children who were securely attached in infancy (e.g. Meins, 1997) may seem inconsistent with the inverse relationship between attachment and mentalization, it is to be expected that in individuals whose attachment is secure, there are likely to be fewer calls over time for the activation of the attachment system. This in turn, given the inhibitory effect of the activation of the attachment system on mentalization related brain activity, might account for the precocious development of mentalization.

The capacity for mentalization in the context of attachment is likely to be in certain respects independent of the capacity to mentalize about interpersonal experiences outside the attachment context (Fonagy and Target, 1997). Our specific measure of mentalisation in the attachment context, reflective function (Fonagy et al., 1998) is predictive of behavioural outcomes that other measures of mentalization do not correlate with. For example, in a quasi-longitudinal study based on interviews and chart reviews with young adults some of whom had suffered trauma, we found that the impact of trauma on mentalization in attachment contexts mediated outcome measured as the quality of adult romantic relationships but mentalization measured independently of the attachment context using the Reading the Mind in the Eyes test did not (Fonagy et al., 2003a). It seems that measuring mentalization in the context of attachment might measure a unique aspect of social behaviour.

The key consideration is probably that securely attached children do not need to activate their attachment system as often and have greater opportunity to 'practice' mentalization in the context of the child-caregiver relationship. Belsky's (1999b) evolutionary model of attachment classification is helpful here. When resources are scarce and insecure attachment strategies are possibly most adaptive, children probably need to monitor the unpredictable caregivers' mental states quite carefully, are forced to find alternative social contexts to acquire social cognitive capacities, and thus they deprive themselves of some developmental learning opportunities of understanding minds in abstract ways independent of physical reality.

The development of an agentive self: The social acquisition of social cognition

An overview of the model of contingent mirroring

The evolutionary neurobiological speculations above imply that children's care giving environments play a key role in their development as social beings. How are we to conceive of the actions of these environmental influences? Our model relies on the child's inbuilt capacity to detect aspects of his world that react contingently to his own actions. In his first months the child begins to understand that he is a physical agent whose actions can bring about changes in bodies with which he has immediate physical contact (Leslie, 1994). Developing alongside this is the child's understanding of himself as a social agent. Through interactions with the caregiver (from birth) the baby learns that his behaviour affects his caregiver's behaviour and emotions (Neisser, 1988). Both these early forms of self-awareness probably evolve through the workings of an innate contingency detection mechanism that enables the infant to analyse the probability of causal links between his actions and stimulus events (Watson, 1994). The child's initial preoccupation with perfectly response-contingent stimulation (provided by the proprioceptive sensory feedback that the self's actions always generate) allows him to differentiate his agentive self as a separate entity in the environment and to construct a primary representation of the bodily self.

> At about 3–4 months, infants switch from preferring perfect contingency to preferring high-but-imperfect contingencies thereafter (Bahrick and Watson, 1985)—the level of contingency that is characteristic of an attuned caregiver's empathic mirroring responses to the infant's displays of emotion. Repeated experience of such affect-reflective caregiver reactions is essential for the infant to begin to be able to differentiate his/her internal self-states: a process we termed 'social biofeedback' (Gergely and Watson, 1996). A congenial and secure attachment relationship can vitally contribute to the emergence of early mentalization capacities allowing the infant to 'discover' or 'find' his/her psychological self in the social world (Gergely, 2001). The discovery of the representational or psychological self (what we may think of as full mentalization) is probably based in the same mechanism coming to understand and regulate emotion and be securely attached.

Let us take the development of an understanding of affects as an example. We assume that at first infants are not introspectively aware of different emotion states. Rather, their representations of these emotions are primarily based on stimuli received from the external world. Babies learn to differentiate the internal patterns of physiological and visceral stimulation that accompany different emotions by observing their caregivers' facial or vocal mirroring responses to these (e.g. Legerstee and Varghese, 2001; e.g. Mitchell, 1993). Firstly, the baby comes to associate his control over the parents' mirroring displays with the resulting improvement in his emotional state, leading, eventually, to an experience of the self as a regulating agent. Secondly, the establishment of a second order representation of affect states creates the basis for affect regulation and impulse control: affects can be manipulated and discharged internally as well as through action, they can also be experienced as something recognizable and hence shared. If the parent's affect expressions are not contingent on the infant's affect this will undermine the appropriate labelling of internal states which may, in turn, remain confusing, experienced as unsymbolized and hard to regulate.

If the capacity to understand and regulate emotion is to develop two conditions need to be met: (a) reasonable congruency of mirroring whereby the caregiver accurately matches the infant's mental state and (b) 'markedness' of the mirroring, whereby the caregiver is able to express an affect while indicating that she is not expressing her own feelings (Gergely and Watson, 1999). Consequently two difficulties may arise: (a) in the case of incongruent mirroring the infant's representation of internal state will not correspond to a constitutional self state (nothing real) and a predisposition to a narcissistic structure might be established perhaps analogous to Winnicott's notion of 'false-self' (Winnicott, 1965) and (b) in cases of un-marked mirroring the caregiver's expression may be seen as externalisation of the infant's experience and a predisposition to experiencing emotion through other people (as in a borderline personality structure) might be established (Fonagy et al., 2002). An expression congruent with the baby's state, but lacking markedness, may overwhelm the infant. It is felt to be the parent's own real emotion, making the child's experience seem contagious and escalating rather than regulating his state.

The secure caregiver soothes by combining mirroring with a display that is incompatible with the child's feelings (thus implying contact with distance and coping). This formulation of sensitivity has much in common with Bion's (1962) notion of the role of the mother's capacity to mentally "contain" the affect state that feels intolerable to the baby, and respond in a manner that acknowledges the child's mental state, yet serves to modulate unmanageable feelings (see below). Well-regulated affect in the infant parent couple is thought to be internalized by the child to form the bases of a secure attachment bond and internal working model (Sroufe, 1996). Ratings of the quality of reflective function of each parent during pregnancy were found independently to predict the child's later security of attachment in the London Parent-Child Project (Fonagy et al., 1992). However, this finding is somewhat limited since only the AAI RF measure was examined in relation to infant attachment (Fonagy et al., 1991; Fonagy et al., 1994). Thus the parents' capacity to mentalize was measured in relation to their own childhood and their capacity to do likewise with their child had been assumed rather than observed.

The stages of acquiring mentalization (a Theory of Mind)

The emergence of mentalizing function follows a well-researched developmental line that identifies 'fixation points':

(a) During the second half of the first year of life, the child begins to construct causal relations that connect actions to their agents on the one hand and to the world on the other. Infants around 9 months begin to look at actions in terms of the actor's underlying intentions (Baldwin et al., 2001). This is the beginning of their understanding of themselves as teleological agents who can choose the most efficient way to bring about a goal from a range of alternatives (Csibra and Gergely, 1998). At this stage agency is understood in terms of purely physical actions and constraints. Infants expect actors to behave rationally, given physically apparent goal states and the physical constraints of the situation that are already understood by the infant (Gergely and Csibra, 2003). There is no implication here that the infant has an idea about the mental state of the object. He/she is simply judging rational behaviour in terms of the physical constraints that prevail and that which is obvious in terms of the physical end state which the object has reached. We have suggested a connection between the focus on understanding actions in terms of their physical as opposed to mental outcomes (a teleological stance) and the mode of experience of agency that we often see in the self-destructive acts of individuals with borderline personality disorder (BPD) (Fonagy et al., 2000). Thus slight changes in the physical world can trigger elaborate conclusions concerning states of mind. Patients frequently cannot accept anything other than a modification in the realm of the physical as a true index of the intentions of the other.

(b) During the second year, children develop a mentalistic understanding of agency. They understand that they and others are intentional agents whose actions are caused by prior states of mind such as desires (Wellman and Phillips, 2000) and that their actions can bring about changes in minds as well as bodies (e.g. by pointing Corkum and Moore, 1995). Shared imaginative play is enjoyable and exciting for toddlers and may be the basis for the development of collaborative, co-operative skills (Brown et al., 1996). Fifteen months old children can distinguish between an action's intended goal and its accidental consequences (Meltzoff, 1995). At this stage the capacity for emotion regulation comes to reflect the prior and current relationship with the primary caregiver (Calkins and Johnson, 1998). Most importantly, children begin to acquire an internal state language and the ability to reason non-egocentrically about feelings and desires in others (Repacholi and Gopnik, 1997). Paradoxically, this becomes evident not only through the increase in joint goal directed activity but also through teasing and provocation of younger siblings (Dunn, 1988). However, functional awareness of minds does not yet enable the child to represent mental states independent of physical reality and therefore the distinction between internal and external, appearance and reality is not yet fully achieved (Flavell and Miller, 1998), making internal reality sometimes far more compelling and at other times inconsequential relative to an awareness of the physical world. We have referred to these states as psychic equivalence and pretend modes respectively (see below).

(c) Around three to four years of age, understanding of agency in terms of mental causation begins to include the representation of epistemic mind states (beliefs). The young child thus understands himself as a representational agent, he knows that people do not always feel what they appear to feel, they show emotional reactions to an event that are influenced by their current mood or even by earlier emotional experiences which were linked to similar events (Flavell and Miller, 1998). The preschool child's mental states are representational in nature (Wellman, 1990). This transforms their social interactions so their understanding of emotions comes to be associated with empathic behaviour (Zahn-Waxler et al., 1992) and more positive peer relations (Dunn and Cutting, 1999). Most children come to understand that human behaviour can be influenced by transient mental states (such as thoughts and feelings) as well as by stable characteristics (such as personality or capability) and this creates the basis for a structure to underpin an emerging self-concept (Flavell, 1999). They also come to attribute mistaken beliefs to themselves and to others, which enriches their repertoire of social interaction with tricks, jokes and deception (Sodian and Frith, 1992; Sodian et al., 1992). A meta-analytic review of in excess of 500 tests showed that by and large children younger than three fail the false-belief task and as the child's age increases they are increasingly likely to pass (Wellman et al., 2001), suggesting that mentalizing abilities take a quantum leap forward around age four. The early acquisition of false belief is associated with more elaborate capacity to pretend play (Taylor and Carlson, 1997), greater connectedness in conversation (Slomkowski and Dunn, 1996) and teacher rating of social competence (Lalonde and Chandler, 1995). Notably, also at this time the child shifts from a preference for playing with adults to playing with peers (Dunn, 1994). We understand this shift as bringing to a close the time when mentalization was acquired through the agency of an adult mind and opening a lifelong phase of seeking to enhance the capacity to understand self and others in mental state terms through linking with individuals who share one's interest and humour.

(d) In the sixth year, we see related advances such as the child's ability to relate memories of his intentional activities and experiences into a coherent causal-temporal organisation, leading to the establishment of the temporally extended self (Povinelli and Eddy, 1995). Full experience of agency in social interaction can emerge only when actions of the self and other can be understood as initiated and guided by assumptions concerning the emotions, desires and beliefs of both. Further theory of mind skills that become part of the child's repertoire at this stage include second order theory of mind (the capacity to understand mistaken beliefs about beliefs), mixed emotions (e.g. understanding being in a conflict), the way expectations or biases might influence the interpretation of ambiguous events, and the capacity for subtle forms of social deceptions (e.g. white lies). As these skills are acquired the need for physical violence begins to decline (Tremblay, 2000; Tremblay et al., 1999) and relational aggression increases (Cote et al., 2002; Nagin and Tremblay, 2001).

Relationship influences on the acquisition of mentalization

Our claim that attachment relationships are vital to the normal acquisition of mentalization challenges nativist assumptions. The nativistic position assumes that children's social environments can trigger but cannot determine the development of theory of mind (Baron-Cohen, 1995; Leslie, 1994). There is some evidence that the timetable of theory of mind development is fixed and universal (Avis and Harris, 1991). However, the bulk of the evidence is inconsistent with the assumption of a universal timetable. More recent studies find ample evidence for substantial cultural differences, not just in the rate of emergence of theory of mind skills but also the order of their emergence (Wellman et al., 2001). Many findings suggest that the nature of family interactions, the quality of parental control (e.g. Vinden, 2001), parental discourse about emotions (e.g. Meins et al., 2002), the depth of parental discussion involving affect (Dunn et al., 1991) and parents' beliefs about parenting (e.g. Ruffman et al., 1999) are all strongly associated with the child's acquisition of mentalization. The role of family members in this developmental achievement is further highlighted by the finding that the presence of older siblings in the family appears to improve the child's performance on a range of false-belief tasks (e.g. Ruffman et al., 1998). In sum, the ability to give meaning to psychological experiences evolves as a result of our discovery of the mind behind others' actions, which develops optimally in a relatively safe and secure social context.

Much that is known about correlates and predictors of early ToM development is consistent with the assumption that the attachment relationship plays an important role in the acquisition of mentalization. For example, family-wide talk about negative emotions, often precipitated by the child's own emotions, predicts later success on tests of emotion understanding (Dunn and Brown, 2001). The capacity to reflect on intense emotion is a marker of secure attachment (Sroufe, 1996). Similar considerations may explain the finding that the number of references to thoughts and beliefs and the relationship specificity of children's real-life accounts of negative emotions correlate with early ToM acquisition (false belief performance) (Hughes and Dunn, 2002). Similarly, parents whose disciplinary strategies focus on mental states (e.g. a victim's feelings, or the non-intentional nature of transgressions) have children who succeed in ToM tasks earlier (e.g. Charman et al., 2002)

Relationship influences on the development of mentalization are probably limited and specific rather than broad and unqualified. Three key limitations to simplistic linking of mentalization and positive relationship quality should be kept in mind (Hughes and

Leekham, 2004): (1) The possession of the capacity to mentalize is neither a guarantee that it will be used to serve pro-social ends, nor a guarantee of protection from malign interpersonal influence. The acquisition of the capacity to mentalize may, for example, open the door to more malicious teasing (e.g. Dunn, 1988), increase the individual's sensitivity to relational aggression (Cutting and Dunn, 2002), or even mean that they take a lead in bullying others (Sutton et al., 1999). (2) While, as we have seen, broadly, positive emotion promotes the emergence of mentalization (Dunn, 1999), negative emotion can be an equally powerful facilitator. For example, children engage in deception that is indicative of mentalizing in emotionally charged conflict situations (Newton et al., 2000). (3) The impact of relationships on the development of mentalization is probably highly complex involving numerous aspects of relational influences (e.g. quality of language of mental states, quality of emotional interaction, themes of discourse, amount of shared pretend play, negotiations of conflict, humour in the family, discourse with peers, etc) probably affecting several components of the mentalizing function (joint attention, understanding of affect states, capacity for emotion regulation, language competence, competence with specific grammatical structures such as sentential complements, etc.) (Hughes and Leekham, 2004).

Subjectivity before mentalization

How does the child experience subjectivity before he recognises that internal states are representations of reality? In describing the normal development of mentalizing in the child of two to five years (Fonagy and Target, 1996; Target and Fonagy, 1996), we suggest that there is a transition from a split mode of experience to mentalization. We hypothesize that the very young child equates the internal world with the external. What exists in the mind must exist out there and what exists out there must also exist in the mind. At this stage there is no room yet for alternative perspectives. "How I see it is how it is". The toddler's or young pre-school child's insistence that "there is a Tiger under the bed" is not allayed by parental reassurance. This 'psychic equivalence', as a mode of experiencing the internal world, can cause intense distress, since the experience of a fantasy as potentially real can be terrifying. The acquisition of a sense of pretend in relation to mental states is therefore essential. While playing, the child knows that internal experience may not reflect external reality (e.g. Bartsch and Wellman, 1989; Dias and Harris, 1990), but then the internal state is thought to have no implications for the outside world ("pretend mode").

Normally at around four years old, the child integrates these modes to arrive at mentalization, or reflective mode, in which mental states can be experienced as representations. Inner and outer reality can then be seen as linked, yet differing in important ways, and no longer have to be either equated or dissociated from each other (Gopnik, 1993). The child discovers that 'seeing-leads-to-knowing'; if you have seen something in a box, you know something about what's in the box (Pratt and Bryant, 1990). They can begin to work out from gaze direction what a person is thinking about, thus making use of the eyes of another person to make a mentalistic interpretation (Baron-Cohen and Cross, 1992). There are, however, circumstances under which pre-mentalistic forms of subjectivity re-emerge to dominate social cognition years after the acquisition of full mentalization. We shall consider these in section 5.

Mentalization normally comes about through the child's experience of his mental states being reflected on, prototypically through secure play with a parent or older child, which facilitates integration of the pretend and psychic equivalence modes. This interpersonal process is perhaps an elaboration of the complex mirroring the parent offered earlier. In playfulness, the caregiver gives the child's ideas and feelings (when he is "only pretending") a link with reality, by indicating an alternative perspective outside the child's mind. The parent or older child also shows that reality may be distorted by acting upon it in playful ways, and through this playfulness a pretend but real mental experience may be introduced.

If the child's capacity to perceive mental states in himself and others depends on his observation of the mental world of his caregiver, clearly children require a number of adults with an interest in their mental state, who can be trusted (i.e. with whom an attachment bond exists), to support the development of their subjectivity from a pre-mentalizing to a fully mentalizing mode. In this regard, in past initiatives, perhaps we have placed too much emphasis on parents (particularly mothers). It follows from the evolutionary model presented in section 2 and here that the child's brain is experience

expectant from a range of benign adults willing to take the peda-
gogic stance towards their subjectivity. Thus, teachers, neighbours,
older siblings as well as parental figures could play important roles
in optimizing the child's capacity for mentalization. Children can
perceive and conceive of their mental states to the extent that the
behaviour of those around them has implied that they have them.
This can happen through an almost unlimited set of methods rang-
ing from shared pretend playing with the child (empirically shown
to be associated with early mentalization), and many ordinary interactions (such as conversations and peer interaction) will also involve
shared thinking about an idea.

Disorganized attachment and the unmentalized (alien) self

In children whose attachment is disorganized mentalization may
be evident, but it does not play the positive role in self-organization
that it does in securely or even in insecurely attached children. The
child with disorganised attachment is forced to look not for the
representation of his own mental states in the mind of the other,
but the mental states of that other which threaten to undermine his
agentive sense of self. These mental states can create an alien presence
within his self-representation, so unbearable that his attachment
behaviour becomes focused on re-externalising these parts of the
self onto attachment figures, rather than on the internalization of a
capacity for containment of affects and other intentional states.

Disorganized infants, even if interpersonally perceptive, fail to
integrate this emotional awareness with their self-organization. There
may be a number of linked reasons for this: a) the child needs to use
disproportionate resources to understand the parent's behaviour,
at the expense of reflecting on self-states; b) the caregiver of the
disorganized infant is likely to be less contingent in responding to
the infant's self-state, and further to show systematic biases in her
perception and reflection of his state; c) the mental state of the caregiver
of the disorganized infant may evoke intense anxiety through
either frightening or fearful behaviour towards the child, including
inexplicable fear of the child himself. These factors combine, perhaps,
to make children whose attachment system is disorganized become
keen readers of the caregiver's mind under certain circumstances,
but (we suggest) poor readers of their own mental states.

Trauma related loss of the capacity to conceive of mental states

Adults with a history of childhood attachment trauma often seem unable to understand how others think or feel. We have hypothesized that childhood maltreatment undermines mentalization. When combined with the enfeebled affect representation, poor affect control systems and disorganised self structure that can result from a deeply insecure early environment, trauma has profound effects: (a) It inhibits playfulness which is essential for the adequate unfolding of the interpersonal interpretive function (Dunn et al., 2000); (b) it interferes directly with affect regulation and attentional control systems (Arntz et al., 2000); (c) most importantly, in vulnerable individuals, it can lead to an unconsciously motivated failure of mentalization. This failure is a defensive adaptive manoeuvre: the child seeks to protect himself from the frankly malevolent and dangerous states of mind of the abuser by decoupling his capacity to conceive of mental states, at least in attachment contexts (Fonagy, 1991). (d) We believe that adult social functioning is impaired by childhood and adolescent adversity to the extent that adversity causes a breakdown of attachment related mentalization (Fonagy et al., 2003a). There is considerable evidence that maltreated children have specific mentalization deficits and that individuals with BPD are poor at mentalization following severe experiences of maltreatment (Fonagy et al., 1996). Children cannot learn words for feelings (Beeghly and Cicchetti, 1994), and adults have more difficulty recognising facial expressions, the more severe their childhood maltreatment (Fonagy et al., 2003a). What is the clinical picture like when trauma brings about a partial and temporary collapse of mentalization? We observed an apparent lack of imagination about the mental world of others, a naiveté or cluelessness about what others think or feel that can verge on confusion, and a corresponding absence of insight into the way that the traumatized person's own mind works.

Many maltreated children grow up into adequately functioning adults. While maltreatment places children at increased risk for developing psychopathology, only a small proportion will prospectively need mental health services (Widom, 1999). It is possible that early maltreatment reduces the individual's opportunity fully to develop mentalizing skills, leaving them with inadequate capacities to identify and avoid risks for further interpersonal trauma. In dysfunctional attachment contexts, particularly when children are victims of abuse, they may learn to interpret parental initiation of communicative attention-directing behaviours as a cue that potentially harmful interactions are likely to follow. In consequence, they may defensively inhibit the mentalistic interpretation of such cues; this may finally lead to the defensive disruption of their own metacognitive monitoring procedures in all subsequent intimate relationships (Fonagy et al., 2003b).

The equation of inner and outer

The collapse of mentalization in the face of trauma entails a loss of awareness of the relationship between internal and external reality (Fonagy and Target, 2000). Modes of representing the internal world re-emerge that developmentally precede an awareness that thoughts, feelings and wishes are part of the mind. The 2–3 year old as we saw, not yet experiencing his mind as truly representational, assumes in the mode of psychic equivalence that what he thinks also exists in the physical world. Post-traumatic subjective experience (the flashback) is similarly compelling, resistant to argument and feels dangerous until it becomes mentalized. Often survivors of trauma simply refuse to think about their experience because thinking about it means reliving it. Aspects of the notion of psychic equivalence evidently overlap with descriptions of paranoid-schizoid forms of thinking particularly as formulated by Wilfred Bion in the 'Elements of Psychoanalysis' (Bion, 1963), and symbolic equation as formulated by Hanna Segal (1957).

Separation from reality

As we saw, the pretend mode is a developmental complement to psychic equivalence. Not yet able to conceive of internal experience as mental, the child's fantasies are dramatically divided off from the external world. Small children cannot simultaneously pretend (even though they know it is not real) and engage with normal reality; asking them if their pretend gun is a gun or a stick spoils the game. Following trauma and the constriction of mentalization we see the intrusion of the pretend mode, particularly in dissociative experiences. In dissociated thinking, nothing can be linked to anything—the principle of the 'pretend mode', in which fantasy is cut off from the real world, is extended so that nothing has implications (Fonagy and Target, 2000). Patients report 'blanking out', 'clamming up' or remembering their traumatic experiences only in dreams. The most characteristic feature of traumatization is the oscillation between psychic equivalence and pretend modes of experiencing the internal world.

'I believe it when I see it'

A third pre-mentalistic aspect of psychic reality is the re-emergence of a teleological mode of thought. This mode of understanding the world antedates even language. Infants as young as 9 months are able to attribute goals to people and to objects that seem to behave purposefully, but these goals are not yet truly mental, they are tied to what is observable. The return of this teleological mode of thought is perhaps the most painful aspect of a subjectivity stripped of mentalization.

Following trauma, verbal reassurance means little. Interacting with others at a mental level has been replaced by attempts at altering thoughts and feelings through action. Trauma, certainly physical and sexual abuse, is by definition teleological. It is hardly surprising that the victim feels that the mind of another can only be altered in this same mode, through a physical act, threat or seduction. Following trauma we all need physical assurances of security.

The impact of attachment trauma on mentalization: The hyperactivation of attachment

Attachment is normally the ideal 'training ground' for the development of mentalization because it is safe and non-competitive. This biological configuration, which is so adaptive in the context of normal development, becomes immensely destructive in the presence of attachment trauma. Attachment trauma hyperactivates the attachment system because the person to whom the child looks for reassurance and protection is the one causing fear. The devastating psychic impact of attachment trauma is the combined result of the inhibition of mentalization by attachment and the hyperactivation of the attachment system by trauma. This context demands extraordinary mentalizing capacities from the child, yet the hyperactivation of the attachment system will have inhibited whatever limited capacity he has.

The coincidence of trauma and attachment creates a biological vicious cycle. Trauma normally leads a child to try to get close to the attachment figure. Where the child depends on an attachment figure who maltreats them, there is a risk of an escalating sequence of further maltreatment, increased distress and an ever-greater inner need for the attachment figure. The inhibition of mentalization in a traumatising, hyperactivated attachment relationship is always likely to lead to a prementalistic psychic reality, largely split into psychic equivalence and pretend modes. Because the memory of the trauma feels currently real there is a constant danger of re-traumatisation from inside. The traumatised child often begins to fear his own mind. The inhibition of mentalization is also clearly an intrapsychic adaptation to traumatic attachment. The frankly malevolent mental state of the abuser terrifies the helpless child. The parents' abuse undermines the child's capacity to mentalize, because it is no longer safe for the child, for example, to think about wishing, if this implies recognising his parent's wish to harm him. Because he cannot use the model of the other to understand himself, diffusion of identity and dissociation often follows.

The impact of attachment trauma on mentalization: The biology of being frazzled

The impact of trauma on mentalization is intermittent. As above, sometimes mentalization disappears because an attachment relationship intensifies. At other times, being stressed (for example touching on a sensitive issue) can trigger what feel like wild, unjustified reactions. Six years ago, in a hallmark paper entitled "The biology of being frazzled", Amy Arnsten (1998) explained why (see also Arnsten et al., 1999; Mayes, 2000). At the risk of simplifying highly complex pioneering neuroscientific work, Arnsten's Dual Arousal Systems Model delineates two complementary, independent arousal systems: the prefrontal and posterior cortical and subcortical systems. The system that activates frontal and pre-frontal regions inhibits the second arousal system that normally 'kicks in' only at quite high levels of arousal, when pre-frontal activity goes "offline" and posterior cortical and subcortical functions (e.g. more automatic or motor functions) take over.

The switch-point between the two arousal systems may be shifted by childhood trauma. Undoubtedly, as mentalization is located in the prefrontal cortex, this accounts for some of the inhibition of mentalization in individuals with attachment trauma, in response to increases in arousal that would not be high enough to inhibit mentalization in most of us. Anticipating some of the clinical implications of our thinking, in the light of this phenomenon it is important to monitor the traumatised patient's readiness to hear comments about thoughts and feelings. As arousal increases, in part in response to interpretative work, traumatised patients cannot process talk about their minds. Interpretations of the transference at these times, however accurate they might be, are likely to be way beyond the capacity of the patient to hear. The clinical priority has to be work to reduce arousal so that the patient can again think of other perspectives (mentalize). Mentalization-based treatment—practice.

The consequences for psychodynamic therapeutic technique of this reframing of BPD as a failure to develop a robust self-structure are considerable particularly as many practitioners may currently practice in a way that assumes cognitive and emotional capacities in patients that they simply don't have. In BPD mentalization is enfeebled and almost absent in moments of arousal and at these times actions represent the maladaptive restoration of a rudimentary mentalizing function chiefly aimed at creating the illusion of self coherence. Actions become a desperate attempt to protect the fragile self against the onslaught of overwhelming threat of disintegration or persecution from within, often quite innocently triggered by an other (thus the reaction may often seem disproportionate to the provocation). The experience of humiliation or threat, which the individual tries to contain within the alien part of the self, comes to represent an existential threat and is therefore abruptly externalised. If it is not, suicide may become the only solution in an attempt to save the self. But if the alien self is placed outside and perceived as part of the other, it is disowned and, if it cannot be controlled via a coercive interaction, may be seen as possible to destroy once and for all through verbal attacks or violence. So the other is essential not just to create the illusion of coherence but also to be there to be destroyed. This re-equilibrates the individual. In this sense attacks on the other are a gesture of hope, a wish for a new beginning, a desperate attempt to restore a relationship, even if in reality they may have a tragic end. This is why borderline patients require rather than enjoy relationships. Relationships are necessary to stabilise the self-structure but are also the source of greatest vulnerability because in the absence of the other, when the relationships break down, or if the other shows independence, the alien self returns to wreak havoc (persecute from within) and to destabilise the self-structure. Vulnerability is greatest in the context of attachment relationships because the activation of attachment relationships representations (Internal Working Models, Bowlby, 1973) are most likely to have been traumatic and thus to be least imbued with mental state representations.

Core techniques

The focus in MBT is on stabilising the sense of self and we have defined some core underpinning techniques to be used in the context of group and individual therapy. In order to implement these effectively greater activity on the part of the therapist is required with more collaboration and openness than is implied in the classical analytic stance. The 'blank analytic screen' has no role in the treatment of these patients. In psychodynamic treatment of borderline patients, the therapist has to become what the patient needs him to be, the vehicle for the alien self, the carrier of alternative but not destabilising perspectives. And yet to become the alien self is to be lost to the patient as a provider of different perspectives and therefore of no help to him. The therapist must aim to achieve a state of equipoise between the two—allowing himself to do as required yet trying to retain in his mind as clear and coherent an image of his own state of mind along side that of the patients as is possible to achieve. This is what we have called the mentalizing stance of the therapist (Bateman and Fonagy, 2003) .

Enhancing mentalization

A therapist needs to maintain a mentalizing stance in order to help a patient develop a capacity to mentalize. Self-directed mentalistic questions are a useful way of ensuring that a focus on mentalizing is maintained. Why is the patient saying this now? Why is the patient behaving like this? What might I have done that explains the patient's state? Why am I feeling as I do now? What has happened recently in the therapy or in our relationship that may justify the current state? These are typical questions that the therapist will be asking himself within the mentalizing therapeutic stance and is perfectly at liberty to ask them out loud in a spirit of enquiry. This approach pervades the entire treatment setting. So, in group therapy techniques focus on encouraging patients to consider the mental states and motives of other members as well as their own—'Why do you think that she is feeling as she does'.

Crucially, the therapist is not looking for complex 'unconscious' reasons, rather the answers that common sense or folk psychology would suggest to most reasonable people. Folk psychology is the natural and intuitive understanding of human action on the basis of mental states that we employ ubiquitously in our interactions with each other as well as in our efforts to understand ourselves. Folk psychology includes the various mental concepts we naturally employ, such as desires, feelings, goals, beliefs. But folk psychology is much more than that; it encompasses the narrative structures in which these everyday psychological concepts are embedded, namely, the sequential stories that compose an autobiographical sense of self. In this broad sense, as Bruner (1990) aptly put it, folk psychology "is a culture's account of what makes human beings tick" (p. 13). We believe that even as professional clinicians, we rely far more on folk psychology than scientific psychology in our interactions with patients (Allen and Fonagy, 2002).

Focusing the therapist's understanding of his or her interactions with the patient on the patient's mental state will allow the therapist to link external events, however small, to powerful internal states which are otherwise experienced by the patient as inexplicable, uncontrollable and meaningless. A focus on psychological process and the 'here and now' rather than on mental content in the present and past is implicit in this approach. An important indicator of underlying process and the 'here-and now' is the manifest affect which is specifically targeted, identified, and explored within an interpersonal context in MBT. The challenge for the professional working with the patient is to maintain a mentalizing therapeutic stance in the context of countertransference responses that may provoke the therapist to react rather than to think. Understanding within an interpersonal context why the situation arose in the first place, why such an externalisation became necessary, is the likely immediate solution to this challenge.

Interpretation and bearing in mind the deficits

Bearing in mind the limited processing capacities of borderline patients in relation to attachment issues, patients cannot be assumed to have a capacity to work with conflict, to express feelings through verbalisation, to use metaphor, to resist actions, and to reflect on content, all of which form part of standard psychoanalytic process. These attributes depend on a stable self-structure and ability to form secondary (symbolic) and perhaps tertiary representations (e.g. your feelings about my thoughts about your wishes) which buffer feelings, explain ideas, and give context and meaning to interpersonal and intrapsychic process. Borderline patients' enfeebled mentalizing capacity and emergence of psychic equivalence means that feelings, fantasies, thoughts, and desires are experienced with considerable force because they cannot be symbolised, be held in a state of uncertainty, and given secondary representation with meaning. Under these circumstances the use of metaphor and the interpretation of conflict is more likely to induce bewilderment and incomprehension than to heighten the underlying meaning of the discourse and so the use of these techniques is minimised in MBT.

Yet the deficit in the capacity for mentalization can be masked by an apparent intellectual ability that lures therapists, especially during assessment, into believing that borderline patients understand the complexity of alternative perspectives, accept uncertainty, and can consider difference. Sadly, these assessments are made before the therapist has become an attachment figure for the patient and deficits seen in BPD are to a large measure specific to attachment relationships. Once the attachment system is activated by the reliability and safety of the therapeutic setting, the patient's mentalization is likely to deteriorate and his or her deficits become more evident. Most obvious is the apparent lack of constancy, what may be described as the paradoxically ephemeral nature of apparently deeply held beliefs. In fact at one moment a borderline patient may hold a particular view and yet at another time maintain the opposite is true and continuity of feeling, belief, wish, and desire may be lost between therapeutic sessions. Whilst in some patients this would lead to conflict because two ideas, even if opposing, can be held in mind at the same time, contemplating genuine alternatives is often experienced as toxic to the self-structure of the borderline patient and so is avoided. Here lies the root of what is described as 'black and white thinking' in the CBT literature and is referred to as 'splitting' by psychoanalysts. Constancy of belief and consistent experience of others elude the borderline patient, resulting in idealisation at one moment and denigration the next. The task of the therapist is to establish continuity between sessions, to link different aspects of a multi-component therapy, to help the patient recognise the discontinuity, and to scaffold the sessions without holding the patient to account for sudden switches in belief, feeling, and desire. The borderline patient does not lie but is unable to hold in mind different representations and their accompanying affects at any one time. All are equally true, and the therapist must accept the balance between opposing perspectives and work with both even though they appear contradictory.

Use of transference

In many respects our approach to transference owes much to that of Otto Kernberg, John Clarkin, Frank Yeomans and their group (Kernberg, Clarkin, and Yeomans, 2002) (Clarkin, Yeomans, and Kernberg, 1998) (Clarkin, Foelsch, and Kernberg, 1996) (Clarkin et al., 1999) (Kernberg, 1992). We clearly share a dynamic approach to the understanding of mind and a therapeutic approach that stresses understanding, interpretation and a focus on affect. However, there are also important differences and nowhere are these differences more clear cut than in our approach to the transference. In Transference Focussed Psychotherapy (TFP) patients are seen as re-establishing dyadic relations with their therapists that reflect rudimentary representations of self-other relationships of the past (so called part-object relationships). Thus TFP considers the externalisation of these self-object-affect triads to be at the heart of therapeutic interventions. For the MBT model, the role-relationships established by the patient through the transference relationship are considered preliminary to the externalisation of the parts of the self the patient wishes to disown. In order to achieve a state of affairs where the alien part of the self is experienced as outside rather than within, the patient needs to create a relationship with the therapist through which this externalisation may be achieved. Once it is achieved, and unwanted parts of the self are felt to be reassuringly outside rather than within, the patient has no interest in the relationship with the therapist and may in fact wish to repudiate it totally. Focussing the patient's attention on the relationship can be felt by them as undermining their attempts at separating from the disowned part of themselves and consequently be counterproductive.

It is therefore important that exploration within the transference is built up over time and there is a de-emphasis on reconstruction. Transference distortion is used as a demonstration of alternative perspectives—a contrast between the patient's perception of the therapist or of others in the group and that of others. At first, reference to different perspectives and internal influences that may be driving them should be simple and to the point. Both patient and therapist have to start from a position of 'not knowing' but trying to understand. Direct statements about the relationship between the patient and therapist may stimulate anxiety and be experienced as abusive. Only towards the middle or end of therapy when stable internal representations have been established is it likely to be safe to use the 'heat' of the relationship between patient and therapist in a more direct way to explore different perspectives.

Transference is not seen as the primary vehicle for change in the patient's representational system. We are not suggesting therapists avoid transference, which is essential for effective treatment, but that its use is incremental and moves from distance to near depending on the patient's level of anxiety. Most patients with severe BPD rapidly become anxious in intimate situations and too sharp a focus on the patient/therapist relationship leads to panic that is manifested as powerful and, sometimes uncontrollable, expressions of feeling. This leads to a dissociative experience and a sense that their own experience is invalid. If such transference interpretations are made the patient is immediately thrown into a pretend mode and gradually patient and therapist may elaborate a world, which however detailed and complex, has little experiential contact with reality. Alternatively the patient either angrily and contemptuously drops-out of therapy feeling that their problems have not been understood, or mentally withdraws from treatment, or establishes a false treatment which looks like therapy but is in fact two individuals talking to themselves.

Retaining mental closeness

Retaining mental closeness is the primary vehicle of MBT. It is done simply by representing accurately the current or immediately past feeling state of the patient and its accompanying internal representations and by strictly and systematically avoiding the temptation to enter into conversation about matters not directly linked to the patient's beliefs, wishes, feelings etc. The initial task in MBT is to stabilise emotional expression because without improved control of affect there can be no serious consideration of internal representations. Even though the converse is true to the extent that without stable internal representations there can be no robust control of affects, identification and expression of affect is targeted first simply because it represents an immediate threat to continuity of therapy as well as potentially to the patient's life. Uncontrolled affect leads to impulsivity and only once this is under control is it possible to focus on internal representations and to strengthen the patient's sense of self.

The therapist must be able to distinguish between his own feelings and those of the patient and be able consistently to demonstrate this distinction to the patient. Specifically, feelings belonging to the therapist must not be attributed to the patient or interpreted as such. This repeats the developmental trauma of the patient who, as we have suggested, takes others feelings and representations in as part of himself but these fail to map onto his own state leading to destabilisation of the self-structure or an illusory stabilisation.

A mismatch or discrepancy between the representation of the patient's state by the therapist and the actual state of the patient compels patients and therapists to examine their own internal states further and to find different ways of expressing them if communication is to continue. In addition, the therapist has to be able to examine his own internal states and be able to show that they can change according to further understanding of the patient's state. Similar descriptions have been advanced by those who place therapeutic emphasis upon breaches, negotiations and repairs of the therapeutic alliance (Safran and Muran, 2000).

Working with current mental states

There can be little therapeutic gain from continually focusing in the past. Recovering memories is now recognised as a somewhat risky aim with BPD patients (Brenneis, 1997); Sandler, 1997 #3058]. We would wish to add to these risks, the possibility of encouraging borderline patients to enter a pretend—psychic equivalent mode of relating, where they (unbeknownst to the therapist) no longer use the same circumspect subjective criteria of historical accuracy which most of us do but rather assume that because they experience something in relation to a childhood (usually adult) figure, it is bound to be true. To avoid these risks the focus of MBT needs to be on the present state and how it remains influenced by events of the past rather than on the past itself. If the patient persistently returns to the past, the therapist needs to link back to the present, move the therapy into the 'here and now', and consider the present experience.

Intense feelings about remembered experiences are felt in the present and should be dealt with as a current experience. They are not explored as a justified or unjustified reaction to a past event. Rather, the therapist assumes that regardless of the past significance of the experience, something (internal or external) in the current life of the patient triggered the memory and the trigger, rather than the memory must be the focus of the exploration.

Bridging the gaps

The absence of adequate second-order (symbolic) representations of self-states creates a gap between the primary affective experience of the borderline patient and its meaning as well as a continuous and intense desire for understanding what is experienced as internal chaos. This gap has to be bridged in therapy with a view to strengthening the secondary representational system.

In MBT, the therapist focuses on simple interchanges that show how he believes the patient is experiencing him, and avoids describing a complex mental state to the patient. Interpreting a more complex psychological process, however accurate or inaccurate it may be either pushes the patient into pretend mode or creates instability in which the patient becomes more and more uncertain and confused about himself as the contradictions and uncertainties are pointed out. Change is generated in borderline patients by brief, specific interpretation and clear answers to questions. Clever ideas from the therapist too early in therapy stimulate pretend mode and are used by the patient to stabilise himself in a labyrinth of thought with no connection, depth, or personal meaning and the gravest danger for the therapist is filling the gap in this way rather than bridging it. The patient appears to make rapid gains in therapy as he takes on and develops comments and interpretations from the therapist. But this is an illusion and leads to 'pretend' therapy which is ultimately shallow and barren (although, in our experience at least, not uncommon with this group of patients). There are a number of clues that make it clear that this evident high degree of mentalization is more apparent than real. First it has an obsessive character. Second it becomes apparent over time that there can be dramatically different mental models of things which are readily exchangeable. The patient appears unaware of this contradiction and expresses surprise if challenged by the therapist. In general it is best not to confront the patient with inconsistency, at least initially, since, in pretend mode, they have no access to their previous understanding of others. Third their elaboration is overly rich and frequently assumes complex and improbable unrealistic aspects. Talking to them about their own thoughts and feelings leads to rapid agreement without obvious scrutiny and when reflectiveness occurs it doesn't seem to have any ramifications. Finally, there is no 'felt feeling' or mentalised affectivity (Fonagy et al., 2002). The concept pertains to the integration of emotional experience with knowledge of its origin, relevance meaning. The patient who talks about affect which is not felt at the same time is severing the internal connection between second order representations and constitutional self states. The sessions become empty.

Summary of the evidence for the effectiveness of mentalization based therapy for borderline personality disorder

We have undertaken a long-term follow-up study to evaluate the effect of mentalization based treatment in partial hospital (MBT-PH) compared to treatment as usual (TAU) for borderline personality disorder (BPD) 8 years following entry to a randomized controlled trial and 5 years after all mentalization based treatment (MBT) was complete. Characteristics of the subjects, the methodology of the original trial, and detail of treatment have been described (Bateman and Fonagy 1999, 2006), as have the full findings at 8-year follow (Bateman and Fonagy, 2008). What follows is a summary of that material.

MBT-PH consists of 18-month individual and group psycho-therapy in a partial hospital setting offered within a structured and integrated programme provided by a supervised team. Expressive therapy using art and writing groups is included. Crises are managed within the team; medication is prescribed according to protocol by a psychiatrist working in the therapy programme. The understanding of behaviour in terms of underlying mental states forms a common thread running across all aspects of treatment. The focus of therapy is on the patient's moment-to-moment state of mind. Patient and therapist collaboratively try to generate alternative perspectives to the patient's subjective experience of themselves and others by moving from validating and supportive interventions to exploring the therapy relationship itself as it suggests alternative understanding. This psychodynamic therapy is manualised (17) and in many respects overlaps with transference-focused psychotherapy (18).

We reported 18-month (end of intensive treatment) and 36-month outcomes of patients treated for BPD following randomisation to MBT-PH or TAU (15, 16). MBT-PH and TAU for 18-months were well-characterized. Subsequent treatment was monitored. However, the MBT-PH group continued to receive some out-patient group mental-izing treatment (MBT-OP) between 18–36 months. No TAU patients received the experimental treatment during this 36-month period. Differences between groups found at the end of intensive treatment were not only maintained during 18–36 months but increased substantially. We attributed this to the rehabilitative processes stimulated by the initial MBT-PH treatment. But equally it might have been a result of the maintenance MBT-OP treatment albeit that this group had considerably less treatment than the control group.

All MBT treatment ended 36 months after entry into the study. We wanted to determine whether treatment gains were maintained over the subsequent 5 years, i.e. 8 years after randomization. The primary outcome for this long term follow-up study was number of suicide attempts. But in the light of the limited improvement related to social adjustment in follow-along studies we were concerned to establish whether the social and interpersonal improvements found at the end of 36 months had been maintained and whether additional gains in the area of vocational achievement had been made in either group. We also looked at continuing use of medical and psychiatric services including emergency room (ER) visits, length of hospitalization, out-patient psychiatric care and community support; use of medication and psychological therapies, and overall symptom status. This paper reports on these long term outcomes for patients who participated in the original trial.

The MBT-PH/OP group continued to do well 5 years after all MBT treatment had ceased. The beneficial effect found at the end of MBT-OP treatment for BPD is maintained for a long period, with differences found in suicide attempts, service usage, global function and ZAN-BPD scores at 5 years post-discharge. It is consistent with the possible rehabilitative effects that we observed during the MBT-OP period. This is encouraging because positive effects of treatment normally tend to diminish over time. The TAU group received more treatment over time than the MBT group, perhaps because they continued to have more symptoms. However in both groups GAF scores continue to indicate deficits, with some patients continuing to show moderate difficulties in social and occupational functioning. Nevertheless, when compared to the TAU group, MBT patients were more likely to be functioning reasonably well with some meaningful relationships as defined by a score higher than 60.

More striking than how well the MBT group did was how badly the TAU group managed within services despite significant input. They look little better on many indicators than they did at 36 months after recruitment to the study. A few patients in the MBT sample had made at least 1 suicide attempt during the post-discharge period but these were almost ten times more common in the TAU group. Associated with this were more ER visits and greater use of polypharmacy. However, although number of hospital days was greater for the TAU group than the MBT group, the percentage of patients admitted to hospital over the post-discharge period was small (25–33%). This pattern of results suggests not that TAU is necessarily ineffective in its components but that the package or organization is not facilitating possible natural recovery.

Naturalistic follow-up studies suggest spontaneous remission of impulsive symptoms within 2–4 years with apparently less treatment (21, 22). In line with these findings all patients showed improvement, although not as much in terms of suicide attempts as might be expected. The lower level of improvement observed in this population may be because they represent a more chronic group. Most patients had a median time in specialist services at entry to the trial of 6 years. Whilst this study does not indicate the untreated course of the disorder, the results suggest that quantity of treatment may not be a good indicator of improvement and may even prevent patients taking advantage of felicitous social and interpersonal events (23). It is possible that TAU inadvertently interfered with patient improvement as well as MBT accelerating recovery.

There is an anomaly in the results in that there is a marked difference between the size of the effects as measured by the ZAN-BPD and the GAFs in terms of social and interpersonal function. One possible explanation for this is that the scales offer a slightly different metric to different aspects of interpersonal function. In the GAF, suicidal preoccupation and actual attempts have a large loading and even presence of suicidal thoughts reduces the score substantially. This was the case for a small number of patients in the MBT group and accounts for their larger variance on GAF scores. In contrast the interpersonal subscale of the ZAN-BPD covers two symptoms in the interpersonal realm of BPD, namely intense, unstable relationships and frantic efforts to avoid abandonment which showed marked improvement in the MBT group. A GAF of greater than 60 clearly marks a change back to improved function and more patients in the MBT group achieved scores above this level. A strong correlate of improvement in the MBT group is vocational status. It is unclear whether this is a cause or consequence of improvement. It is likely that symptomatic improvement and vocational activity represent a virtuous cycle. Although we have no evidence to this effect, we suggest MBT may be specifically helpful in improving patient ability to manage social situations by enabling individuals to distance themselves from the interpersonal pressures of the work situation, anticipating other people's thoughts and feelings, and being able to understand their own reactions without over-activation of their attachment systems (24, 25).

The strengths of this study lie in the presence of a long-term control group, in the reliability of care records, and in our data collection for suicide attempts which used the same rigorous criteria as at the outset of the trial. Other follow-up studies have been confounded by lack of controls or TAU patients being taken in to the experimental treatment at the end of the treatment phase. However the long term follow-up of a small sample and allegiance effects, despite attempts being made to blind the data collection, limit the conclusions. In addition some of the measures we used at the outset of the trial were not repeated in this follow-up. We considered the ZAN-BPD to be a more useful outcome measure that would reflect the current state of the patients better than self-report questionnaire methods. Finally the original MBT-PH intervention contained a number of components in addition to psychological therapy. It is therefore unclear whether psychodynamic therapy was the essential component. In order for MBT be accepted as an evidence-based treatment for BPD larger trials using core components of the intervention are necessary. These are now being undertaken. Whilst this study demonstrates that borderline patients improve in a number of domains following MBT and that those gains are maintained over time, global function remains somewhat impaired. This may reflect too great a focus during treatment on symptomatic problems at the expense of concentration on improving general social adaptation.

References

Alexander, R.D. (1989). Evolution of the human psyche. In P. Mellars & C. Stringer (Eds.), *The human revolution: behavioural and biological perspectives on the origins of modern humans* (pp. 455–513). Princeton: Princeton University Press.

Allen, J.G. (2001). *Traumatic Relationships and Serious Mental Disorders.* Chichester: Wiley.

Allen, J., & Fonagy, P. (2002). The development of mentalizing and its role in psychopathology and psychotherapy. (Technical Report No 02-0048). The Menninger Clinic, Research Department, Topeka, KS.

Arnsten, A.F.T. (1998). The biology of being frazzled. *Science, 280,* 1711–1712.

Arnsten, A.F.T., Mathew, R., Ubriani, R., Taylor, J.R., & Li, B.M. (1999). alpha-1 noradrenergic receptor stimulation impairs prefrontal corical cognitive function. *Biological Psychiatry, 45,* 26–31.

Arntz, A., Appels, C., & Sieswerda, S. (2000). Hypervigilance in border-line disorder: a test with the emotional Stroop paradigm. *J Personal Disord, 14*(4), 366–373.

Avis, J., & Harris, P. (1991). Belief-desire reasoning among Baka children: evidence for a universal conception of mind. *Child Development, 62,* 460–467.

Bahrick, L.R., & Watson, J.S. (1985). Detection of intermodal proprioceptive-visual contingency as a potential basis of self-perception in infancy. *Developmental Psychology, 21,* 963–973.

Baldwin, D.A., Baird, J.A., Saylor, M.M., & Clark, M.A. (2001). Infants parse dynamic action. *Child Development, 72*(3), 708–717.

Baron-Cohen, S. (1995). *Mindblindness: An Essay on Autism and Theory of Mind.* Cambridge, MA: Bradford, MIT Press.

Baron-Cohen, S., & Cross, P. (1992). Reading the eyes: Evidence for the role of perception in the development of a theory of mind. *Mind and Language, 6,* 173–186.

Bartels, A., & Zeki, S. (2000). The neural basis of romantic love. *Neuroreport, 11*(17), 3829–3834.

Bartels, A., & Zeki, S. (2004). The neural correlates of maternal and romantic love. *Neuroimage, 21*(3), 1155–1166.

Bateman, A., & Fonagy, P. (1999). The effectiveness of partial hospitalization in the treatment of borderline personality disorder–a randomised controlled trial. *American Journal of Psychiatry, 156,* 1563–1569.

Bateman, A.W., & Fonagy, P. (2003). The development of an attachment-based treatment program for borderline personality disorder. *Bulletin of the Menninger Clinic, 67*(3), 187–211.

Bateman, A.W., & Fonagy P. (2006). *Mentalization Based Treatment for Borderline Personality Disorder: A Practical Guide.* Oxford: Oxford University Press.

Bateman, A.W., & Fonagy, P. (2008). 8-year follow-up of patients treated for borderline personality disorder–mentalization based treatment versus treatment as usual. *American Journal of Psychiatry, 165,* 631–638.

Bartsch, K., & Wellman, H.M. (1989). Young children's attribution of action to beliefs and desires. *Child Development, 60,* 946–964.

Beeghly, M., & Cicchetti, D. (1994). Child maltreatment, attachment, and the self system: Emergence of an internal state lexicon in toddlers at high social risk. *Development and Psychopathology, 6,* 5–30.

Belsky, J. (1999a). Interactional and contextual determinants of attachment security. In J. Cassidy & P.R. Shaver (Eds.), *Handbook of attachment: Theory, research and clinical applications* (pp. 249–264). New York: Guilford.

Belsky, J. (1999b). Modern evolutionary theory and patterns of attachment. In J.Cassidy & P.R. Shaver (Eds.), *Handbook of attachment: Theory, research and clinical applications* (pp. 141–161). New York: Guilford.

Belsky, J., & Fearon, R.M. (2002). Infant-mother attachment security, contextual risk, and early development: A moderational analysis. *Development and Psychopathology, 14,* 293–310.

Bion, W.R. (1962). A theory of thinking. *International Journal of Psychoanalysis, 43,* 306–310.

Bion, W.R. (1963). *Elements of psycho-analysis.* London: Heinemann.

Birch, S.A., & Bloom, P. (2003). Children are cursed: an asymmetric bias in mental-state attribution. *Psychol Sci, 14*(3), 283–286.

Bogdan, R.J. (1997). *Interpreting minds.* Cambridge, MA: MIT Press.

Brenneis, C. (1997). *Recovered Memories of Trauma: Transferring the Present to the Past.* Madison, CT: International Universities Press.

Bronfman, E., Parsons, E., & Lyons-Ruth, K. (1999). *Atypical Maternal Behavior Instrument for Assessment and Classification (AMBIANCE): Manual for coding disrupted affective communication, version 2. Unpublished manuscript.* Cambridge, MA: Harvard Medical School.

Brown, J.R., Donelan-McCall, N., & Dunn, J. (1996). Why talk about mental states? The significance of children's conversations with friends, siblings, and mothers. *Child Development, 67,* 836–849.

Brown, R., Hobson, R.P., Lee, A., & Stevenson, J. (1997). Are there "autistic-like" features in congenitally blind children? *J Child Psychol Psychiatry, 38*(6), 693–703.

Bruner, J. (1990). *Acts of Meaning.* Cambridge: Harvard University Press.

Cabeza, R., & Nyberg, L. (2000). Neural bases of learning and memory: functional neuroimaging evidence. *Curr Opin Neurol, 13*(4), 415–421.

Calkins, S., & Johnson, M. (1998). Toddler regulation of distress to frustrating events: Temperamental and maternal correlates. *Infant Behavior & Development, 21,* 379–395.

Cavell, M. (1991). The subject of mind. *International Journal of Psycho-Analysis, 72,* 141–154.

Cavell, M. (1994). *The Psychoanalytic Mind.* Cambridge, MA: Harvard University Press.

Champagne, F.A., Chretien, P., Stevenson, C.W., Zhang, T.Y., Gratton, A., & Meaney, M.J. (2004). Variations in nucleus accumbens dopamine associated with individual differences in maternal behavior in the rat. *J Neurosci*, 24(17), 4113–4123.

Charman, T., Ruffman, T., & Clements, W. (2002). Is there a gender difference in false belief development? *Social Development*, 11, 1–10.

Chugani, H.T., Behen, M.E., Muzik, O., Juhasz, C., Nagy, F., & Chugani, D.C. (2001). Local brain functional activity following early deprivation: a study of postinstitutionalized Romanian orphans. *Neuroimage*, 14(6), 1290–1301.

Cicchetti, D., Rogosch, F.A., & Toth, S.L. (2000). The efficacy of toddler-parent psychotherapy for fostering cognitive development in offspring of depressed mothers. *J Abnorm Child Psychol*, 28(2), 135–148.

Clarkin, J.F., Yeomans, F.E., & Kernberg, O. (1998). *Psychodynamic psychotherapy of borderline personality disorder: a treatment manual.* New York: Wiley.

Clarkin, J.F., Kernberg, O.F., & Yeomans, F. (1999). *Transference-Focused Psychotherapy for Borderline Personality Disorder Patients.* New York, NY: Guilford Press.

Claussen, A.H., Mundy, P.C., Mallik, S.A., & Willoughby, J.C. (2002). Joint attention and dosrganised atachment status in infants at risk. *Development and Psychopathology*, 14, 279–291.

Conway, M.A. (1992). A structural model of autobiographical memory. In M.A. Conway, H. Spinnler & W.A. Wagenaar (Eds.), *Theoretical Perspectives on Autobiological Memory.* (pp. 167–194). Dordrecht, The Netherlands: Kluwer Academic Publishers.

Conway, M.A. (1996). Autobiographical knowledge and autobiographical memories. In D.C.Rubin (Ed.), *Remembering our past: Studies in autobiographical memory* (pp. 67–93). New York: Cambridge University Press.

Conway, M.A., & Holmes, A. (2004). Psychosocial stages and the accessibility of autobiographical memories across the life cycle. *J Pers*, 72(3), 461–480.

Corkum, V., & Moore, C. (1995). Development of joint visual attention in infants. In C. Moore & P. Dunham (Eds.), *Joint Attention: Its Origins and Role in Development* (pp. 61–83). New York: Erlbaum.

Cote, S., Tremblay, R.E., Nagin, D., Zoccolillo, M., & Vitaro, F. (2002). The development of impulsivity, fearfulness, and helpfulness during childhood: patterns of consistency and change in the trajectories of boys and girls. *Journal of Child Psychology and Psychiatry and Allied Disciplines, 43*(5), 609–618.

Csibra, G., & Gergely, G. (1998). The teleological origins of mentalistic action explanations: A developmental hypothesis. *Developmental Science, 1*(2), 255–259.

Cutting, A.L., & Dunn, J. (2002). The cost of understanding other people: social cognition predicts young children's sensitivity to criticism. *J Child Psychol Psychiatry, 43*(7), 849–860.

Davidson, D. (1983). *Inquiries into Truth and Interpretation*. Oxford: Oxford University Press.

Dennett, D. (1987). *The intentional stance*. Cambridge, MA: MIT Press.

Dias, M.G., & Harris, P.L. (1990). The influence of the imagination on reasoning by young children. *British Journal of Developmental Psychology, 8*, 305–318.

Dunn, J. (1988). *The Beginnings of Social Understanding*. Oxford: Basil Blackwell Ltd and Cambridge, MA: Harvard University Press.

Dunn, J. (1994). Changing minds and changing relationships. In C. Lewis & P. Mitchell (Eds.), *Children's Early Understanding of Mind: Origins and Development* (pp. 297–310). Hove, UK: Lawrence Erlbaum.

Dunn, J. (1999). Making sense of the social world: Mindreading, emotion and relationships. In P.D. Zelazo, J.W. Astington & D.R. Olson (Eds.), *Developing theories of intention: Social understanding and self control*. (Vol., pp. 229–242). Mahwah, NJ: Lawrence Erlbaum Associates.

Dunn, J., & Brown, J. (2001). Emotion, pragmatics and developments in emotion understanding in the preschool years. In D. Bakhurst & S. Shanker (Eds.), *Jerome Bruner: Language, culture, self*. Thousand Oaks: CA: Sage.

Dunn, J., Brown, J., & Beardsall, L. (1991). Family talk abut feeling states and children's later understanding of others' emotions. *Developmental Psychology, 27*, 448–455.

Dunn, J., & Cutting, A. (1999). Understanding others, and individual differences in friendship interactions in young children. *Social Development., 8*, 201–219.

Dunn, J., Davies, L.C., O'Connor, T.G., & Sturgess, W. (2000). Parents' and partners' life course and family experiences: links with parent-child relationships in different family settings. *J Child Psychol Psychiatry, 41*(8), 955–968.

Fearon, R.M., & Belsky, J. (2004). Attachment and attention: protection in relation to gender and cumulative social-contextual adversity. *Child Dev, 75*(6), 1677–1693.

Flavell, J., & Miller, P. (1998). Social cognition. In D. Kuhn & R. Siegler (Eds.), *Cognition, perception, and language. Handbook of child psychology.* (5 ed., Vol. 2, pp. 851–898). New York: Wiley.

Flavell, J.H. (1999). Cognitive development: children's knowledge about the mind. *Annu Rev Psychol, 50*, 21–45.

Fonagy, P. (1991). Thinking about thinking: Some clinical and theoretical considerations in the treatment of a borderline patient. *International Journal of Psycho-Analysis, 72*, 1–18.

Fonagy, P. (2001). *Early intervention and the development of self-regulation.* Paper presented at the Keynote address at the meeting of the Australian Association for Infant Mental Health, Perth, Australia, 30th August 2001.

Fonagy, P. (2003). The development of psychopathology from infancy to adulthood: the mysterious unfolding of disturbance in time. *Infant Mental Health Journal, 24*(3), 212–239.

Fonagy, P., Gergely, G., Jurist, E., & Target, M. (2002). *Affect Regulation, Mentalization and the Development of the Self.* New York: Other Press.

Fonagy, P., Leigh, T., Steele, M., Steele, H., Kennedy, R., Mattoon, G., et al. (1996). The relation of attachment status, psychiatric classification, and response to psychotherapy. *Journal of Consulting and Clinical Psychology, 64*, 22–31.

Fonagy, P., Steele, H., Moran, G., Steele, M., & Higgitt, A. (1991). The capacity for understanding mental states: The reflective self in parent and child and its significance for security of attachment. *Infant Mental Health Journal, 13*, 200–217.

Fonagy, P., Steele, M., Moran, G.S., Steele, H., & Higgitt, A. (1992). The integration of psychoanalytic theory and work on attachment: The issue of intergenerational psychic processes. In D.Stern & M.Ammaniti (Eds.), *Attaccamento E Psiconalis* (pp. 19–30). Bari, Italy: Laterza.

Fonagy, P., Steele, M., Steele, H., Higgitt, A., & Target, M. (1994). Theory and practice of resilience. *Journal of Child Psychology and Psychiatry, 35*, 231–257.

Fonagy, P., Stein, H., Allen, J., & Fultz, J. (2003a). *The relationship of mentalization and childhood and adolescent adversity to adult functioning.* Paper presented at the Biennial Meeting of the Society for Research in Child Development, Tampa, FL.

Fonagy, P., & Target, M. (1996). Playing with reality: I. Theory of mind and the normal development of psychic reality. *International Journal of Psycho-Analysis, 77,* 217–233.

Fonagy, P., & Target, M. (1997). Attachment and reflective function: Their role in self-organization. *Development and Psychopathology, 9,* 679–700.

Fonagy, P., & Target, M. (2000). Playing with reality III: The persistence of dual psychic reality in borderline patients. *International Journal of Psychoanalysis, 81*(5), 853–874.

Fonagy, P., & Target, M. (2002). Early intervention and the development of self-regulation. *Psychoanalytic Inquiry, 22*(3), 307–335.

Fonagy, P., Target, M., & Gergely, G. (2000). Attachment and borderline personality disorder: A theory and some evidence. *Psychiatric Clinics of North America, 23,* 103–122.

Fonagy, P., Target, M., Gergely, G., Allen, J.G., & Bateman, A. (2003b). The developmental roots of borderline personality disorder in early attachment relationships: A theory and some evidence. *Psychoanalytic Inquiry, 23,* 412–459.

Fonagy, P., Target, M., Steele, H., & Steele, M. (1998). *Reflective-Functioning Manual, version 5.0, for Application to Adult Attachment Interviews.* London: University College London.

Frith, U., & Frith, C.D. (2003). Development and neurophysiology of mentalizing. *Philosophical Transactions of the Royal Society of London B, Biological Sciences, 358,* 459–473.

Gallagher, H.L., & Frith, C.D. (2003). Functional imaging of 'theory of mind'. *Trends Cogn Sci, 7*(2), 77–83.

Gergely, G. (2001). The obscure object of desire: 'Nearly, but clearly not, like me. Contingency preference in normal children versus children with autism. In J. Allen, P. Fonagy & G. Gergely (Eds.), *Contingency Perception and Attachment in Infancy, Special Issue of the Bulletin of the Menninger Clinic* (pp. 411–426). New York: Guilford.

Gergely, G., & Csibra, G. (2003). Teleological reasoning in infancy: The naive theory of rational action. *Trends in Cognitive Sciences, 7,* 287–292.

Gergely, G., & Csibra, G. (2005). Social construction of the cultural mind: imitative pedagogy as a mechanism for social leanirng.

Gergely, G., & Watson, J. (1996). The social biofeedback model of parental affect-mirroring. *International Journal of Psycho-Analysis, 77,* 1181–1212.

Gergely, G., & Watson, J. (1999). Early social-emotional development: Contingency perception and the social biofeedback model. In P. Rochat (Ed.), *Early social cognition: Understanding others in the first months of life* (pp. 101–137). Hillsdale, NJ: Erlbaum.

Gopnik, A. (1993). How we know our minds: The illusion of first-person knowledge of intentionality. *Behavioral and Brain Sciences, 16,* 1–14, 29–113.

Greene, J., & Haidt, J. (2002). How (and where) does moral judgment work? *Trends Cogn Sci, 6*(12), 517–523.

Grienenberger, J., Kelly, K., & Slade, A. (2005). Maternal reflective functioning, mother-infant affective communication, and infant attachment: Exploring the link between mental states and observed caregiving behaviour in the intergenerational transmission of attachment. *Attachment and Human Development, 7*(3), 299–311.

Gusnard, D.A., Akbudak, E., Shulman, G.L., & Raichle, M.E. (2001). Medial prefrontal cortex and self-referential mental activity: relation to a default mode of brain function. *Proc Natl Acad Sci USA, 98*(7), 4259–4264.

Harman, C., Rothbart, M.K., & Posner, M.I. (1997). Distress and intention interactions in early infancy. *Motivation and Emotion, 21,* 27–43.

Hobson, P. (2002). *The cradle of thought: Explortions of the origins of thinking.* Oxford: Macmillan.

Hofer, M.A. (2004). The Emerging Neurobiology of Attachment and Separation: How Parents Shape Their Infant's Brain and Behavior. In S.W. Coates & J.L. Rosenthal (Eds.), *September 11- "When the Bough Broke", Attachment Theory, Psychobiology, and Social Policy: An Integrated Approach to Trauma.* New York: Analytic Press.

Hrdy, S.B. (2000). *Mother nature.* New York: Ballentine Books.

Hughes, C., & Dunn, J. (2002). When I say a naughty word. Children's accounts of anger and sadness in self, mother and friend: Longitudinal findings from ages four to seven. *British Journal of Developmental Psychology., 20,* 515–535.

Hughes, C., & Leekham, S. (2004). What are the links between theory of mind and social realtions? Review, reflections and new directions for studies of typical and atypical development. *Social Behavior, 13,* 590–619.

Insel, T. (1997). A neurobiological basis of social attachment. *American Journal of Psychiatry, 154,* 726–735.

Insel, T.R. (2003). Is social attachment an addictive disorder? *Physiol Behav, 79*(3), 351–357.

Jacobsen, T., & Hofmann, V. (1997). Children's attachment representations: longitudinal relations to school behavior and academic competency in middle childhood and adolescence. *Dev Psychol, 33*(4), 703–710.

Jacobson, E. (1954). The self and the object world: Vicissitudes of their infantile cathexes and their influence on ideational affective development. *The Psychoanalytic Study of the Child, 9*, 75–127.

Jaworski, J.N., Francis, D.D., Brommer, C.L., Morgan, E.T., & Kuhar, M.J. (2005). Effects of early maternal separation on ethanol intake, GABA receptors and metabolizing enzymes in adult rats. *Psychopharmacology (Berl)*.

Kernberg, O.F. (1992). Aggression in Personality Disorders and Perversions. New Haven & London: Yale University Press.

Kernberg, O., Clarkin, J.F., & Yeomans, F.E. (2002). A primer of Transference Focused PSychotherapy for the Borderline Patient. New York: Jason Aronson.

Kochanska, G., Coy, K.C., & Murray, K.T. (2001). The development of self-regulation in the first four years of life. *Child Development, 72*, 1091–1111.

Koren-Karie, N., Oppenheim, D., Dolev, S., Sher, S., & Etzion-Carasso, A. (2002). Mother's insightfulness regarding their infants' internal experience: Relations with maternal sensitivity and infant attachment. *Developmental-Psychology, 38*, 534–542.

Lalonde, C., & Chandler, M.J. (1995). False belief understanding goes to school: On the social-emotional consequences of coming early or late to a first theory of mind. *Cognition and Emotion., 9*, 167–185.

Legerstee, M., & Varghese, J. (2001). The role of maternal affect mirroring on social expectancies in 2–3 month-old infants. *Child Development, 72*, 1301–1313.

Leslie, A.M. (1994). TOMM, ToBy, and agency: core architecture and domain specificity. In L. Hirschfeld & S. Gelman (Eds.), *Mapping the mind: Domain specificity in cognition and culture* (pp. 119–148). New York: Cambridge University Press.

Liszkowski, U., Carpenter, M., Henning, A., Striano, T., & Tomasello, M. (2004). Twelvemonth-olds point to share attention and interest. *Developmental Science., 7*, 297–307.

MacLean, P. (1990). *The triune brain in evolution: role in paleocerebral functions*. New York: Plenum.

Maddock, R.J. (1999). The retrosplenial cortex and emotion: new insights from functional neuroimaging of the human brain. *Trends Neurosci,* 22(7), 310–316.

Mayberg, H.S., Liotti, M., Brannan, S.K., McGinnis, S., Mahurin, R.K., Jerabek, P.A., et al. (1999). Reciprocal limbic-cortical function and negative mood: converging PET findings in depression and normal sadness. *Am J Psychiatry,* 156(5), 675–682.

Mayes, L.C. (2000). A developmental perspective on the regulation of arousal states. *Seminars in Perinatology, 24,* 267–279.

Meins, E. (1997). *Security of attachment and the social development of cognition.* London: Psychology Press.

Meins, E., & Fernyhough, C. (1999). Linguistic acquisitional style and mentalising development: The role of maternal mind-mindedness. *Cognitive Development, 14,* 363–380.

Meins, E., Fernyhough, C., Russel, J., & Clark-Carter, D. (1998). Security of attachment as a predictor of symbolic and mentalising abilities: a longitudinal study. *Social Development, 7,* 1–24.

Meins, E., Fernyhough, C., Wainwright, R., Clark-Carter, D., Das Gupta, M., Fradley, E., et al. (2003). Pathways to understanding mind: construct validity and predictive validity of maternal mind-mindedness. *Child Dev, 74*(4), 1194–1211.

Meins, E., Fernyhough, C., Wainwright, R., Das Gupta, M., Fradley, E., & Tuckey, M. (2002). Maternal mind-mindedness and attachment security as predictors of theory of mind understanding. *Child Development, 73,* 1715–1726.

Meins, E., Ferryhough, C., Fradley, E., & Tuckey, M. (2001). Rethinking maternal sensitivity: Mothers' comments on infants mental processes predict security of attachment at 12 months. *Journal of Child Psychology and Psychiatry, 42,* 637–648.

Meltzoff, A.N. (1995). Understanding the intentions of others: Re-enactment of intended acts by 18-month-old children. *Developmental Psychology, 31,* 838–850.

Mitchell, R.W. (1993). Mental models of mirror self-recognition: Two theories. *New Ideas in Psychology, 11,* 295–325.

Mitchell, S.A. (2000). *Relationality: From attachment to intersubjectivity.* Hillsdale, NJ: Analytic Press.

Mundy, P., & Neal, R. (2001). Neural plasticity, joint attention, and a transactional social-orienting model of autism. In L. Masters

Glidden (Ed.), *International review of mental retardation: Autism (Vol 23)* (pp. 139–168). San Diego, CA: Academic Press.

Nagin, D.S., & Tremblay, R.E. (2001). Parental and early childhood predictors of persistent physical aggression in boys from kindergarten to high school. *Archives of General Psychiatry, 58*(4), 389–394.

Neisser, U. (1988). Five kinds of self-knowledge. *Philosophical Psychology, 1*, 35–59.

Newton, P., Reddy, V., & Bull, R. (2000). Children's everyday deception and performance on false-belief tasks. *British Journal of Developmental Psychology., 18*, 297–317.

Nitschke, J.B., Nelson, E.E., Rusch, B.D., Fox, A.S., Oakes, T.R., & Davidson, R.J. (2004). Orbitofrontal cortex tracks positive mood in mothers viewing pictures of their newborn infants. *Neuroimage, 21*(2), 583–592.

Oppenheim, D., & Koren-Karie, N. (2002). Mothers' insightfulness regarding their children's internal worlds: The capacity underlying secure child-mother relationships. *Infant-Mental-Health-Journal, 23*, 593–605.

Panksepp, J. (1998). *Affective neuroscience: The foundations of human and animal emotions.* Oxford: Oxford University Press.

Plotsky, P.M., Thrivikraman, K.V., Nemeroff, C.B., Caldji, C., Sharma, S., & Meaney, M.J. (2005). Long-Term Consequences of Neonatal Rearing on Central Corticotropin-Releasing Factor Systems in Adult Male Rat Offspring. *Neuropsychopharmacology.*

Povinelli, D.J., & Eddy, T.J. (1995). The unduplicated self. In P. Rochat (Ed.), *The Self in Infancy: Theory and Research* (pp. 161–192). Amsterdam: Elsevier.

Pratt, C., & Bryant, P.E. (1990). Young children understand that looking leads to knowing (so lovng as they are looking into a single barrel). *Child Development, 61*, 973–982.

Repacholi, B.M., & Gopnik, A. (1997). Early reasoning about desires: Evidence from 14- and 18-month-olds. *Developmental Psychology, 33*, 12–21.

Rochat, P., & Striano, T. (1999). Social-cognitive development in the first year. In P. Rochat (Ed.), *Early social cognition.* Mahwah, NJ: Lawrence Erlbaum.

Ruffman, T., Perner, J., Naito, M., Parkin, L., & Clements, W. (1998). Older (but not younger) siblings facilitate false belief understanding. *Developmental Psychology, 34*(1), 161–174.

Ruffman, T., Perner, J., & Parkin, L. (1999). How parenting style affects false belief understanding. *Social Development, 8*, 395–411.

Rutter, M., & O'Connor, T.G. (2004). Are there biological programming effects for psychological development? Findings from a study of Romanian adoptees. *Dev Psychol, 40*(1), 81–94.

Safran, J.D., & Muran, J.C. (2000). Negotiating the Therapeutic Alliance. New York: Guilford Press.

Schechter, D.S., Coots, T., Zeanah, C.H., Davies, M., Coates, S., Trabka, K., et al. (2005). Maternal mental representations of the child in an inner-city clinical sample: Violence-related posttraumatic stress and reflective functioning. *Attachment and Human Development, 7*(3), 313–331.

Schölmerich, A., Lamb, M.E., Leyendecker, B., & Fracasso, M.P. (1997). Mother-infant teaching interactions and attachment security in Euro-American and Central-American immigrant families. *Infant Behavior and Development, 20*, 165–174.

Segal, H. (1957). Notes on symbol formation. *International Journal of Psycho-Analysis, 38*, 391–397.

Siegel, D.J. (1999). *The developing mind: Toward a neurobiology of interpersonal experience.* New York: Guilford.

Simpson, J.A. (1999). Attachment theory in modern evolutionary perspective. In J. Cassidy & P.R. Shaver (Eds.), *Handbook of attachment: Theory, research and clinical applications* (pp. 115–140). New York: Guilford.

Slade, A. (2005). Parental reflective functioning: An introduction. *Attachment and Human Development, 7*(3), 269–281.

Slade, A., Grienenberger, J., Bernbach, E., Levy, D., & Locker, A. (2005). Maternal reflective functioning, attachment and the transmission gap: A preliminary study. *Attachment and Human Development, 7*(3), 283–298.

Slomkowski, C., & Dunn, J. (1996). Young children's understanding of other people's beliefs and feelings and their connected comunication with friends. *Developmental Psychology, 32*, 442–447.

Sodian, B., & Frith, U. (1992). Deception and sabotage in autistic, retarded and normal children. *J Child Psychol Psychiatry, 33*(3), 591–605.

Sodian, B., Taylor, C., Harris, P.L., & Perner, J. (1992). Early deception and the child's theory of mind: false trails and genuine markers. *Child Development, 62*, 468–483.

Sroufe, L.A. (1996). *Emotional development: The organization of emotional life in the early years.* New York: Cambridge University Press.

Sutton, J., Smith, P.K., & Swettenham, J. (1999). Social cognition and bullying: Social inadequacy or skilled manipulation? *British Journal of Developmental Psychology, 17,* 435–450.

Target, M., & Fonagy, P. (1996). Playing with reality II: The development of psychic reality from a theoretical perspective. *International Journal of Psycho-Analysis, 77,* 459–479.

Taylor, M., & Carlson, S.M. (1997). The relation between individual differences in fantasy and theory of mind. *Child Dev, 68*(3), 436–455.

Taylor, M., Esbensen, B.M., & Bennett, R.T. (1994). Children's understanding of knowledge acquisition: the tendency for children to report that they have always known what they have just learned. *Child Dev, 65*(6), 1581–1604.

Tremblay, R.E. (2000). The origins of violence. *ISUMA*(Autumn), 19–24.

Tremblay, R.E., Japel, C., & Perusse, D. (1999). The search for the age of onset of physical aggression: Rousseau and Bandura revisited. *Criminal Behavior and Mental Health, 9,* 8–23.

van IJzendoorn, M.H. (1995). Adult attachment representations, parental responsiveness, and infant attachment: A meta-analysis on the predictive validity of the Adult Attachment Interview. *Psychological Bulletin, 117,* 387–403.

Vinden, P.G. (2001). Parenting attitudes and children's understanding of mind: A comparison of Korean American and Anglo-American families. *Cognitive Development, 16,* 793–809.

Waters, E., Merrick, S.K., Treboux, D., Crowell, J., & Albersheim, L. (2000). Attachment security from infancy to early adulthood: a 20 year longitudinal study. *Child Development, 71*(3), 684–689.

Watson, J.S. (1994). Detection of self: The perfect algorithm. In S. Parker, R. Mitchell & M. Boccia (Eds.), *Self-Awareness in Animals and Humans: Developmental Perspectives* (pp. 131–149): Cambridge University Press.

Wellman, H. (1990). *The Child's Theory of Mind.* Cambridge, MA: Bradford Books/MIT Press.

Wellman, H.M., Cross, D., & Watson, J. (2001). Meta-analysis of theory-of-mind development: the truth about false belief. *Child Dev, 72*(3), 655–684.

Wellman, H.M., & Phillips, A.T. (2000). Developing intentional understandings. In L. Moses, B. Male & D. Baldwin (Eds.), *Intentionality: A
Key to Human Understanding*. Cambridge, MA: MIT Press.

Widom, C.S. (1999). Posttraumatic stress disorder in abused and
neglected children grown up. *Am J Psychiatry, 156*, 1223–1229.

Winnicott, D.W. (1956). Mirror role of mother and family in child development. In D. W. Winnicott (Ed.), *Playing and reality* (pp. 111–118).
London: Tavistock.

Winnicott, D.W. (1965). *The maturational process and the facilitating
environment*. London: Hogarth Press.

Winston, J.S., Strange, B.A., O'Doherty, J., & Dolan, R.J. (2002). Automatic and intentional brain responses during evaluation of trustworthiness of faces. *Nat Neurosci, 5*(3), 277–283.

Zahn-Waxler, C., Radke-Yarrow, M., Wagner, E., & Chapman, M. (1992).
Development of concern for others. *Developmental Psychology, 28*,
126–136.

Zhang, T.Y., Chretien, P., Meaney, M.J., & Gratton, A. (2005). Influence
of naturally occurring variations in maternal care on prepulse inhibition of acoustic startle and the medial prefrontal cortical dopamine
response to stress in adult rats. *J Neurosci, 25*(6), 1493–1502.

CHAPTER FOUR

Psychoanalytic group therapy with severely disturbed patients: Benefits and challenges

Caroline Garland

Introduction

The early stages of psychoanalytic enquiry into borderline conditions began with clinical descriptions of a group of patients who occupied a position midway between neurosis and psychosis. The enquiry then went on to follow two rather different paths. One of these was concerned with detailed psychoanalytic investigations of what were thought to be characteristically borderline or psychotic *mechanisms of functioning*, encountered in a wide variety of conditions, including severe neurosis. These states have been described illuminatingly by, amongst many others, Steiner (1979) and Rey (1994), both of whom worked for many years with such patients at the Maudsley Hospital, as well as by Bion (1967) and Rosenfeld (1987). The other approach, in the 1960s and 70s, was influenced by Otto Kernberg's introduction of object relations theory to North America. His systematic approach to psychoanalytic observations of these patients resulted in the description of *borderline organisations of the personality* (e.g. 1975) on which he based an approach to their treatment. Subsequent research has been greatly affected by the dominance of the trend in psychiatry towards employing descriptive research diagnostic syndromes

81

as the basic starting point of any enquiry—predominantly the DSM definitions of borderline personality disorder. (See Gunderson, 2005, for a fuller account.) And of course, since then many other investigators including Fonagy and Target, 1996, Bateman and Fonagy, 2004 and 2006, and Hobson and Patrick, 2005, using differing angles of approach, and differing therapeutic approaches, have contributed greatly to the understanding of borderline conditions. The present paper will focus on *borderline mechanisms of functioning* as seen in the patients in a psychoanalytically-orientated therapy group, and will conclude with some recommendations and provisos.

The nature of the patients and their psychopathology

Borderline patients have troubled histories. Often they have been projected into, both mentally and physically, via various kinds of deprivation, neglect and abuse. Consequently for them to occupy a stable identity, or equilibrium, in relation to the world, feels impossible or dangerous. They tend to oscillate, as their name implies, between two states, while managing at the same time to be neither entirely one nor the other: shut in (imprisoned) or shut out (abandoned, rejected); too close (suffocated) or too far away (isolated); too personal or too remote; too large and powerful, or too small and helpless; neither entirely male, or entirely female, heterosexual or homosexual. Frantic attempts to 'take over' or get inside the object (therapist) are followed by equally desperate attempts to escape from or destroy it. From the patient's perspective, the object is perceived to shift rapidly back and forth. At one moment it appears as the provider of a helpful and containing structure and at the next, it becomes something ensnaring, dangerous and persecuting. Thus extremes of dependency and need are evoked, followed rapidly by a sense of entrapment or claustrophobia. The concreteness and the extreme and visible nature of these rapidly fluctuating states suggest that during infancy, childhood and adolescence, the processes that ordinarily allow the development of symbolization or emotional containment have either not occurred, or have been extremely difficult for these patients. Representing, comprehending and linking, planning—in short, thinking—and the making and sustaining of relationships are all impossible if experience cannot be represented to the self in the form of memory, dream, story or symbol. In particular, forming and maintaining affectionate, sharing or trusting relationships is difficult or impossible. In Kleinian terms this represents a pathological version of the paranoid-schizoid position.

The outcome, to quote Rey, is that, "They (borderline patients) are demanding, controlling, manipulating, threatening and devaluing towards others. They accuse society and others for their ills and are easily persecuted. This may be associated with grandiose ideas about themselves ... When threatened by feeling small and unprotected and in danger they may defend themselves by uncontrollable rages and various forms of impulsive behaviour." (p. 9) Splitting and projective identification—the need to project into others unbearable parts of the self—together with sustained and extreme difficulties in integration make these amongst the most demanding of our patients.

All this forms part of the problem in issues of clinical management and in making treatment decisions. Nevertheless even though most of these patients have suffered at the hands of others, it is neither helpful nor effective to treat them as though they were victims. The identity of chronic sufferer, or chronic complainer, can be used to intimidate, control and project into those who try to work with them. An aggressively aggrieved victim can force others into a powerless sympathy, in which the hope of treatment aimed at change is lost.

An alternative: Treatment in a group setting

As is clear, individual work with such patients will be demanding and time-consuming in terms of both management and treatment, often provoking considerable frustration in the therapist or nursing staff. As one possible therapeutic approach, probably complementary to others, I shall describe some elements of work carried out at the Tavistock Clinic with borderline and/or schizoid patients in a *group* setting. How realistic is it to take on not just one such patient, but seven or eight at a time in such a way as to provide containment without imprisonment, tolerance without indulgence, and understanding without intrusion?

I hope to show through clinical material how some borderline patients may be able to use group treatment as a means of understanding and modifying their own and each other's behaviour. In a group setting, over time and within a stable setting, this is something they can work at *with, and for, each other.* Under these circumstances they become able to observe and moderate in themselves and in each other that most important feature of BPD, the chronic instability and impulsivity in interpersonal relations. Correspondingly, for some, though not all, there is a reduced tendency to respond impulsively or act out. Although the presence and the temperament, the theoretical background and experience of the therapist are crucial, interpretation of unconscious material is less important in a group of this kind than is the maintenance of the understanding, strong, yet flexible setting. To provide this, and to contain the group process adequately, the therapist needs to be able to identify the childhood origins of troublesome and fluctuating states of mind, such as the rapid alternation in individuals between agoraphobic and claustrophobic states. This background understanding can help the therapist to frame interpretations or comments that are sufficiently precise for the patients—that is to say the group itself—to be helped to tolerate a more sustained contact with earlier childhood anxiety situations, which will include intense depressive, persecutory and confusional qualities. This is hard work. By flexible I mean that it will some of the time almost inevitably involve the therapist in work on the edge of the normal therapeutic boundary.

One of the models I have found helpful is Bion's (1967) differentiation between psychotic and non-psychotic parts of the personality. This provides a way of understanding the different types of functioning seen in 'borderlines' themselves—and seen to some extent in the group as a whole as well. For example, as will be seen in my clinical material, Sharon is possessed by a desperate and unthinking need to get <u>out</u> of the group, followed by a realistic recognition that it has helped her. Eventually she is able to make a decision to return. This kind of repeated experience shows that some borderline patients, given the opportunity, are able to mobilize the healthier (non-psychotic) parts of the personality not only in order to hold in and manage the more psychotic parts, but as well to use those same healthier capacities to bring the unworkable, ill, even psychotic parts of their functioning to a place where they can be understood, and possibly treated. Others are unable to do this, even though they might want to. Clearly from the point of view of clinical management the importance of being able to tell the difference is great, since there is a limit to what any therapy group is able to contain—and my clinical material will show some of the problems of over-optimism, even, with hindsight, omnipotence, in this respect.

Containment

Clearly, the issue of containment for the patients is crucial, both of a physical and a emotional kind. Borderline patients are not easily seen in private consulting rooms, particularly not when seven or eight such patients are seen together. And physical containers of course provide psychological holding as well. Physical containment is offered by what (ideally) are the nested structures of NHS, Hospital or Clinic, CMHT, the unit, and in the case of in-patients the ward, the therapy room. Henri Rey called the hospital 'the stone mother'. Individual doctors, psychologists and therapists may come and go, retire, become ill, go on holiday or on maternity leave, but the hospital endures. It survives the patient's storms. As we know, many of our patients have had considerable early experience of institutions (Children's Homes, Social Services, foster parents) which link in terms of both structure and process with aspects of the Health Service. Thus there is a 'genetic' or 'family' resemblance, and an emotional continuity present, and this will be reflected in the nature of the transference to the group setting. A well-functioning group will have the ability to contain and process some of these (often split) transferences and can in that way function as a healthy institution.

The physicality of the buildings and the structure of the NHS also provide important containment for the therapist. Borderline patients are quick to sense anxiety in the therapist, who is of course the main source of psychological containment, in partnership with his or her intellectual and theoretical stance—that provided by a substantial personal therapy and good training. Continued contact with colleagues (including seminars, case conferences, workshops, conferences) is important. However, even though there may exist a hard-working community of professionals engaged in the work of managing and understanding such patients, in the last resort it is the therapist's own internal resources that are tested when he or she must remain open to the intense emotional pressure exerted by the patient, or patients. I emphasize 'remaining open' to the patient's internal state, because a closed or unreceptive manner aggravates any potential turmoil. It is a difficult balancing act: not so closed defensively (sometimes masquerading as 'professional') that the patient feels shut out and frantic; not so open as to be overwhelmed and unable to function. Anyone who has worked with severe disturbance knows how important these factors are and also how difficult they are to sustain. Why then should it be easier to have several rather than one or two of the kind of patient I have described? Why does it not result in chaos and/or Bedlam?

Why group treatment?

I am going to outline some principles about group treatment in general, and go on to describe those that apply in particular to work with borderlines. Of course it is extremely important for the therapist to be clear about the value (and the limitations) of group therapy as a treatment modality with advantages of its own over and above its obvious cost-effectiveness. Patients offered group treatment may often feel they are being fobbed off with something second best. Individual treatment is seen as first-class travel, with the advantages of privacy and exclusivity. (However the intimacy of individual treatment may also threaten the borderline patient with intense claustrophobia.) A therapist offering a group can be seen as pushing bucket-shop modes of treatment, and the anxiety is often, in the state of intense need experienced by the patient at the consultation, that having to 'share' a therapist with six or seven others may aggravate the sense of deprivation. Here then is my general rationale for group treatment.

a) General principles

1. Every individual's mental life, his internal world, is founded upon the structures he has formed as a result of his biologically and constitutionally-influenced responses to his actual early experience. This of course means the couple, or family, and later the school and the wider world. These early structures, or internal object relations, are also infused with phantasy as to the nature of the self in relation to these powerful objects. There is in this early phantasy a continuous process of projection and introjection of aspects of these relationships, all of which contribute to

the formation of the individual's character, strengths and vulner-abilities. This process is largely unconscious, and is particularly resistant to change. It is the bedrock of the personality.

2. The group becomes a microcosm in which these object relationships can be lived out. In group therapy, internal object relations and primitive phantasies are externalised in the room in relation to the other members of the group, including the therapist. A variety of internal structures, each a product of both experience and constitution and distorted by unsatisfactory or inadequate early experience, becomes visible in the group arena. However, having then to tolerate and manage the ensuing difficulties <u>with each other</u> is an equal task for every patient in the room. When this kind of work goes well, it offers the chance of providing alternative modes of response, even of shifting internal structures in a more durable way, strengthening some and reducing others—a move from *narcissism* towards *social-ism*. Learning from experience is difficult for the most psychologically intact. It is easier to learn from the objectification of experience provided by a chance to take up the position of observer *in vivo*, not simply in theory.

3. Since not everyone can speak at the same time, turns have to be taken, and the shifting and rotating nature of the triangles (actor, reactor, observer) present in a group is equivalent to practice in dealing with complex Oedipal issues. Each member has the opportunity to observe, notice and reflect on what is happening, to take up a 'third position' (Britton, 1989) as well as being at other moments part of the action that is observed by others. What may at first feel like being excluded can, in time, come to be felt as a valuable opportunity to take stock of the action. In taking up the position of observer, advantages as well as disadvantages can be discovered, finding through varying identifications differing ways of being. In the same way, habitual observers become more confident in taking up the position of protagonist, at claiming their own right to be not just 'in on the act' but one of the actors. Thus identifications can become more flexible and offer a greater degree of freedom.

4. Dependence upon the therapist alone is diminished because of the existence not only of fellow patients, but of 'the group' itself. Dependence on 'the group' can often be tolerated where

dependence on the therapist is resented and denied, leading to an envious rejection of the therapist's greater understanding and psychologically-educated point of view. Group patients are strikingly better able to bear plain speaking from fellow members than they can from a therapist. Moreover, fellow patients often put things more directly and bluntly than a therapist could risk. "Why don't you face it, you're an alcoholic," may not rate as a psychologically sophisticated interpretation but nevertheless be both accurate and effective in the particular circumstances.

b) Borderlines in groups
5. In borderline patients, that bedrock I have described is inadequate and unstable. Often their early experience has been ill-attuned, or neglectful to the point of traumatic, resulting in a failure of the capacity to engage in the normal give and take of relationships. Yet many borderline patients also have within them a capacity for a psychologically acute and finely tuned observation of others' behaviour. They can 'read between the lines' better than most, even if the reading is often selective. When they feel the heat is on them, this capacity is easily overwhelmed by impulsively avoidant and/or chaotic behaviour; but when the heat is on <u>another</u>, there is revealed a capacity to observe and understand the situation with empathy and accuracy. In short, borderline patients seem able to tune into *each other's difficulties* more acutely can than many therapists, and without the interference of the hierarchical structure of therapist/patient, adult/child, *well-balanced and successful* vs. *crazy lost cause.*
6. This capacity in such patients to 'read' others can *join up* to form something surprisingly robust, even stable, called by them *'the group'*. Each member develops a relationship with, even an attachment to *'the group'* which seems to survive the disturbances and hostilities that erupt between the individuals within it. 'The group' continues to have an existence for each member whether or not he or she attends in any particular week, offering a kind of containment above and beyond that which can be provided by the individual therapist. Members trust each other even if they quarrel, <u>because</u> they understand each other. This description of course is of 'the good group'. There also exists 'a bad or malignant

group', which is feared and hated, and which can be experienced as quite as claustrophobic as an individual therapist, however much needed and depended on. Indeed it is partly the dependence itself that renders the object so suffocating, because the patient feels imprisoned with his own frantic needs. 'The group' too may have its psychotic and non-psychotic ways aspects, or ways of functioning. Nevertheless, good group or bad, it continues to exist. It is there in a permanent way to be loved or hated, clung to or avoided. It is also a shared experience, physically and emotionally, in itself a rarity for this kind of patient. The group exists in the mind of each member of the group, and it connects them to and with each other.

7. So a group offers a very particular structure in which each member can feel himself to be not only a patient, but also to have an important role in others' treatments. In symbolic terms, when a patient can exist as a part of the breast, the providing object, as well as feeling himself to be a frantic, perhaps starving infant, there is a mitigation of envy. Inevitably when very deprived people receive therapy from those who are less deprived, the envy that is aroused may be conscious and realistic as well as unconscious. Yet even unconscious envy can be modified, that of the other infants and of the breast itself, for being the source and provider of all goodness, full of what the infant desires and needs: it is an indisputable fact that each and every group patient is both baby and also part of the breast that nourishes and supports the other babies—the therapeutic presence. Psychic nourishment is easier to take in when one also has the opportunity to become capable of providing it for others.

Clinical material

This is a process account of material from a long-standing group, seven of whose eight members were at the more disturbed end of the spectrum. Two had spent many years of their childhood and adolescence in Care and as adults suffered from eating disorders; one of these was also a frequent and chaotic cutter. Another with a severe eating disorder, also a cutter, had had four pregnancies terminated before she joined the group. Another had been taken from her schizophrenic mother and placed in foster care, where she was perversely abused and ill-treated by the foster father, the leader of the local church group; another, a young man, with a menacing schizoid air got into frequent fights, including with the police, and had appeared in court on many occasions. Yet another was severely depressed, silent and suicidal; In spite of these unpromising beginnings, I hope to convey some idea of the degree of engagement that can characterise relations between such group patients who have come to know each other well, as well as to give examples of how effectively how group members can understand and interpret their own and each others' behaviour if given room to do so by the therapist.

Two events had taken place in the week preceding this session. First, I had seen this last member, Mike, an intelligent and sensitive but severely depressed young man, for an individual session the day before the group met. He had at his assessment interview one month earlier expressed clear suicidal intentions and after discussion with his GP, and with the local CMHT, he was admitted as a voluntary patient in the psychiatric wing of the local hospital. I had been worried both that the group was too much for him, and also that he was too much for the group, but at the point at which I took him on the group was all that could be made available. Nevertheless the degree of self-destructiveness apparent was hard for other patients to manage. He remained largely silent in my interview with him, but by the end it was agreed between us that he would continue to attending the group, and as well would come to once monthly individual meetings with me.

Second, Sharon (a childhood in Care, eating-disordered, a cutter) and Joe (brought up in Care, aggressive and a powerfully built fighter, expert in Karate) had had a bitter row before the most recent break about Sharon's having called Joe 'a prat'. She'd said she found him spooky, disturbing, that she thinks he's weird. He'd been upset and angry and had banged out of the room in the penultimate session of term, not returning for the final session. Sharon herself had in turn been upset by his response because in her world, to call someone a prat is merely ordinarily insulting. Everyone's a prat really. Joe had demanded to know why I was willing to let people get away with insulting him in the group. It was not what he was here for. Recently he'd been trying to distance himself from rows, confrontations and fights. He'd had enough of all that in his karate club. In the first week of the following term, the row erupted again and Sharon hissed she was never going to come back, this group is rubbish and anyway, he is a prat. Joe, encouraged by the others, had then tried very hard to be sensible about it all, saying through clenched teeth that he thought he'd over-reacted before Christmas. Sharon continued to hiss and mutter at him, at the same time feeling guilty and angry. I commented that I thought they recognised something about each other, the capacity for violence, which frightened them both. Sharon then rang me during the week to underline her message: she is NEVER EVER coming back—Joe's an idiot (i.e. promoted from, or perhaps demoted from 'prat'), and so are YOU (i.e. me), and she had had it up to here. She then rang off, cutting me off in mid-sentence. An hour later a further message from her arrived, saying she'd forgotten to ask me something, and will I call her.

I called Sharon the next day, the day of the group. She was in bed, apparently not feeling well. I left a message with the young boy that had answered the phone, asking him to tell his mother that her call had been returned. When I gave my name, the boy responded by saying "Oh, she said if it's you, to tell you she'll be there this afternoon ....." Here we can see the intensity of the agora-claustrophobic dilemma: *got to get out of here,* followed swiftly by *got to get back in.*

The session

When I arrive, Sharon, Elsie, Alexa and Mike are there. They've all just arrived. Sharon pulls a sheepish face at me and I smile a brief acknowledgement. Mike is silent, staring at his hands and picking at the skin on his fingers as usual, but I felt he looked very slightly less tense than the week before.

Elsie and Alexa said variously: "Hello Mike! Glad you're here, Sharon, we thought we'd seen the last of you. What a relief." Alexa adds, "I'd have been furious if you hadn't come. Rose is on her way, I've just seen her driving round and round looking for somewhere to park."

They go on to ask how come Sharon changed her mind. This is followed by silence. Sharon gestures a thumb towards me and pulls a face. "I phoned Er. You say," she says to me. I keep quiet. The others want to know what happened, and it gets told in muffled half-sentences. "I wasn't going to come back NEVER. I was so angry. It was my kids what got me to come. Said I was bein' stupid. An' I shouldn't just walk out on things, cos' I was doin' better than I used to. An' then SHE phoned me. I was so angry, SO ANGRY wiv her I wanted to cut meself, you know, like I used to. I called Er an idiot."

The others are excited, alarmed, delighted. "DID you, what did she say?" A little pause. Then: "She said to come anyway." I said that I thought the person Sharon really had it in mind to cut was me, to cut me up and to cut the group by not coming. She said *Yeah*. The others persisted—so what made her come in the end? After a silence I said I thought Sharon had found she could be angry with me in a direct way, completely furious, and that we could both survive it, and that was a relief to her. Living through these things and coming out the other side was what was important, and I thought that was true for many of the relationships in the room, not just Sharon's with me. "Yeah, where izee anyway??" she said. Joe is noticeable by his continued and unusual absence. There is another silence.

Alexa asks, "What happened with Mike—you saw him yesterday?" They ask him about it but he doesn't respond. I say to Mike that I'd like to tell the group about our meeting. Is that all right with him? Worrying, he still doesn't answer, but his face is slightly less furrowed and contorted than usual. I function as an auxiliary ego in saying that Mike is facing something difficult because the lease on his flat comes to an end at the end of the month and the landlord is not renewing it. He has to leave. The psychiatrist at the hospital where he is now an in-patient has said once he's discharged she will get him into a men's hostel in the local Borough if he wants her to. They ask him, does he want her to? Mike remains silent, picking at his fingers. The group becomes anxious.

Rose has come in during this passage. She listens and becomes troubled by the idea of the loss of his flat. I add that there was something else that Mike said that was important, and it was that he did not trust me. The atmosphere is very tense and serious. I had asked him if he knew why, and he had answered, "Because everything comes to an end." I ask the group what they think about that.

"Yes, but it doesn't come to an end all at once. Not completely, not till you die. I mean Mike, you're losing your flat but you'll then get somewhere else to live." "Mike, I wish you'd <u>talk</u> and then we could like really get to know you." Alexa (who herself has made a suicide attempt after a fourth abortion) said "I'm just glad I'm still alive now even though it's going to end some time." I think with hindsight one can hear in these exchanges their fear of Mike's silent but clear suicidality.

Jane comes in at this point. She has lost an extraordinary amount of weight over the break and looks transformed, and everyone is amazed and complimentary about it, in a flurry of comments. She says it was the 'flu, she just couldn't eat. (I am unconvinced by this.) She is relieved to see Sharon and there is a recap of how Sharon got to be there after all this week. Then Jane goes quiet. I feel there is something she cannot talk about, but it is not the moment to open this up. Rose is still very preoccupied with the loss of the flat—what does Mike *feel* about it? There is silence from Mike, who can only pick his fingers and stare at the floor.

Elsie and Alexa say how important home is, and specially the centre of home, namely their own beds. Alexa says her bed smells like home. She only really feels absolutely safe and secure under her own duvet. When her cat, Small, was still alive, Small would climb under the duvet and purr very loudly, and that was when she felt safest and happiest. Rose says that she wants to know what Mike feels because she feels very upset about the loss of her own flat (having moved her base to the country village where her Lesbian partner lives). It's not she doesn't like the cottage, but there's nowhere in it that is really *hers*. She has driven down from the Midlands that afternoon to be at the group, and she is going to go and visit her old flat. All her old teddies are there, looking at her reproachfully. She is laughing, but crying at the same time. Alexa says she should take them up to the country with her but she says she can't, she feels too stupid. They tease her about their mournful little eyes following her as she goes out of the door back to the country. Rose then says suddenly she'd thinks she'll stay the night in her own flat. It's not just her partner's cottage, she also feel excluded from her Mum's home—one of her brothers and one of her sisters (she is one of six) have moved back in and her mother is ever so pleased and busy with them, and she feels there's nowhere now that's really home for her.

I say that the group too has changed, with two new members in it since last term, and that too doesn't feel like home, like the old group, when I am so occupied with the difficulties of the new members here. She nods, sniffing. Alexa says that hearing Rose talk about what it's like for her at her partner's is weird, because she's got her little brother living with her now and she absolutely *hates* it if he wants to change anything. She feels she mustn't be so hard on him. She's got to let him have a bit of space where he can make his own kinds of mess. I am thinking about the loss of space in the group, and how much room there is now for anyone's mess.

In the middle of this Joe suddenly bursts in, panting and hot, and begins to peel off layers of clothes—ragged, but clean sports clothes, sweat shirts, socks; he unlaces his trainers and eventually sits there in just a tee shirt, socks and baggy, torn leggings. Everyone is looking at him, but he is silent, still over-heated, and so they go on talking about Mike's enforced move. Joe says then that it's obvious things are happening with Mike and he was very sorry to miss him talking. Alexa says he wasn't talking, and relays to Joe the situation with the flat. Then Rose and Alexa ask Joe why he's so late. (Sharon is looking pointedly out of the window, chewing gum and looking bored.)

Joe says, *I just forgot!* I forgot it was the group day. I was having this animated conversation with Rose and then I suddenly remembered it was therapy day and I just got over here on my bike at maximum speed. The others look at him—is this a hallucination, a joke, or just Joe? Rose asks, giggling slightly, *well what did I say??* Joe then told a long saga, much of which was the lead-up to what Rose was saying to him in his head. He'd been holding auditions for his end-of-year drama production, and his teacher, on whom he relies a great deal, was absent so he was having to make decisions about the actors himself, which he was finding very difficult. The problem was that one of them was very good looking, but the good-looking one wasn't as right for the part as the other actor. He found himself beginning to be preoccupied with the good-looking one, wanting to follow him after the audition to find out where he lived. He said, "I just went into gay mode, and decided that's what I really wanted, a relationship with this young actor, but then I started to think but I *also* want children and that's more or less ruled out if I'm living with a man, 'cos you can't have children then. And then I thought of Rose, and how gay and Lesbian parents can have children these days, and then Rose started saying to me but Joe you're not ready to have children yet, you've got to get yourself sorted out first, *I've* already spent five years in this group …"

He is being serious as he recounts this long vivid day-dream, which nevertheless has elements of a quite useful awareness of reality in it, as well as evidence of the existence of the group in his mind even when he is not present. The others are smiling at him quite fondly, and listening to his saga which has no full-stops in it. Then he suddenly said that he had found himself crying last night, because he felt very deeply that he missed his Mum—he loves his Mum and they had had a good time together in Ireland at Christmas, got on very well even though his dreadful step-father was there too, somehow they'd all got on with it together.

Rose asked him if this was recent, this feeling of missing his Mum—"I mean do you think it's because we had a break from the group over the holidays?" Joe said no, he often misses her. He did even when he was very small in Care. He can remember telling Dr. T. (his assessor) how he used to rock himself to sleep in Care, crying at night till he was 13 or 14. He told the group about his mother's weekend visits, how she would visit and be with him and then leave, and he would feel terribly lonely. Perhaps all that's being so vivid now for him because he's in therapy, he knows therapy is supposed to open you up (the others are nodding).

This is the first time he's talked about being brought up in Care when Sharon has actually been in the room. She too was brought up in Care. She is looking at him very intently, legs and arms wrapped round her body, one hand round her face. She says suddenly that she'd had no-one to collect her at the weekends. Some of the kids just didn't. When everyone else had gone off she'd be on her own, just one or two others, kicking around the empty building. The staff had found her something called a "social aunt and uncle" and they would come and take her out but she never talked. She went mute at the age of five for over a year. She was sent to a psychiatrist but she never talked to him.

Alexa bursts out how shocking it is that she was sent to a psychiatrist when it must be perfectly obvious to anyone who knows ANYTHING about children WHY she's mute, that she's missing her Mum. (This seems to me to contain an oblique reference to Mike's mute state.) Sharon said crossly, "No I wasn't, I never wanted to see her anyway!" Joe said anyway he didn't think it was so shocking— at least it's an *attempt* to help, some offer of something, so at least she had a chance to tell someone what she felt. Sharon said again she never spoke to the psychiatrist. (Is Mike listening, I wonder?) But she continued to visit her social aunt and uncle, after she got talking a bit, and even saw them sometimes when she was quite grown-up. They was good to her. (This is a quite lengthy passage from Sharon, who is often largely silent.) Then she spoke directly to Joe, looking sideways at him: "How long was you in Care?" They swap notes. I am holding my breath. Many years for each of them: Joe from 0–8, then 12–14, and Sharon from 2–16. There is a silence—this is felt by the group to be a very long time, the whole of a childhood, an adolescence.

Sharon says suddenly looking at Joe, "I know I got pissed off wiv you, but I need you to like me, Joe, I know it's silly, but you know where I'm coming from. It's why I find you spooky, it's because you're *like me.*"

After a moment Jane says, "It's amazing you can say that, Sharon, I think that's really brave." Joe says, "Well, I need that from you too, Sharon." Sharon looks at me and says, "Az wo' you said, wonni', vere was fings we could understand 'bou' each uvver …." She goes on to say that she thinks the group is difficult, but she knows she needs it, it's done her more good in 18 months than all them years of counselling. She's changed, her kids keep telling her. The others are watching the two of them, Sharon and Joe, very intently.

Joe speaks to Sharon. He said that one of the things he's begun to recognise is that the reason abuse is so difficult is that it makes you feel special, even though it's harmful. That's why he likes Buddhism. It tries to help you let go of your ego, because if you can let go of that you lose the feeling that you're special, even specially *bad*—in some ways even feeling specially bad is something people want when there's no other way of feeling special or even all right.

The others are quiet, trying to digest this. After a while Alexa says in a very quiet voice she thought the group was going to be really difficult with these new people in it, but perhaps the group has never been as important to her before.

Session two

The following week, Rose is not there, because she and her partner are house-hunting, looking for somewhere to buy together (this is conveyed in a phone message). Alexa (looking scruffy and uncared for, as though she is sleeping rough) asks Mike if he has had to move out, and after a long silent struggle, he says a single word, his first after four months in the group: "Tuesday". Everyone looks at each other, pleased, and Sharon looks at me and smiles. However, both Alexa and Jane begin to cry a lot in this session, apologetically, wanting very much to be seen to be good and be strong, because they've been there longest of all and they want to show the others that the group can help them if they just stick at it. But Alexa says she has been having unprotected sex again, with two men she doesn't really know, and she is very afraid of being pregnant, which would make her feel quite awful in relation to Rose, and her struggles to conceive via IVF.

Elsie, more neurotic than borderline, is in her seventies and a different generation from the others. She talks then about how much she regrets never having taken risks in her life, either practical or emotional. Now she feels she is going to die, to end her life, feeling she has wasted it. Jane is clearly in a state—is she unwell? Alexa suddenly starts getting cramps. It makes her feel and look relieved. She thinks her period is about to start which would mean she can face Rose and tell her how terrible she would have felt if she had been pregnant. Rose does not like this. She feels she can manage her own difficulties in trying to conceive, and if she doesn't manage it she is going to adopt. She doesn't want anyone feeling sorry for her. She's glad Alexa isn't pregnant for Alexa's sake, not for hers. They speak to Elsie about the risks and the pain of getting it wrong, but Elsie now feels she would rather have got into a mess and into a state than having nothing to show for her life. This is a very truthful if painful admission for her, a shift away from her habitual envious rejection of others' capacity for living, however chaotically.

Jane is saying that she is terribly upset, because all her old phobias have returned and she feels she is "back to square one". I say they feel forced into being grown-up before they feel ready by this influx of needy new patients, and they need to remind me that they are in many ways still at square one, as vulnerable and needy as babies too. There is much sniffing and sharing of Kleenex.

Discussion

The process of externalization, which increases the possibility of taking up a 'third position'—discovering what is in oneself through observing and recognising the same processes taking place between others in a *three*-person setting—is immensely useful when it comes to helping patients 'see' what's going on inside them, and what part they are playing in their own difficulties. It is a long way from having a therapist *tell* you exactly the same thing whether in a group or in a *two*-person setting. In a well-functioning group, that work is done by patients in relation to each other within the steady long-term environment that can be provided by a committed therapist. And as in all forms of analytically-based treatment, the reintrojection of lost or projected parts of the mind leads to a greater mental capacity to tolerate pain and distress, and to a fuller and more integrated personality. Unappreciated emotional intelligence is discovered and used. This can lead to some quite unexpected side-benefits, apart from the amelioration of object relations in general—the patient may discover new interests in the external world, such as an increased appetite for taking up work, or sustaining a social life.

However, I called this paper 'benefits and challenges'. Although I hope that my clinical material has given a glimpse of some of the benefits, I am also aware of the great challenges inherent in dealing with a rapid deterioration in psychic functioning. The warning signs of Mike's deterioration were his silence, his obliging me to speak for him. There was then a period of months in which Mike began to recover and to take part, revealing himself as an intelligent and sensitive member of the group, but abruptly—perhaps afraid of 'coming to life' once more, and having to give up the 'solution' to life that he kept in reserve—he quite suddenly withdrew altogether. Three weeks later, in spite of being on a 15 minute watch in the psychiatric ward of the hospital, he committed suicide—some six months after the material I have reported. The shock for the group, and for me, was immense, and its reverberations felt for years. I went on wonder if in some respects it had functioned as a suicide by proxy, in that the amount of destructive acting out by Joe, Sharon and Alexa diminished, always with a warning to each other *you don't want to finish up like Mike.*

The psychotic part of the personality operates on the basis of a need for immediate solutions to various forms of breakdown in ego-functioning. Yet an instant solution or 'repair' is inevitably omnipotent. It may be achieved on the basis of sacrificing a piece of reality; even—through suicide—the ego itself. This is a subjective version of 'sanity' clung to by the damaged ego at the expense of the reality principle. In this case it was a version of sanity that was preferred to the difficult reality of putting his life together once again bit by bit. This degree of illness cannot be contained by the group for long. It is of course hard when you are ill yourself to cope with others' illness. It makes demands upon the less ill members for a degree of integration and maturity that cannot always be available. With hindsight, there may be occasions when a patient as ill as this should be withdrawn from the group. However, in this particular group, the remaining members (seven out of eight) continued to grow in strength and capacity to take on work, to bear and raise children, and in one case to begin and sustain a lengthy professional training. In some respects perhaps, the more disturbed and ill aspects of their own functioning were felt to have been projected into Mike and taken away with him. Yet the group continued for another five years without the need for further sacrifices. It makes the issue of selection for this kind of treatment of primary importance.

Conclusions

The mutual openness and understanding that can be achieved between even damaged members of a group venture involves not only knowing about illness in others, but also involves the obligation to recognise aspects of the same kinds of illness in the self. Given permission to voice thoughts and feelings that are normally private, sometimes hidden, in a setting which is specifically designed to offer this opportunity, human beings (even damaged or ill human beings) reveal themselves to be subtle, sophisticated and sensitive instruments for the recognition and reading of each others' behaviours. The task of putting into words—'publication' of the self through verbalising these discoveries—is one of the routes towards internal change; and this in turn fosters change in ways of relating to others.

However, such a group must operate along certain lines.

1. It should be long–term: my own slow-open group ran for over fifteen years. No patient should expect to spend less than three to four years in treatment.
2. It must have a reasonably stable membership: be either a closed or a very slow-open group.
3. It must be actively managed by the therapist, who needs to be someone who likes this kind of work and this kind of patient.

4. Back-up support must be available. Such a group will work best as part of a whole treatment system because of the variability in patients' needs at different times. It is for instance useful to have an 'in-patient' option should it be necessary.
5. The therapist cannot be everything to everyone all of the time.

Shifting and modifying characteristic modes of relating is the hardest of tasks for human beings, and there is a built-in aversion to the kind of pain involved in real change. Some group patients will wish, and will fight, to use the setting for the purposes of re-enactment rather than for change. Relinquishing behaviours can be painful and frightening, and the existing modes of relating may offer gratifications that new ones do not possess. Yet if attendance can be sustained—and this may require flexibility and hard work on the part of the therapist—change can be seen to take place.

Finally, there is the central fact that <u>the group itself</u> comes to be an important object in its own right, and own way. However it is an object that differs from the seven or eight other people in the room in a number of ways.

1. It belongs equally to every patient in the room.
2. It has a continuous existence. The group is alive, whether good or bad, in the mind of each patient. Thus every patient has an existence in the mind of every other patient and containment and the maintenance of the therapeutic setting becomes a joint activity.
3. The group can be a <u>loved object</u>, by virtue of the attendance of each of its members.
4. The group can be a <u>hated object</u>, assaulted and avoided, but refound in an alive state when the patient feels less full of rage and distress once more.
5. It is a <u>maternal object</u>: it remains open to the patient and it provides emotional nourishment in the form of tolerance and understanding. This is its 'lap' function.
6. It is a <u>paternal object</u>: it provides insight through verbal comment and interpretation, which offers the possibility of thinking again: of pausing the action before impulsively acting it out, much as the action is paused on the screen of a word-processor for consideration and editing before being printed out. This is its 'organizer' function.

7. These two functions operate together via the person of the therapist, and via the patients themselves; that is to say via the existence of the <u>object that is the group</u>.

8. Every member of the group can relate to it in a number of ways. As I have indicated, being able to function as both baby <u>and</u> breast, both impulsive child <u>and</u> thinking organizing adult, fosters the reintrojection and integration of split parts of the personality in the patient. Each patient possesses as well as illness a capacity for helpful, considerate and thoughtful (non-psychotic) functions of the personality. Being a 'patient' (bringing the ill parts of the personality for treatment) is made more tolerable by each member's also being able to function as 'non-psychotic' in relation to the others.

A more ordinary developmental process begins to take place in the group's members as they project more normal parts of the self into the group for public consideration of their meaning and significance. Although the subsequent reintrojection is subject to ups and downs, negative therapeutic reactions, there is a sense in which the original deteriorating vicious cycles can begin to be supplanted by something more benign. These sorts of developments are necessary for the individual to locate him or herself in those human groups on which, in turn, the ability 'to work and to love' depends. The ability to operate as a member of a family, social or work group is one of the central tasks of healthy personality functioning. And the converse is also true: for human groups to function normally and well, their members must be able to projects parts of themselves into group organisations to form the networks of cooperation that enable family and social organisations to function.

And as Bion has indicated in his description of the move from *narciss-ism* to *social-ism*, a therapy group is in this way a microcosm of society. The expectation is that those who come to be able to take part in it will be, perhaps only marginally, perhaps only from time to time, but still *better* able to take part in the complex negotiations, the give and take, of society itself.

References

Bateman, A. & Fonagy, P. (2004). *Psychotherapy for Borderline Personality Disorder: mentalization-based treatment*. Oxford: Oxford University Press.

Bateman, A. and Fonagy, P. (2006). *Mentalization-Based Treatment for Borderline Personality Disorder: a Practical Guide*. Oxford: Oxford University Press.

Bion, W. (1967, reprinted 1984). *Second Thoughts: selected papers on psychoanalysis*. London: Karnac.

Britton, R. (1989). The missing link: Parental sexuality in the Oedipus complex. In: J. Steiner (Ed.), *The Oedipus Complex Today*. (pp. 83–101). London: Karnac.

Gunderson, J.G. (2005). Chapter 1, pp. 1–33 in *Borderline personality disorder: a clinical guide*. American Psychiatric Publishing.

Hobson, R.P., Patrick, M., et al. (2005). Personal relatedness and attachment in infants of mothers with borderline personality disorder. *Development and Psychopathology, 17*, 329–347.

Kernberg, O. (1975). *Borderline Conditions and Pathological Narcissism*. New York: Jason Aronson.

Rey, H. (1994). *Universals of psychoanalysis in the treatment of psychotic and borderline states*. (Ed. J. Magagna). London: Free Association Books.

Rosenfeld, H. (1987). *Impasse and Interpretation*. London: Tavistock Publications.

Steiner, J. (1979). The border between the paranoid-schizoid and the depressive positions in the borderline patient. *Brit. J. Med. Psychol. 52*, 385–391.

CHAPTER FIVE

The fiend that sleeps but does not die: Toward a psychoanalytic treatment of the addictions

Stephen M. Sonnenberg

In this essay the author describes his views on the psychoanalytic treatment of the addictions. He describes addiction as a serious mental disorder, which is appropriately included as a topic in this conference. Next, he conveys the scope of this major public health problem, and discusses the reasons why psychoanalysis has made so small a contribution to its understanding. This essay discusses addiction in high functioning analytic patients, and offers a definition of what constitutes high functioning individuals. Case examples from thirty years ago, and from the present, illustrate how today, with more advanced knowledge, more successful analytic treatment of addiction is possible. The author describes modifications in standard analytic technique which are helpful, and which result in analysands who remain abstinent indefinitely.

Introduction

At first blush one might wonder whether the treatment of the addictions belongs in this conference where we are exploring such difficult clinical situations as the treatment of schizophrenia, borderline personality disorder, and suicidality. I contend that it very much fits, because addicted analysands often behave in suicidal ways, in some cases might well qualify diagnostically as schizophrenics or border-lines, and in general fundamentally challenge the treating psycho-analyst to work effectively.

What is of particular interest to me is that while I have been prac-ticing psychoanalysis for thirty-five years, it has only been in the last five years that I have been able to recognize that right along my psychoanalytic practice has been filled with analysands who suffer from serious addictions. At the core of this presentation I shall offer two cases. The first will illustrate how years ago, like many of my colleagues, I missed the presence of addiction in my analysands. The second is designed to illustrate how today I have a far different per-spective on addiction than earlier in my professional life, and will include a description of what I believe is an effective strategy for treatment.

Scope of the problem

Addiction represents a major challenge to psychoanalysis, psychi-atry, psychology, social work, and other mental health disciplines because of the enormity of the health problem it represents. In what I believe to be a vast underestimation, the World Health Organization (2008) states that there are over 90 million substance abusers world wide. Whether each of these is an addict depends to some extent on which of the many definitions one favours. My definition equates abuse and addiction, because I do not believe that physical depend-ency is the crucial characteristic of the addict from a psychoana-lytic perspective. Rather, I look for self-destructive behavior based on poor judgment; driven, compulsive drug seeking; and a range of sometimes subtle, sometimes not so subtle cognitive processing deficiencies. In sum, what I am describing is what is sometimes described as the hijacked brain, a concept which I embrace as clini-cally very helpful (Hyman, 2005).

In addition to these many substance abuse problems there are addictive disorders which do not involve substances. One such category is internet addiction (Block, 2008), with three subcate-gories already described: gaming, sexual preoccupation, and use of websites like MySpace and You Tube, or email instant messag-ing. Other non-substance addictions include sexual addiction, gambling addiction, exercise addiction, and in my view workaholism. Estimates about how many people are affected by such addictions are very unreliable.

Finally, there are serious substance addictions which do not involve drugs or alcohol. Here I would mention food addiction and cigarette smoking. I realize that many would place this last in the category with drugs.

What is most striking to me is that without taxing our imaginations too much I believe we can make the case that even the most seemingly benign of these conditions carries with it serious health consequences, which actually shorten life in very significant ways. So for that reason I think of these various forms of addiction as falling within the category of severe disturbance.

 Another critical point is that today the experts among us who study addiction recognize that we know very little about the entity (Miller and Carroll, 2006a). This is so despite the fact that huge amounts of money and scientific effort have been expended to investigate this public health crisis. Among the points that experts make is that substance and non-substance abuse are not associated with a particular personality structure (Carroll and Miller, 2006). In fact, most recently, addiction has been described as occurring along side the full range of life problems and personality styles (Carroll and Miller, 2006). Addiction can be a pernicious health problem for a relatively high functioning person and for a derelict living on the street. In my view much of the disagreement about addiction in the relatively sparse psychoanalytic literature is a reflection of different populations studied, different interventions offered, and different venues in which studies take place (Director, 2002; Dodes, 1996; Khantzian, 1987; Krystal, 1982; Wurmser, 1974).

It is curious that psychoanalysts have contributed so little to investigating addiction. I believe that historically analysts were taught that addicts were not treatable psychoanalytically, so that even when an addiction came into clinical focus the analyst observer was motivated to ignore it. To understand more about this history within psychoanalysis one has to go back to Freud. To begin with, early in his scientific explorations Freud (1890, p. 299) referred to addiction and alcoholism as morbid habits, similar to sexual aberrations, associated addiction with masturbation, called masturbation a primal addiction (Freud, 1897), and suggested that addiction could not really be cured (Freud, 1898). None of this motivated the beginning student of psychoanalysis to develop an interest in addiction.

Then, in his six *Papers on technique* (1911–1915 [1914]), Freud described a treatment method, which was destined to deter psychoanalysts from undertaking the treatment of addiction, and to ensure failure, and subsequent disinterest, if they were to try. What I have in mind is Freud's prescription in these papers that the analyst function with abstinence, anonymity, neutrality, and the absolute preservation of confidentiality. Curiously, despite writing on technique Freud believed that the value of written material in the training of psychoanalysts was limited, favouring the personal analytic experience as the critical measure which might equip someone to become an analyst (Strachey, 1958). Additionally, Freud offered examples within and outside the *Papers on technique* which indicated that in his own work he did not adhere to what came to be cited as his technical canon. In the technique papers, for example, in writing on premature termination Freud was anything but neutral and abstinent (pp. 129–130). Freud also recorded that he fed the Rat Man (Freud, 1909; Lipton, 1977, 1979), and many other examples of his departure from his written technical prescription have been reported (Lynn and Vaillant, 1998). But what might have been Freud's preference was outweighed by his technique papers, and the way what he wrote has been interpreted and taught by those who claim to be his most loyal followers (Eissler, 1953). Later, in my second clinical example, by contrast, I will demonstrate why those who follow these rules strictly are unlikely to have success treating addicts, and will then be likely to avoid such clinical encounters.

It follows what I have so far said that since addiction is a very broad category, and those who develop addiction represent a very diverse population, that for this to be a meaningful essay I have to make clear the population of addicts I have treated and studied. Since 1977, when I graduated from a psychoanalytic training institute in the United States, I have usually had a full analytic practice. That means I usually worked with between nine and twelve analysands at a time. Back a few decades my definition of analysis was more rigid: at least four sessions each week on the couch. Today my definition is far more flexible, and I'll leave it to your imagination to consider the range of patients I calculate that I have in analysis. But I will state unequivocally that my practice is still completely psychoanalytic, and that means that with each analysand there is an observable psychoanalytic process, involving mindfulness, mentalization, introspection, self-analysis, and the analysis of the transference-countertransference encounter. Obviously, an analysand's capacity to engage in these forms of thinking, feeling, and observing, changes over the life of his or her analysis. But after the opening phase, and the establishment of a therapeutic alliance (which can take from months to years), every patient in my practice comes for psychoanalytic exploration.

In this essay I am focusing on a particular group of individuals, that I describe as high functioning. For a good working definition of what I am calling high functioning I want to refer you to the *Diagnostic and statistical manual of mental disorders, Fourth edition* (DSM), a publication of the American Psychiatric Association. Members of my high functioning group of analysands have scores of eighty and above on the Global Assessment of Functioning Scale (GAF) as it is described in that volume, on initial evaluation. That means that "symptoms [if present] are transient and expectable reactions to psychosocial stressors ... [and there is] no more than slight impairment in social, occupational, or school functioning ..." (American Psychiatric Association, 1994, p. 32). So this is a well functioning group of individuals, despite their addictions. I do want to add that when I look at an analysand through a psychoanalytic lens, examining affect regulation in relation to psychic conflict and such phenomena as mindful self-analytic capacity, I bring into focus a perspective which is far different from the behavioural emphasis of American psychiatry, especially as it is depicted in the DSM.

The case of James Edwards

The first case I will describe was treated by me over thirty years ago. At the time I was a young but experienced analyst. The patient was referred to me by colleagues in another city, from which he had moved to Washington, D.C., where I was living. He was a high ranking United States government employee, who occupied a Sub-Cabinet level position. When we first spoke on the phone he reported depression over the break-up of his second marriage.

When I met with James I heard a remarkable story. He was forty-seven years old, and African-American. He had risen from poverty and deprivation in a ghetto in a major United States city. When he was quite young his mother, who had previously been doting, encouraging, and loving, began to drink and run around with men outside her marriage. In response to mother's behavior father, a critical and angry man to begin with, protested vigorously, but in vain. He would lose his temper and hit mother, which was obviously counterproductive. When James was twelve, his mother left the family, and lived with her alcoholic boyfriend in a neighbouring state. For the next few years James rarely saw mother, but based on their sporadic contact was aware that she was deteriorating. Father took up with another woman, and James had to fend for himself. Members of his extended family lent a hand, but he was largely unsupervised. When he was fifteen his girlfriend became pregnant, he married her, and soon was the father of twins. That marriage lasted for twenty years, and James became father to a second set of twins and a fifth child.

Against great odds James fought to keep his family together, and get an education. He worked at menial jobs within universities in order to gain tuition remission. He was also a gifted musician, studied part-time at a local conservatory, and eventually earned a college degree, and became a pioneer in the area of community arts advocacy. He developed programs involving the teaching of fine and creative arts to ghetto children and ghetto mental health patients.

Twelve years before I met him James' marriage ended. He and his first wife did not wish to remain together, but remained on cordial terms. Soon after his divorce James met and married his second wife, and they had a son. When he was offered his high level job in D.C. he, his wife, their son, and his fifth child from his first marriage, also a son, moved to Washington. In his new position he was to use his skills as a community arts activist and organizer.

From the time of his move his second wife rejected him. She hated where they lived, complaining that it was away from the "Black action." Eventually, a few months before I met James, she moved out. He felt depressed, helpless, and abandoned. He was furious at his wife, and in our extended consultation reported that he drank "immoderately" in an effort to "take the edge off" his rage. He reported that at such times instead of feeling calmer he felt angrier, and would call his wife and rage at her over the phone. This, in turn, led him to feel guilty and more depressed, and he ended up blaming himself for her departure.

Early in the analysis James demonstrated a transference reaction to me in which he saw me as being like his father: He believed I would find fault in his behavior and reject him, which paralleled the way he experienced his father after mother's departure. He related father's harshness during that period, during which James was on the receiving end of frequent and regular beatings. He also demonstrated the belief that his experience with his wife was identical to what his mother had done to him. He believed that both women had left him because of his own shortcomings, particularly his anger. Early in the analysis he came to appreciate ways in which in the present he was re-experiencing his childhood helplessness when his mother had left him, and his father had angrily beaten him. He realized that in some ways he could actually feel happy at the possibility of a divorce, if only he could fully understand and put an end to the ways in which he was using the present to re-experience and rework the past, especially motivated by his guilt at what he saw as his responsibility for the decline of both his parents.

On the surface this analysis went extremely well over its course of seven years. However, what I will now convey, through the use of process material, and a candid reappraisal of how I worked with James, sheds a very different light on what went on.

He did not appear for his first analytic session, which was scheduled after a period of detailed and careful consultation. The next day he appeared and after clearing up a few loose ends he lay down on the couch. He began:

> "I missed yesterday because the night before I was furious at my wife, I started to drink, I drove to her house and I yelled at her, I hit her, then I blacked out. It was the worst episode of its kind I ever had, though for a number of years, especially the last two years, this has been happening ... I just can't accept that a Black woman can treat a Black man like that ... when I was twelve my aunt seduced me and introduced me to sex ..."

> I responded that this was the first time he had told me of this sexual experience, and that he "was in the right place, that we could talk about this." He then became tearful, cried throughout the rest of the session, expressing gratitude that I had said what

I had. He said "I need help ... so much of what I feel toward my wife is a rage at my aunt and my mother, at women in the past ..."

During the months that followed James began to talk about the racism he experienced in his work. He felt that he needed the support of his wife to deal with that, and was disappointed and angry that she was not there to give it to him. Eventually, he became more specific about how his peers in his Cabinet department viewed him. They were, in his view, privileged white men, were disrespectful of his expertise, of his mission, and of the unique education he had gained through his own hard work over many years. He began to make anti-white statements, and I responded by asking him how he thought I might respond to what he was saying. He insisted that he trusted me, that he believed I was on his side, and that I believed that what he had to say was accurate and appropriate. When he reported that he was afraid his boss, the Cabinet member, was going to squeeze him out and fire him, he said that he believed I understood and agreed with his concerns. I knew he was correct, and reacted quietly with a sense that he had gotten the message I wished him to receive.

Then, several months later, he spoke about his uncertainty about the analysis. He had spent the hour talking about how empty and sad he felt inside, how miserable he felt about his wife and his sons in Washington, and as the session drew to a close he said "I wonder what I'm doing in analysis, I feel so unsure about how to use it, so strange on the couch, I don't know where I'm heading." I interpreted this as an expression about the general uncertainty of his future, but did not ask about what it might have meant regarding his concrete experience of analysis.

The next week he came in and was enraged at his boss. He told me that there had been some kind of a leak to the press about some important departmental issue, and that the Cabinet Secretary had said "there's a nigger in the woodpile somewhere ..." The Secretary then caught himself, looked at James, swallowed hard, and said "... to use an expression you would use ..." James was furious, but during the next few minutes of his hour we saw a demonstration of what we had come to expect of him: He turned on himself, and wondered if he had behaved properly in the face of what was obviously an unpardonable insult on the part of his boss.

What followed was that for the next two weeks every session began with a report that James had been drinking heavily at night, had consistently contacted his wife and screamed at her for not supporting him, and had blacked out at the end of each encounter. He then would associate to the way his father monitored his conduct, and routinely beat him out of what James knew was displaced rage at mother for abandoning father and him. And each time, as his associations turned to his guilt and shame at his behavior, I interpreted his turning on himself.

James' most successful child was a college professor, who was informed by his estranged wife of what was going on, and visited his father in Washington. The two had a joyous reunion, and son was supportive of father. But this respite had almost no lasting effect, because right after father and son parted James began to drink, and ended the night screaming at his wife over the phone, and blacking out. I made an attempt to interpret these blackouts as a defense against recalling the extent of his aggression, which was freed up by his consumption of alcohol to be felt and expressed. James politely agreed that might be possible, and when I sought the opinion of two analytic colleagues about my interpretation they thought that I was on the right track.

Some time later James came to an hour describing a conversation he had with a neighbour who is a psychiatrist and a psychotherapist. He felt that this man is troubled, and just doesn't understand how he feels, who he is. He is afraid to say anything to that neighbour, for fear of insulting him. I ask if there's something here that he feels about me, that there's something about myself or the two of us that I just don't get. I asked if he feared insulting me if he told me what he really thought. James responded "I'm a compulsive drinker when there's alcohol around ... I need to talk about the way I drink ... I feel like your interpretations, when you talk about my guilt and shame over my rage, and the way I turn on myself, that's not so pertinent, relevant, correct ..." That statement closed his hour, and got lost the next day when he described, in retrospect conveniently reinforcing and affirming my confidence in the approach I had taken for a very long time, an episode of hostile aggression from childhood. He remembered shooting his mother in the stomach with a BB gun during one of her rare visits after her departure. This description was filled with guilt and shame, and reinforced my view that it was in that area of investigation that this analysis belonged.

What I want to emphasize now is that James' analysis continued for seven years. At the time I would not have said that his cognitive function was impaired, that his ability to be self-reflective and thoughtful was less than excellent. Eventually, the notion that he turned on himself became an important aspect of how he understood himself, and he was able to recognize that when he was exposed to racist attitudes, which was a regular occurrence in his world, he responded to that stressor with rage, before turning on himself out of a sense of guilt and shame. He eventually reconciled with his wife, and though their marriage remained tumultuous, it persevered. He came to possess an integrated understanding of the scars he felt from his very dysfunctional childhood, and he could stop himself and recognize when he would superimpose the past on the present.

What James never brought under control was his addiction to alcohol. While he could speak about his personal history and psychodynamics in a way which made sense, he never stopped drinking when he was stressed. The result was that he did not perform well in the very demanding Sub-Cabinet level job he had, and given his high and sensitive political profile, a quiet and honourable job change, away from Washington, was arranged. There was a big going away party, and James was publicly praised. But, predictably, in retrospect, James failed at three subsequent jobs, each time taking a new position with less responsibility and less pay. In the end he reached retirement age a man who had failed to live up to his potential, as a talented public servant, a husband, or a father. He had kept in touch with me over the years, and because of occasional phone conversations I knew all this. In the end James still turned on himself, and to my knowledge never felt that I had let him down. Of course, this was consistent with his defensive style. Until I came to understand, years later, that James' alcoholism had never been treated, that he had never stopped drinking, and that he had never reclaimed his hijacked brain, I could not formulate what had gone undone. Now I believe that for all he had learned, he had never possessed the capacity to think in a deeply self-analytic way about what he had potentially learned.

The case of stuart holcombe

Now, having described a case from three decades ago, in which I failed to recognize and address my analysand's addiction, I will report on a very different clinical situation. For the last thirteen years I have lived and practiced in Austin, Texas, a medium sized city in central Texas, which is the state capital and the home of the very large and quite excellent University of Texas. For all intents and purposes until very recently I was the only training analyst in Austin, which means that almost all my analysands were mental health professionals, known as such to each other and the broader mental health community. For that reason I must avoid writing about one of my own analysands. However, I am fortunate in that I also have a large supervising and consulting practice, which includes people who live far from Austin, and one case on which I have consulted for five years serves to beautifully illustrate what I have learned about the treatment of the addictions. Nevertheless, I do want to emphasize that the case is well disguised, and of course the name of the analysand is fictional.

Let me begin by telling you about the analyst with whom I consult. From 1969 through May of 1995 I lived in Washington, D.C. One academic activity I enjoyed in Washington was my service on the faculty of the Uniformed Services University of the Health Sciences (USUHS), also known as the "military medical school." Part of my work at the medical school involved supervising psychiatry residents studying at the various military hospitals in the Washington metropolitan area. One particularly outstanding resident was a man who had been a career soldier, serving first as an enlisted man, then while on active duty going to college and eventually graduating from USUHS. He began training in internal medicine, before switching to psychiatry. It was then that we first worked together. His name is Joseph Waterbury. Years went by, I had moved away, and Joseph became a psychoanalyst. He would send me a Christmas card every year, with a photo updating me on the growth of his family, and occasionally we crossed paths at a conference or congress. Five years ago, in 2003, he called me, asking if I would consult with him on a particularly difficult case. He reminded me that now he had left the military, and was in private practice. He added that because he had worked at the Bethesda Naval Hospital while on active duty, he had taken care of many VIPs. This pattern continued when he went into private practice. He had many high profile analysands, some were elected officials, some were appointed officials, and some from within the military and the press corps. The person he wanted to discuss with me, a man named Stuart Holcombe, was an investigative journalist. One reason he wanted to speak with me was that I no longer lived in D.C., and while in theory that didn't matter he liked the idea that I was in some ways more removed from the scene of the treatment and the home of the analysand than a local consultant. He also wanted to speak with me because he knew that I am a writer, and he felt that at times, when his analysand's writing was not going well, I might have some special insights to share with him. I was flattered that this former resident supervisee would call on me at this time in his life, when he himself had accomplished so much, and we began to meet weekly over the phone.

Joseph told me that ten years earlier, in 1993, he was consulted by Stuart, who presented with a chief complaint of depression. During an initial period of evaluation Stuart related the following story. He was the third son of his parents, who were educated and privileged. Before he was born his oldest sibling had died in a freak drowning accident. He asserted that he was a replacement child, but that he could never make up for the loss experienced by his parents. In Stuart's opinion his inability to temper the disappointment and profound sense of loss which permeated the family resulted in distant relationships with both his parents. He said that he grew up feeling alone and isolated. His surviving older brother was seven years his senior, and also depressed, so that brother was unable to mitigate Stuart's profound aloneness.

Growing up as he did in a family in which each parent and his older brother were self-absorbed in their unprocessed grief, Stuart had no models on which to base his efforts to have friends outside the family. He did, however, grow up a very curious fellow, always trying to figure out why his family situation was so static, so unchanging. However, he was never drawn to psychology as a vehicle for developing the understanding he lacked.

Stuart had been a good student, and left home for the first time when he attended one of America's leading universities. However, there he proved to be a directionless student, and eventually dropped out before receiving his degree. At that point he went to Washington, with the plan that he would try to establish himself as an independent investigative journalist. Things went very slowly at first, but shortly before he consulted with Joseph he enjoyed his first success. He had gotten wind that the Washington branch of a religious cult was being investigated by the D.C. Police for child abuse, and he decided that he would attempt to infiltrate the cult. At that point Joseph was quite young, still of college age, and many of the cult members were his chronological contemporaries. He attended cult functions, pretended to be very interested in what the cult leaders preached, and eventually took up residence in a group home operated by the cult. There, he met a woman of similar age, and they seemed to fall in love. He also encountered proscriptions on his conduct of that relationship, rules which included threats of physical punishment and excommunication should he fail to cooperate. He actually became quite frightened, and when he found himself unable to convince his girlfriend to leave the cult with him, he slipped away late one night. He was very surprised when cult leaders pursued him, ordered him back to the group home, and threatened him if he publicly spoke about the cult.

Stuart was not a well socialized person, and because of that was more resistant to the kinds of group pressures to which he was being exposed. Someone with more social skill might have been more frightened, and would have been more tempted to return to the group. Instead, he stayed away, and wrote his story, which included many details of his own experience of intimidation and abuse within the cult. His reward was that a major national news magazine bought the story, and from then on Stuart was thought of as a hard charging, gifted journalist. His immediate response to that was to become depressed, and that motivated him to ask around for suggestions about who he might see for help. Since Joseph was well know in Washington journalistic circles, his name came up more than once as Stuart the investigator located a potential therapist. Eventually, Stuart called Joseph for an appointment.

In that first meeting Joseph recalled Stuart as an unusual man. He had already earned the reputation of a skilled reporter, but to Joseph he seemed withdrawn and irritable. Stuart explained that as a rule he is perceived as aloof, even as unfriendly, and that his withdrawn exterior masks his profound discomfort in any situation in which he is required to socially mix. He added that this first interview with Joseph seemed to him to be one of those awkward social situations. Joseph decided that he would need to see Stuart several times before he could formulate his clinical impression and make a sensible treatment recommendation, but after three more meetings, and still unsure of what to recommend, he explained his uncertainty to Stuart, but recommended a trial of psychoanalysis. Stuart, always the curious one, agreed.

At the first analytic session Joseph began to question his therapeutic plan. For Stuart not only appeared vacant when entering the consulting room and lying on the couch, but once supine he fell into silence. This lasted most of the session. That pattern continued for several weeks, during which Joseph worked hard to help Stuart understand the source of his withdrawal once the analysis had begun. Once again, all that the analytic pair came up with was that withdrawal by Stuart was a function of his discomfort in interpersonal or social situations. Joseph silently hypothesized that when on the trail of a story Stuart was quite different, because in that situation he felt confident when acting as the aggressor.

Eventually, there was a change in Stuart's behavior in the consulting room. He began to reflect more on his childhood, and on how his upbringing was instrumental in shaping his adult personality. But to Joseph there was always something about Stuart that he could not understand, and as the opening phase of analysis continued Stuart explained more about his moods. He knew that when he was on the trail of a good story he felt energized, capable, even powerful, but that when there was no story on which he was working his aloofness and unfriendliness came to the fore, accompanied by feelings of depression. One thing he could not do, Stuart asserted, was to generate story ideas on his own, at such times. Investigative challenges had to come to him.

Consistent with the minimal but identifiable progress outlined above, the first five years of analysis were relatively unproductive. There were no new big stories, and no substantial analytic progress. And though there was no evidence for a clear therapeutic alliance, Stuart continued to come to all his sessions, though often remaining silent. Then, one day, Stuart told Joseph that he was on a new story, involving a sex scandal in Washington. He also mentioned, almost as an aside, that he had been snorting cocaine recreationally for the past six months.

Stuart was now quite different in his sessions, talking rapidly about how excited he was to be on the trail of something important on the Washington journalistic landscape. Joseph was energized by Stuart's new found passion, and Stuart used his sessions to describe in detail his uncovering of a scandal that involved important political figures, and their paid sexual partners. Stuart revealed during this time just how much contempt for people he could conjure up in his mind, cynically describing the political leaders his investigation could bring down.

When the investigation ended, again causing Stuart's star to rise in national journalistic circles, he once again fell into a state of depression. Then, he confessed to Joseph that he was infatuated with one of the high priced prostitutes he had met while investigating the sex scandal. He knew that this was a potentially poisonous relationship, and he was restraining himself from acting on his impulse to contact the woman. But this was not easy for him, especially because he had never had sexual relations with a woman, nor had he ever gone out on a date other than with his girlfriend in the sect (which, upon reflection, was nothing more than Stuart's journalistic contrivance). For the first time Stuart talked with Joseph about his sexual history, and about feeling very excited, tempted, and stressed.

Soon talk of Stuart's infatuation stopped, as did descriptions of depression, stress, and cocaine abuse. The analysis went back into the doldrums, Stuart was sad and immobilized, and Joseph was bored. But as Stuart's luck would have it, soon a new Washington scandal distracted him from his depression, and his former infatuation, if it still remained in dormancy in his mind. This scandal involved crime in local prisons, and with the network of informants within government that Stuart had built up during his investigation of cult activity in Washington, and sexual misbehaviour among government leaders, he was well positioned to pursue this new investigation vigorously.

By this time Joseph had been seeing Stuart four times a week, on the couch, for about seven years. He had seen Stuart up, and down, but now, aware of Stuart's use of cocaine, he listened for signs of euphoria, grandiosity, or paranoia. His careful attunement was rewarded, because when Stuart's investigation had been completed, he confessed to Joseph in more detail than ever before what he felt during an investigation, and how he dealt with it. Here's what happened.

Stuart discovered that there was an organized drug ring in neighbouring state prisons and Washington's own equivalent of a state prison. The ring included correctional officers and inmates, the former serving as drug couriers and distributors, and the latter as the contacts to the suppliers. Large sums of money were changing hands, and the betrayal of their inmate business partners by the correctional officers resulted in several inmates going public, and calling in the press. But Stuart had gotten a big jump on his journalist competitors, and was turning out great reporting while others were still getting oriented to the potential revelations. However, Stuart was chagrined, because despite his natural excitement which accompanied his working on this great scandal, he found that he was experiencing very high levels of stress, and that he craved cocaine more and more. Eventually, he was snorting it uncontrollably, many times a day. He brought it with him to the prisons he visited, and risked getting caught in public when he snorted it in his car in what were relatively exposed circumstances. He became fearful of this, and confessed to Joseph his fear that he was an addict. But within a couple of weeks he reported that this concern had receded, that he was once again using cocaine only recreationally.

For three more years Joseph worked with Stuart, trying to activate and energize an analytic process. But he was unsuccessful, and out of conscious desperation, along with optimism generated by the fact that this withdrawn man came to all his sessions, Joseph called me in as a consultant. I am often amazed at how, at such times, unexpected things happen in analyses. Such occurrences always make me feel that unstated and mostly unconscious communications between the members of the analytic pair motivate the analysand to behave in ways which open up the analysis, and the analyst, in unconscious anticipation of such events, to prepare for them by bringing in a consultant.

Joseph began our work together by giving me the detailed history I have just conveyed, and I immediately raised the possibility that Stuart was revealing only the tip of the pathological iceberg. I speculated that stress and cocaine addiction were playing a central role in Stuart's life, and that Stuart was even coming to sessions intoxicated.

At this point I urged Joseph to diligently look for signs of Stuart's substance abuse, in and out of analytic sessions. I explained to Joseph that addictions were difficult to spot in high functioning people like Stuart. Such individuals do not usually come for analysis complaining of being addicted. If anything, they play down their own helplessness in the face of their use of an addicting substance, claiming that it is a recreational pursuit, and fully under control, if they mention it at all in the initial evaluation or the subsequent analysis. I added that current thinking about addiction is that such behavior most often occurs when the individual is under stress (Koob, 2006), and that for Stuart either work on a story, or not having a story to investigate, constitutes a state of high stress. I encouraged Joseph to view Stuart as having very poor judgment, related to his cocaine addiction, and the euphoria it induced in his poorly functioning, hijacked brain (Hyman, 2005).

I review the literature for Joseph

At this point in the consultation process I imparted some very specific information to Joseph, information to which I have previously referred in this essay. I explained that it is my observation that because psychoanalytic education emphasizes that addiction is untreatable by analysis (Freud, 1890, 1897, 1898), analysts tend to ignore the information they receive from analysands suggesting that there is a true addiction problem. Also, I added, past failures of one's own or of analytic colleagues in treating addiction reinforce a reluctance to undertake the analytic treatment of addicts.

I went on to say that in training analysts are imbued with a set of principles of analytic technique which serve simultaneously as ethical guidelines, creating a self-reinforcing system which inhibits us as we attempt to work creatively and analytically with addicted analysands (Freud, 1911–1915 [1914]); Sonnenberg, 2008). What I had in mind, and explained in detail, is that card-carrying analysts have been overexposed in training to injunctions to practice with strict adherence to abstinence, neutrality, anonymity, and the pledge of absolute confidentiality, all reinforced by the concept of undesirable parameters which supposedly poison the analytic process (Eissler, 1953). The result of all these lessons is an analytic healer who intuitively anticipates failure because he or she is inhibited by the technical-ethical considerations just mentioned: Common sense then encourages him or her to avoid recognition of addiction in a range of clinical situations he or she might encounter, or the need for the analytic treatment of addiction within one's practice. I urged Joseph to begin to think out of the box. I urged him to consider that the pressure to use only interpretation as his method of intervention might prevent him from offering Stuart an effective analytic treatment.

Next, I reviewed for Joseph the observations made by other analysts as regards the treatment of addiction. Not surprisingly, I told him, there is relatively little in the analytic literature about addiction, and certainly no consensus. First, I mentioned the work of Krystal (1982), who notes that addicts are unable to recognize and articulate what they feel, including feelings of pleasure. Another difficulty Krystal identifies is the inability of addicts to regulate their affects, an observation now better understood because of the work of Schore (2003a,b). Krystal emphasizes that addicts have experienced very early difficulties with their mothers, and that addiction represents a symbolic search for a mother they can take in, internalize. Thus, for Krystal, the drug represents a transference object. In addition, Krystal is interested in the role of trauma in the life of the addict, trauma which is both pre-verbal and experienced in adult life. While there is no memory of the early, pre-verbal trauma, Krystal believes it is trauma at the hands of the mother, who mistreated her infant. Krystal advocates an analytic stance in which the analyst plays a mothering role in the interaction with the patient, encouraging the addict to develop capacities for self-care.

Next I touched on the work of Wurmser (1974). Wurmser asserts that the addict cannot tolerate affects such as shame and guilt, and in response to such feelings searches compulsively for drugs. Standing in distinction to Carroll and Miller (2006), who write that addicts come from every possible personality type, Wurmser states that addicts are self-destructive borderlines with narcissistic features. Like Krystal, Wurmser's perspective emphasizes that addicts are incapable of affect regulation, and by default use an addictive substance as a self-help device in the face of an overwhelming unpleasurable feeling, usually involving a narcissistic injury. Wurmser also blames the addict's parents for not providing good models for superego development. Wurmser minimizes the role of dependency in discussing addiction.

I told Joseph that Khantzian (1987) is another analyst who has studied addiction. Unlike Krystal and Wurmser, he rejects either/or positions and embraces many theoretical and developmental perspectives. He focuses on the suffering of the addict, who struggles with multiple layers of psychopathology. Like Krystal, Khantzian emphasizes a caring relationship between therapist and addicted patient, in which the patient learns self-care, and affect recognition and regulation.

I now told Joseph about Dodes (1996), who describes the addict as striving for power when he feels a sense of helplessness. To Dodes compulsive drug use represents such a striving, and his view is that this is the case with other compulsions. Dodes sees addiction as an unconscious compromise formation which can be analyzed. Like Khantzian, and unlike Krystal and Wurmser, Dodes does not focus on early psychopathology in the addict.

Finally, I mention to Joseph the work of Director (2002). She is a relational analyst, who emphasizes that within the analysand-analyst relationship the addict can develop new, more effective ways of interacting with others. This occurs as old, troubling relational dynamics are re-enacted, early painful patterns of relating are iden-tified as the source of these dynamics, and all this is understood. Director asserts that under these conditions the roots of addiction can be mastered.

After having gone through this exercise of identifying for Joseph what other analysts have said before, I emphasize that these col-leagues have put forth many different ideas, but not brought us to the point where we can embrace a psychoanalytic consensus.

I also review for Joseph what non-analyst addiction experts have to say. We do know definitively that addiction is in part a response to genetic influence (Hasin, Hatzenbuehler, Waxman, 2006). We also know that within the central nervous system there are centres which respond to intoxicating substances and experi-ences of pleasure, and we also know something about the neuro-chemistry of the brain's response to addicting substances which cross the blood brain barrier (Koob, 2006; Childress, 2006). I again emphasize that this knowledge helps us to understand that in addiction certain central nervous system functions are usurped, and learning and memory do not work as they do under other cir-cumstances. This means that judgment is poor, that the brain is hijacked (Hyman, 2005). I stress that while we know a great deal, we are not able to mount an effective treatment protocol for addic-tion, and that psychoanalysts are as much in the dark as other men-tal health practitioners.

I continue to summarize the critical thinking of those I consider the experts in this field (Miller and Carroll, 2006a). I point out that despite the identifiable risk factors, such as genes, drug use is a gradually emerging, self-perpetuating, chosen behavior (Miller, 2006). Drug use is not an isolated psychological phenomenon, but occurs imbedded within personal and broader societal phenomena, including family discord, poor health, poverty, child abuse, and various forms of psychopathology, such as mood disorders (Carroll and Miller, 2006; Miller and Carroll, 2006a,b). Broader social issues are of great importance, and we must be sure that when we treat someone for addiction we are aware of how the analysand's family, social network, and total environment promote or discourage the addiction. All this must be considered as we deal with Stuart. One very critical point that the experts on addiction make is that quality relationships can be crucial in preventing addiction and promoting abstinence. Especially critical is the relationship with an understanding, empathic, non-shaming therapist (Miller and Carroll, 2006a,b).

These experts also emphasize that addiction treatment should be integrated with other aspects of healthcare, and not isolated in addiction designated specialty clinics (Miller and Carroll, 2006b). I tell Joseph that my view of analysis is that it is part of an holistic healthcare system. Other critical dimensions of treatment are the enhancement of motivation to conquer the addiction (Miller, 2006), and the encouragement of abstinence (Alcoholics Anonymous, 2007).

Finally, I tell Joseph about observations I have made in my own work with analysands who struggle with addiction. In distinction to the conventional clinical wisdom that addiction accompanies dysphoria, I have observed something different. First, I see it as emerging in situations where analysands are experiencing stress. Some of these analysands have experienced acute traumatic stress at some point in their lives, others have experienced what is sometimes referred to as strain trauma in childhood, that is the trauma associated with chronic, though not dramatic, mistreatment from parents who range from overtly cruel to unempathic. This observation is also consistent with what addiction experts observe (Koob, 2006).

But even more important, in my view, is that I have observed that addiction is more likely to be a problem in high functioning analysands who are good at creating and experiencing pleasure, as opposed to analysands who are better characterized as dour.

In my clinical experience dour analysands, individuals who would describe their lives as a series of unrewarding challenges are less likely to become addicted to anything as compared to analysands who experience life as a series of challenging experiences which hold the promise of pleasurable endings. Consistent with that view are my hypotheses that addictions, both substance and non-substance, operate psychologically and physiologically in the same ways, at their most fundamental levels, and that substance and non-substance addictions are ubiquitous human phenomena, and forms of normal pleasure seeking gone wild. These addictions occur more frequently when an individual used to experiencing pleasure cannot achieve that usual end, and that is experienced as a stressor. In sum, I told Joseph, for the addiction prone, high functioning analysand about whom I am speaking, based on temperament and life experience the pleasure principle and the reality principle overlap, and the result is poor judgment and an inability to delay gratification when pleasure is not readily forthcoming (Sonnenberg, 2008).

At this point I refrain from explaining to Joseph what specific measures I would employ with Stuart, and ask him to take his time in reassessing the situation, and developing a treatment strategy. I do say that the analysis of Stuart is at a crossroads, and that what has been an inauthentic relationship between him and Stuart now has the potential to become an authentic one. I say that there is room in my mind for optimism. But all this is contingent on getting Stuart to acknowledge his addiction, which I am almost certain is the unacknowledged variable in this analytic situation.

Joseph tells me at this point that while he is encouraged by my thoughts and optimism, he feels that he has spent ten years with an analysand who has probably been withholding a great deal of information from him. I reiterate that in my experience that is inevitably the case with high functioning analysands who struggle with addiction.

Back to the analysis

The next week, following four more sessions with Stuart, Joseph tells me that the two of them have spoken candidly about what has been going on for a very long time. Stuart has acknowledged that his addiction has been out of control for most of the time of the analysis, and that shame (Vaillant, 1980) and his fear of Joseph throwing him out of treatment has prevented him from being more candid. He now tells Joseph of his long history of marijuana smoking, which actually had much to do with his academic collapse when he went to college. In fact, he now acknowledges that he is dually addicted to marijuana and cocaine, and has even shot up heroin on a few occasions.

Joseph reports that he then told Stuart that he sees this treatment as a very long row to hoe, and he expressed his uncertainty that he and Stuart could really form the kind of honest, open relationship which is required if an analysis is to proceed to a successful conclusion. Stuart responded that he can understand Joseph's doubt, but added that he is critical of Joseph for not being more aggressive in pursuing him when he so often came to sessions intoxicated with marijuana at the beginning of the analysis. He reminds Joseph of his vacant silence during the first months of the analysis, and adds that at the time he thinks he was testing Joseph to determine whether he had any knowledge of addiction, and whether he was capable of responding to him with the necessary assertiveness and concern he so much needed and desired. It seemed to Joseph, and to me, that this more honest exchange held the promise of a far more intimate analytic relationship than what had been the case before, though both of us reserved judgment and maintained cautious optimism, at best.

While at this point I contemplated sharing with Joseph my own views on the analytic treatment of addiction, I stuck with my decision to restrain myself, because I believed that it would be far better for Joseph to build on this disillusioning experience by giving himself the space and time to consider what might be an effective way to structure Stuart's treatment. I maintained that position in part because I know that the treatment method I advocate is controversial, in part because I know that I am a very forceful person and did not want to close off Joseph's avenues for creative thinking, and in part because I believed that both of us would learn the most about how to treat addiction analytically if I respected Joseph's opportunity to absorb what had happened and to resonate with Stuart in constructing an effective analytic environment.

About a month after Stuart, Joseph, and I had reached this very challenging crossroad in Stuart's treatment, Joseph came in with a proposal which Stuart had spoken of during his last couple of sessions. Stuart had been doing his usual investigative exploration of what might be the right next step for him, and he had heard of an analyst in Europe who had devised an intervention for addiction which combined psychodynamic insight and hypnosis. Stuart wanted Joseph's blessing on this, and Joseph wondered what I had to say about it.

I found this proposal very evocative, because I was aware that it harkened back to the time when Freud made his original observations about the relationship of masturbation, which he called the primary addiction, and other addictions, such as alcoholism (Freud, 1890, 1897, 1898). For, at that time, when first considering the possible treatment of addiction, Freud had proposed hypnosis as an appropriate treatment. I was also pleased that Stuart had shown initiative in seeking an effective treatment for his addiction, for that meant to me that he was engaging in a promising process of motivated, self propelled change. I knew that experts in addiction believed this was an important part of a healing process for an addict (DiClemente, 2006). So I told Joseph that while this was not what I would necessarily advocate, it was worth a try.

And off went Stuart, accompanied on this unusual journey to Austria by Joseph. Upon his return alone from Austria here is what Joseph told me. The Austrian analyst who Stuart had identified was a member of the International Psychoanalytical Association, but was also something of a maverick. He had studied Freud's advocacy of hypnosis as a treatment, and he believed that addiction was somehow related to repressed infantile sexual desires and conflicts. In a sense I thought that this view was not totally inconsistent with that of Dodes (1996), who saw addiction as an unconscious compromise formation which could be analyzed, as could any other compromise formation.

So Stuart gave himself over to this analyst, and was hypnotized. What emerged was quite consistent with what other analytic thinkers had to say. Krystal's view of the role of maternal mistreatment and trauma was borne out (1982), as Stuart confirmed under hypnosis that his mother's distance and emotional neglect had left its mark. In keeping with the observations of Vaillant (1980) and Wurmser (1974), under hypnosis Stuart revealed a delicate sensitivity to emotions involving shame and guilt, over his inability to control his addictive impulses. This finding was also in agreement with Dodes' observation that the addict strives for power when he feels a sense of helplessness, which is what he feels in relation to his compulsive drug desires (1996). In keeping with Kantzian's perspective (1987), under hypnosis Stuart revealed a sensitive appreciation of what Joseph had provided, by his steady and non-judgemental acceptance of Stuart's cocaine cravings. Joseph's empathy turned out to be critical in allowing Stuart to remain in treatment for ten years. Finally, supporting Director's view of the centrality of the analytic relationship in allowing the addict to develop new ways of interacting, hypnosis confirmed that Stuart believed that within the analysis he had developed new skills in solving old, re-enacted dynamics, involving his distant mother (2002).

When Stuart was not under hypnosis the Austrian doctor explained what had been observed. These findings, like much that is discovered when an individual undergoes conventional, contemporary analysis, were received by Stuart with the response that everything seemed to confirm what he had expected, what he had just about concluded in his self-reflective, analytic deliberations. He was grateful for the experience in Austria, and decided that what he needed to do was take time off for a different sort of reportorial project. He told Joseph that he wanted to take some time to write a memoir, and that upon its completion he would return to his analysis. Joseph wished him well, and returned to Washington, and to his consultation process with me.

I wondered to Joseph what the future might hold. I wondered if Stuart would ever return to analysis. At this point Joseph decided to present other analysands to me in supervision, particularly because he had other people in analysis who he now recognized as suffering from other, unacknowledged addictions. As we discussed these analysands it seemed appropriate to explain to Joseph what techniques for the analysis of addicts I had developed in my own practice.

I describe my technique to Joseph

I explained to Joseph that I had developed several technical departures which I found useful in analyzing high functioning addicts. I began by reasserting that these individuals never came for treatment asking for help with addiction. Indeed, they always came for other reasons, usually did not even mention addiction or substance or non-substance abuse in the consultation, and when such matters arose they were always referred to as "recreational" activities, always under the analysand's control. When this myth was finally exploded, and an explosion it usually was, the analysand and I had to go through a process of reassessing the analysis, a reconsideration of whether authentic, mutually committed analysis was possible. When it was, I instituted the analytic techniques I next described.

First, it was often necessary to modify the rule of absolute confidentiality. That was the case for any number of reasons, including the possibility that a legal process, such as a drunk driving charge or a professional licensure review, was part of the picture. In other instances I had learned about the analysand's addiction because it had been reported to me by a member of the analysand's family, or a business associate, who expressed a compelling need to be kept informed of the analysand's well-being.

I had given such situations a great deal of thought, particularly from the perspective of the analysand's right to autonomy, to a true sense of agency. Upon reflection I concluded that if an analysand had created a situation in which others needed to know something of the analysand's analytic progress, true agency meant that I could not protect the analysand from that personal responsibility and need to report. I realized that when commanded by compelling outside circumstances I could expect and require the analysand to write such a report as a condition of our working together, and that my attesting to its validity was a further departure from absolute confidentiality. I believe all this is consistent with my view of what constitutes the promotion of autonomous, personally responsible analytic work. I explained all this to Joseph.

The second modification of technique I embraced was insisting that my analysand engage in a twelve step group experience along with analysis. I recognize that this requirement is also a departure from strict confidentiality, since twelve step groups are not, strictly speaking, private experiences. But I explained that I have concluded that the kinds of interactive processes which support autonomous, mature development are induced by group experiences, in addition to what are now well understood individual developmental experiences, whether these latter occur in the natural course of life or in analytic treatment (Beebe and Lachmann, 2002; Miller and Carroll,

2006; Schore, 2003a,b; Siegel, 2007). For that reason, while I don't insist that my addicted analysand go public and join a twelve step group immediately upon starting analysis, sooner or later I insist on that experience as a part of treatment.

A third twelve step related modification is that I insist that for at least some period of time in analysis my analysand remain sober. In the case of a non-substance addiction that means abstaining from the compulsive, addictive activity. Since I believe that the mechanism of action of substance and non-substance addictions are identical, at some fundamental neurobiological level, sobriety, or abstinence, are absolutely essential if the analysand is to be able to restore his or her hijacked brain to a state of clear thinking about the addiction, an essential component of conquering the addiction.

Finally, a fourth modification involves the analysand acknowledging that his or her brain has been hijacked, and that therefore, lacking in good judgment, he or she must acknowledge that not only is sobriety or abstinence essential, but that at least temporarily I am the higher power, the individual with good judgment, to whom he or she must defer. I do not suggest that I must always be thought of in that way by addicted analysands, but that as long as we suspect that their memory and learning capacities are not under good control, it is useful to defer to me as their higher power as regards the conquest of their addiction. Of course, this, too, is a modification in keeping with the twelve step model.

I told Joseph, in a summary of what I had just explained, that all this was consistent with what I was trying to promote with a person with whom I had previously been going through the motions, without an authentic analytic relationship: I was trying to promote real intimacy and cooperation, where before what had existed was a superficial masquerade of an analytic relationship. Joseph understood what I was explaining. I also emphasized to Joseph that I saw all that I did as compatible with the teachings and programs of Alcoholics Anonymous (2007).

Two years after Stuart's hypnosis in Austria, and two years after parting company with Joseph, he returned to Washington and asked Joseph if they could resume their work together. Stuart reported that he had not used cocaine or marijuana in two years. It was then that Joseph said to me what has been incorporated into the title of this essay. He said: "I have spent years, knowingly and more often intuitively, unknowingly, trying to wean Stuart from his addictions. I believe that now that fiend is asleep, but I know it is not dead, I know that it has the potential to return. Here I believe Freud was correct. An addiction may be dormant, indeed, it may never return, but it is not medically appropriate to think of it as permanently conquered. That fiend can reawaken at any time." And so, as conditions for resuming treatment, Joseph insisted that Stuart accept all the treatment conditions and modifications I have just described. Joseph did this willingly, and now, three years later, I can report that Stuart has been cocaine and marijuana free.

I can also state that Stuart's analysis has deepened. There has been a focus on Stuart's early life experience with his distant mother, and his evolving understanding of the ways that traumatic relationship causes him to feel unloved and unlovable, inadequate, helpless, and powerless. This discussion of what some would call a history of strain trauma has resulted in Stuart understanding two very important aspects of his history and his personality. In the past, like many high functioning addicts, Stuart would experience a repetitive, escalating cycle in analysis: when he felt particularly helpless in the face of his addiction, and would engage in addictive behavior, he would feel so ashamed that he would not tell his analyst about what was happening. This led to even more addictive behaviour, and a cycle of helplessness, shame, secrecy, and more addictive behaviour would ensue. Now, Stuart was able to tell his analyst when he was feeling compelling addictive urges, and abort the escalating cycle of addictive behaviour.

A second area of understanding, consistent with the first, is that Stuart came to understand that his early life experience left him unknowing of how to use personal relationships constructively, to feel more regulated when he was frustrated, sad, or disappointed in himself. Now Stuart learned to use the analytic relationship in such a way, and it became a model for other relationships, as well.

This more authentic analysis has led Stuart to a greater appreciation of the ways his drug cravings reflect his temperament, his biology, as well as his psychodynamically influenced efforts to find and take in a good mother. As noted, he has discussed his intense shame at his powerlessness in the face of his addictions, and his desire for a form of powerful self-regulation when in the past he medicated himself with cocaine and marijuana. His analysis has taken on the form of an authentic, two person conversation, as Stuart has been able to express his gratitude to Joseph for his kindness, empathy, and candour, and engage as well in an analytic conversation which has, when appropriate, focused on Stuart's experience of being misunderstood by Joseph. The doubts such moments raise in Stuart, and Stuart's concurrent transference experience which causes him to conflate such situations with the fear that Joseph is like his mother, and neither cares about him nor desires to understand him, has been an important part of analysis since Stuart's return to treatment. All in all, Stuart seems far better able to think self-reflectively, to mentalize, to self-analyze, to self-regulate, and to interact with others in a more intimate, satisfying fashion.

Conclusion and summary

In this essay I have tried to describe my views on the analytic treatment of the addictions. I began by describing my conviction that addiction is a serious mental disorder, which is appropriately included as a topic in this conference on the psychoanalytic therapy of severe disturbance. Next, I described the scope of this major public health problem, and discussed the reasons why psychoanalysis has made so small a contribution to its understanding. I explained that only in the last five of my thirty-five year career as a full time, practicing psychoanalyst have I recognized that addicted individuals have regularly and frequently been my analysands. I explained that I was discussing addiction in high functioning analytic patients, and I offered a definition of what characterized high functioning individuals. I followed this with an appropriate case example from thirty years ago, which illustrated the way in which I was then unable to understand and respond to my analysand's pleas that I recognize and treat his alcoholism. Then, using a contemporary case in which I served as a consultant, I described the course of a more successful treatment. In that description I believe I conveyed my current perspective on addiction, which includes an integration of the views of leading experts from within and outside of psychoanalysis. I spelled out the modifications in standard analytic technique which I employ, and the reasons I believe these methods are helpful. I will emphasize at this time that based on my personal experience, my addicted analysands do well. They come to deeply understand themselves, the biology and the psychology of their addictions, and they are able to conquer their addictive tendencies, and remain abstinent indefinitely. They come to understand the incapacities in thoughtfulness which they experienced when their brains were hijacked, and appreciate the differences in their mental functioning once they are in recovery. A corollary of all this is that these analysands are able to experience a full range of analytic activities and gains, including a deep analytic understanding of themselves, and rich capacities to empathize, mentalize, be mindful, self-regulate, and self-analyze in an ongoing way. Once their addictions are recognized within the analytic relationship they are able to share a committed, intimate, authentic relationship with their analysts, and with those relationships serving as models, deepen the intimacy of their relationships outside of analysis. I hope that in this essay I have provided enough specific information to be helpful to practitioners who in the future self-consciously undertake the psychoanalytic treatment of addicted individuals, and that I have given those with doubts about the efficacy of psychoanalytic treatment for the addicted the confidence and motivation to try to be of help to that population.

And now, the truth shall be told

I am about to conclude this essay, and I have a confession to make. The second case I reported, as I indicated, was not a case of my own, and was disguised. I stated that this was necessary for reasons of confidentiality, and I do want to emphasize that confidentiality was the decisive factor in governing the way I wrote both the case presentations in this essay.

For several additional reasons I chose for the high functioning addict to be successfully analyzed one of the most popular heroes in the history of these islands, of the UK, Sherlock Holmes. Yes, Stuart Holcombe is Sherlock Holmes, workaholic and substance addict, a compulsive and uncontrolled user of cocaine and morphine. Joseph Waterbury, soldier turned internist, turned psychiatrist and psychoanalyst, in none other than John Watson, M.D., formerly attached as a military physician to the Fifth Northumberland Fusiliers. The first big story, which Stuart investigates, involving a religious cult, is loosely based on *A Study in Scarlet* (Doyle, 2003 [1887]), the second, the investigation of a government sex scandal, on *A scandal in Bohemia* (Doyle, 2003 [1891]), and the third, the investigation of prison corruption on *The Sign of Four* (Doyle, 2003 [1890]). Stuart's seeking help from the Austrian psychoanalyst hypnotist, and his subsequent absence from psychoanalytic treatment is based on *The Final Problem* (Doyle, 2003 [1893]), and Nicholas Meyer's *The seven-per-cent- solution* (Meyer, 1993 [1974]). The entire description of Stuart borrows from Austin Mitchelson's *The baker street irregular: the unauthorized biography of Sherlock Holmes* (Mitchelson, 1994). Finally, Joseph's comment on the fiend that is asleep, a line which is incorporated in the title of this essay, comes from *The adventure of the missing three-quarter* (Doyle, 2003 [1904], p. 174).

Knowing that this is a very serious conference, dedicated to helping all of us offer more effective psychoanalytic treatments to severely disturbed individuals, I thought long and hard about whether to go forward with the idea I had, which was to use in this essay a fictional character as one of my two main clinical examples, and to reveal that device only at the end of the essay. I decided to do so only after fully assimilating the extent to which Sherlock Holmes was believed by many readers to be a real, living person, a fact about which Sir Arthur Conan Doyle himself commented (Doyle, 2003 [1923]).

However, there is an additional point which I wish to make explicit, and that concerns why I concealed the identity of the second case until the end of the essay. That point has to do with what I think of as a blended form of Irish and British humour, and my experience of that humour. A very dear friend of mine for fifty years, since my university days, H. Montgomery Davis, died unexpectedly while I was preparing this essay. Monty was a man of the theatre, and was proud of his Orange Irish ancestral roots, his years studying theatre in London, and his world class knowledge of his favourite playwright, the Irishman George Bernard Shaw. In fact, Monty was clearly a hybrid blend of Northern Ireland, Dublin, London, and the United States.

In that friendship I always enjoyed Monty's wry wit, and came to understand that in the experience of his humour I learned a great deal about life, things which I did not readily forget because they were embedded in moments of laughter, of the unexpected punch line. So in thinking about using Sherlock Holmes as a clinical example, and revealing that choice only at the close of the essay, I came to think that I might create a humorous moment, which might also cement in memory a very important clinical lesson: A high functioning addict might appear extremely competent in many ways, but was in fact very severely disturbed. I came to feel that since the addict in question was Sherlock Holmes the lesson might very well stick better than if I wrote about an anonymous, disguised clinical case. I hope my effort has been successful.

In closing, then, I want to thank all of you for your close attention. To those of you who are from the United Kingdom, from these islands, I offer special thanks, for providing me with Sherlock Holmes, a man of great talent and purpose, a true hero of these islands, who for much of his life suffered the scourge of addiction.

References

Alcoholics Anonymous [Internet] (2007). Available from: http://www. alcoholicsanonymous.org/en_information_aa.cfm?PageID=17& SubPage=68

American Psychiatric Association (1994). *Diagnostic and statistical manual of mental disorders. Fourth edition,* p. 32. Washington, DC: American Psychiatric Association.

Beebe, B. & Lachmann, F.M. (2002). *Infant research and adult treatment: Co-constructing interactions.* p. 272. Hillsdale, NJ: Analytic Press.

Block, J.J. (2008). Issues for DSM-V: Internet addiction. *Am J Psychiat* 165:306–307.

Carroll, K.M. & Miller, W.R. (2006). Defining and addressing the problem. In: Miller, Carroll, W.R. & Carroll, K.M. eds. *Rethinking substance abuse: What science shows, and what we should do about it,* pp. 3–7. New York: Guilford Press. p. 320.

Childress, A.R. (2006). What can human brain imaging tell us about vulnerability to addiction and to relapse? In: Miller, WR, Carroll, KM, eds. *Rethinking substance abuse: What science shows, and what we should do about it,* pp. 46–60. New York: Guilford Press.

DiClemente, C.C. (2006). Natural change and the troublesome use of substances: A life-course perspective. In: Miller, W.R. & Carroll, K.M. eds. *Rethinking substance abuse: What science shows, and what we should do about it,* pp. 81–96. New York: Guilford Press.

Director, L. (2002). The value of relational psychoanalysis in the treatment of chronic drug and alcohol use. *Psychoanal Dialog* 12:551–579.

Dodes, L. (1996). Compulsion and addiction. *J Am Psychoanal Assoc* 44:815–835.

Doyle, A.C. (2003 [1887]). *A Study in Scarlet*. In: Doyle A.C. (2003). *The Complete Sherlock Holmes*, Vol. 1, pp. 3–96. New York: Barnes & Noble.

Doyle, A.C. (2003 [1890]). *The Sign of Four*. In: Doyle A.C. (2003). *The complete Sherlock Holmes*, Vol. 1, pp. 97–184. New York: Barnes & Noble.

Doyle, A.C. (2003 [1891]). *A Scandal in Bohemia*. In: Doyle A.C. (2003). *The Complete Sherlock Holmes*, Vol. 1, pp. 185–205. New York: Barnes & Noble.

Doyle, A.C. (2003 [1893]). *The Final Problem*. In: Doyle A.C. (2003). *The complete Sherlock Holmes*, Vol. 1, pp. 557–570. New York: Barnes & Noble.

Doyle, A.C. (2003 [1904]). *The Adventure of the Missing Three-Quarter*. In: Doyle, A.C. (2003). *The Complete Sherlock Holmes*, Vol. 2, pp. 174–190. New York: Barnes & Noble.

Doyle, A.C. (2003 [1923]). *The Truth about Sherlock Holmes*. In: Doyle A.C. (2003). *The complete Sherlock Holmes*, Vol. 2, pp. 679–690. New York: Barnes & Noble.

Eissler, K.R. (1953). The effect of the structure of the ego on psychoanalytic technique. *J Am Psychoanal Assoc* 1:104–113.

Freud, S. (1890h). Psychical (or mental) treatment. *Standard Edition 7*, pp. 281–302. London: Hogarth Press.

Freud, S. (1950a [1887–1902]). Letter 79. Extracts from the Fliess papers. *Standard Edition 1*, pp. 272–273. London: Hogarth Press.

Freud, S. (1898a). Sexuality in the aetiology of the neuroses. *Standard Edition 3*, pp. 259–285. London: Hogarth Press.

Freud, S. (1909d). Notes upon a case of obsessional neurosis. *Standard Edition 10*, p.151–318. London: Hogarth Press.

Freud, S. (1911–1915 [1914]). *Papers on technique. Standard Edition* 12, pp. 83–173. London: Hogarth Press.

Hasin, D., Hatzenbuehler, M. & Waxman, R. (2006). Genetics of substance use disorders. In: Miller, W.R. & Carroll, K.M. editors. *Rethinking substance abuse: What science shows, and what we should do about it*, pp. 61–77. New York: Guilford Press.

Hyman, S.E. (2005). Addiction: A disease of learning and memory. *Am J Psychiatry* 162:1414–1422.

Khantzian, E.J. (1987). A clinical perspective of the cause-consequence controversy in alcoholic and addictive suffering. *J Am Acad Psychoanal and Dynamic Psychiat* 15:521–537.

Koob, G.F. (2006). The neurobiology of addiction: A hedonic Calvinist view. In: Miller, W.R. & Carroll, K.M. ed. *Rethinking substance abuse: What science shows, and what we should do about it*, pp. 25–45. New York: Guilford Press.

Krystal, H. (1982). Adolescence and the tendencies to develop substance dependence. *Psychoanal Inq* 2:581–617.

Lipton, S.D. (1977). The advantages of Freud's technique as shown in his analysis of the rat man. *Int J Psychoanal* 58:255–273.

Lipton, S.D. (1979). An addendum to 'the advantages of Freud's technique as shown in his analysis of the rat man'. *Int J Psychoanal* 60:215–216.

Lynn, D.J. & Vaillant, G.E. (1998). Anonymity, neutrality, and confidentiality in the actual methods of Sigmund Freud: A review of 43 cases, 1907–1939. *Am J Psychiat* 155:163–171.

Meyer, N. (1993 [1974]). *The seven-per-cent solution: Being a reprint from the reminiscences of John H. Watson, M.D. as edited by Nicholas Meyer.* New York: Norton & Company.

Miller, W.R. (2006). Motivational factors in addictive behavior. In: Miller W.R., Carroll, K.M, ed. *Rethinking substance abuse: What science shows, and what we should do about it*, pp. 134–150. New York: Guilford Press.

Miller, W.R. & Carroll, K.M. ed (2006a). *Rethinking substance abuse: What science shows, and what we should do about it.* New York: Guilford Press.

Miller, W.R. & Carroll, K.M. (2006b). Drawing the science together: Ten principles, ten recommendations. In: Miller, W.R. & Carroll, K.M. ed. *Rethinking substance abuse: What science shows, and what we should do about it*, pp. 293–311. New York: Guilford Press.

Mitchelson, A. (1994). *The Baker Street Irregular: The unauthorized biography of Sherlock Holmes.* Studio City, CA: Players Press.

Schore, A.N. (2003a). *Affect Regulation and the Repair of the self.* New York: Norton.

Schore, A.N. (2003b). *Affect Dysregulation and Disorders of the self.* New York: Norton.

Siegel, D.J. (2007). *The Mindful Brain: Reflection and Attunement in the cultivation of well-being.* New York: Norton.

Sonnenberg, S.M. (2008). Psychoanalytic ethics and the treatment of the addictions. A paper presented at the annual ethics conference of the Austin Society for Psychoanalytic Psychology, on April 26, 2008, in Austin, Texas, USA.

Strachey, J. (1958). Editor's introduction to the papers on technique. In: Freud S (1911–1915 [1914]. *Papers on technique*, pp. 85–88, *Standard Edition* 12. London, Hogarth Press, 1955.

Vaillant, G.E. (1980). Natural history of male psychological health: VIII. Antecedents of alcoholism and "orality". *Am J Psychiat* 137: 181–186.

World Health Organization [Internet] (2008). Available from: http://www.who.int/substance_abuse/facts/en/index.html.

Wurmser, L. (1974). Psychoanalytic consideration of the etiology of compulsive drug use. *J Am Psychoanal Assoc* 22: 821–843.

CHAPTER SIX

Some considerations about the psychoanalytic conceptualisation and treatment of psychotic disorders

Franco de Masi

> *"If you ask me what psychoanalysis can do about psychosis, I might give you two opposite answers: one is that psychoanalysis can do very little, the other that it can and must do a lot."*
>
> —Paul C. Racamier

I would like to begin my contribution to the Belfast Conference with some preliminary remarks that coincide with the core of my theoretical position about the treatment of psychotic disorders.

The difficulties in the analytic therapy of psychotic patients are not due to our individual limits, which can emerge during our professional meetings, but *depend mostly on the inherent incompatibility between the psychotic state and traditional analytic thinking.*

It is well known that the psychoanalyst who tries to treat analytically psychotic patients is subjected to many painful failures. At the 41st Congress of the International Psychoanalytical Association in Santiago, Chile, García Badaracco drew attention to this difficulty by noting that very few cases of recovery from psychosis are reported in the analytic literature (Badaracco and Mariotti, 2000). This well justified pessimism about the treatment of such patients should spur us on to augment our therapeutic arsenal and to learn also from our failures.

Failures

I consider that my past personal failures with psychotic patients originated mostly from the fact that I was listening to them in the same way that I was accustomed to do with neurotic patients. I was expecting associations, dreams deserving consideration and interpretation, and the kind of dependent transference similar to the one that even disturbed patients develop.

A major change in my analytical approach to the psychosis happened after the outcome of the analytic treatment of a patient, which I had described in a paper on Super-ego and hallucinations published in the *International Journal of Psychoanalysis* (De Masi, 1997). In this paper, written after eight years of analytic treatment, I emphasized his improvement and the analytic work that allowed him to emerge from his hallucinating world. After the publication of my paper this patient had a new serious psychotic crisis, even more severe than the one which had caused his hospitalisation before the beginning of his analysis.

This unlucky and sudden conclusion of the analytic relationship made me think about the irreducibility of psychotic processes, and led me to wonder how the delusion could have carved out such a path upon which the patient embarked upon again even after eight years of analysis.

In my opinion, the decisive fact remained that, by virtue of the analytic work on the psychotic superego, the patient's internal world had undergone a positive transformation.

I actually remembered that every time I had tried, in the analysis, to raise the issue of the psychotic episode for which he had been admitted to hospital, the patient put up a stubborn resistance, quickly taking flight from the memory of what had happened or trivializing it.

In reconsidering the unlucky outcome of this case, I benefited from a statement found in a paper by Thomas Freeman (2001) who notes that even when the psychotic episode has been overcome, the "crisis" persists as a powerful destabilizing element. Terrified of having to relive it and of becoming psychotic again, the patient is frightened even to remember the circumstances, let alone the development, of the psychotic attack.[1]

As a matter of fact, I recognized that I had not undertaken a systematic, in-depth analysis of the first psychotic episode, but had concentrated instead on his need to repair the damage and on finding ways for him to recover his mental functioning.

I am now convinced of importance to perform, session by session, a systematic analysis of the delusional world, both in its past manifestations and in its tenacious and deceitful action in the present. Unless we can discover how the patient *creates* the psychotic state, the hallucinations, and the delusion, even the best of therapies may be unable to avert a relapse. Like Freud, who considered transference initially as an obstacle and afterwards as a transformational event, we must take the delusional functioning, which is always active underneath in the analytic process, as a normal, ubiquitous event and the key to a possible therapeutic path.

Emotive and dynamic unconscious

When we analyze a psychotic patient we must be able to proceed in the same way as a physicist studying the atom, who does not refer to Newtonian Mechanics because he knows that he is dealing with a wholly different kind of phenomenon.

To show how the growth of the emotional world has been seriously hindered in the psychotic patient, I have made a distinction between *emotive unconscious* and *dynamic unconscious* (De Masi, 2000).

Man does not come into the world with equipment fit to perceive the emotions but he possesses the ability to develop it. As Bion says, in order to develop such apparatus there has to be a mother who

---

[1] The patient's state of mind in relation to the past psychotic attack is dominated, even years later, by terror in case the delusional reality returns. Even chance words spoken in the analytic dialogue that trigger associations to the traumatic event arouse the patient's terror, owing to the sudden invasive feeling of not remembering the event but of reliving it in the present and hence of still being trapped in psychosis.

In this situation, any association to the trauma is immediately blotted out because it is connected with catastrophic anxiety and is therefore likely to reconstruct the delusion. That is why the analyst finds it extremely difficult to succeed in examining the past psychotic episode with the patient.

gives fitting answers to strengthen the baby's emotive preconceptions. The psychotic patient lacks such apparatus and cannot use the emotive unconscious to construct psychic reality and give meaning to human relationships.[2]

I assume (2006) that the psychotic state represents the extreme development of a condition started in childhood in which the child began to live in a parallel world, created in his imagination and kept secret, which enabled him to interact with the environment only superficially. This withdrawal has gradually made him unable to use the unconscious functions in charge of registering and understanding emotions, which are the carriers of intrapsychic communication.

Lack of empathy from the caregiver causes a patient to escape into a dissociated world. Parental pathological intrusions into the baby's mind produces confusions or false identities and increases the child's psychic retreat and a compulsive need to expel unbearable states of mind using others as a repository (Williams, 2004).

The damaged functioning of emotive unconscious produces monsters, i.e., delusions and hallucinations. This process does not work in a mechanical or direct way: in the patient's psychic retreat, delusional imagination becomes a psychopathological structure that dominates and colonizes step by step his mind until its complete invasion.

The dream-delusion

One of the clinical problems of analytic therapy of psychotic patients is how to remove the patient from the power and fascination of the delusional world, which is normally concealed to the analyst and works dangerously in a secretive way. Indeed, one of the difficult clinical issues we are confronted with in the treatment of psychotic patients is their passive acceptance with which they let themselves be trapped in their delusional world.

The aim of the delusional power is to create a new reality that appears superior and desirable; this is the reason why its colonizing action is not clear to the patient who is passively drawn toward it.

---

[2] We can consider the *emotive unconscious* as an implicit knowledge that operates like a procedural memory. The patient bound to become psychotic suffered damage in the acquisition of this procedure during his first development and further deterioration because of the creation of subsequent psychopathological constructions.

In a paper written with Paola Capozzi (2001) we suggested a distinction between *dream-thought* and *dream-delusion*. We think that, in the psychotic patient, while few dreams can be considered as thoughts (like dreams of a neurotic patient) most dreams contain in a nutshell the delusion itself and describe the working and the seductive quality of delusional power.

A clinical example[3]

Angela is a 21 year-old patient whose psychotic onset dates back to when she was 16. She had a mystical delusion and a state of exaltation, which led her to confess that she had sexual intercourses with Jesus. As a child she was shy and withdrawn in her fantasy word. After some two years of therapy a second psychotic episode took place. The patient claimed to be the devil and asked her therapist not to look into her eyes, for fear of contaminating her. The breakdown was treated at the patient's home with the help of a psychiatrist. Her state of severe distress made her miss some sessions: Angela was afraid to leave her home because she was terrified of being killed. Her therapist wondered about the reasons for this new breakdown and discussed this in supervision with me.

In my opinion the therapist had worked too much on a symbolic level (content interpretations) and had been so worried for her patient that sometimes she would not even maintain the time setting. The anxiety conveyed by the patient might have prevented her from capturing the specific elements of the on-going psychotic transformation and from containing them promptly.

I advised her to try and see how Angela entered her delusion and to understand all her communications in this light. The patient attended an art school and, because of artistic talent, she had always been considered a little genius in her family. She had often brought her drawings to sessions and the analyst had commented on their contents. The analytic sequence I report here follows a partial resolution of the psychotic episode, when she has started again to go to therapy regularly. It is at this very time that, I believe, it is possible to help the patient understand how psychosis impinges on her mind. In this vignette Angela shows a special capacity for insight in this respect. During a session she recounts a dream:

"I am travelling by train with my father; it is evening. We must go to a village and, since it is evening, I assume that we are going to spend the

---

[3] This patient's material was brought to me in supervision by Dr. Marina Medioli.

night away from home. During the trip my father works absorbed in his papers and I feel uncomfortable and alone.

Then, I am in a car together with dad and Franzoni[4] at the steering wheel. I recognize Franzoni and I feel very uncomfortable to be in the car with her. I get to a walled-in boarding school. They teach archery. At night I am in a dormitory with other girls, and in the darkness I see a girl who carries a luminous bow and smiles oddly at me. The following morning we all go to the swimming pool and, for fear that my bathrobe may be stolen, I swim in 'dog-style', keeping my bathrobe out of the water."

The patient's associations to the dream are that, when she goes to the public swimming pool, she is afraid that she may have something stolen. She always puts her towel and the locker key by the edge of the pool. When her therapist suggests that the bathrobe is like a skin, the patient confirms that she is afraid of losing her identity. Then the patient mentions the bow and says that the smile of the girl strikes her. Actually it strikes fear into her. Of course, there is also her fear of being killed, but the bow can be easily recognized and seen, as it is luminous.

The session ends and the therapist addresses the patient with the mutual commitment to think more about this dream.

In the following sessions the patient, perhaps for the first time, brings her own contribution to the working through process:

P: *You know, I have thought a lot what the bow in the dream could mean. I have also thought that I could be the girl holding it. I remembered that, besides her strange smile that scared me, her lips were moistened …*

A: *Then we can say that there was a lot of sensuality …*

P: *Yes, I thought the same thing; there is a strong sexual component. The bow evoked the light, and angels and devils came to my mind. Through the arrow that strikes me I become the light.*

A: *There you are. This is the delusional part that strikes, enlightens and captivates you, making you believe that this is the only way of becoming superior, an angel.*

P (chuckles): *Yes, you are right. It is really a crazy thing, I am a human being, not an angel or a devil. I get transformed into them …*

---

[4] Franzoni is a mother convicted for infanticide, and she has become popular in Italy through the mass media.

A: *I was wondering whether Mrs Franzoni might represent an omnipotent part, which kills the son if he is not up to her expectations. In your dream she is the one at the steering wheel ... We may think that when you are isolated and secluded from the rest of the world this exciting part wins you over more easily ...*

P: *Yes, quite so ... And I feel like an angel ... that can always become a devil.*

A: *Sure, and therefore you are afraid that somebody wants to kill you ...*

P: *You know, I continue to go and visit the dogs (Angela has abandoned school and she goes regularly to the dog pound to look after the animals), and I feel that it is something really important for me. I thought over what you told me last time. It is true that through them I am learning how to feel, but not only because I recognize the feelings in the dogs. I realize that they are opening up something inside me, like a lung that can really fill up with air ... I think it is the relationship.*

I have reported these sequences to show how the delusional withdrawal (the patient who becomes the girl with the bow) can be a protective measure against anxiety (against the lack of relationships), but also and mostly a place of pleasure in which the patient feels like a god able to enlighten herself with her omnipotence. In this sense, as I have tried to show in this clinical vignette, psychotic dreams are very helpful because *while the delusion conceals and confuses, the dream communicates.*

This is the *true communication, the true gift that the psychotic patient gives the analyst.* Just because the patient is unaware of the danger of the psychotic transformation, the dream opens a door into the secret retreat where the delusional operation is put in motion. In the scene of the boarding school, a secluded place where archery is taught, the patient describes the exciting sensory enchantment inherent in the delusion, the luminous and sensual bow. By allowing herself to show in the dream her own hallucinatory reality, an idealized and seductive reality she might not be able to resist, the patient lets the analyst come into her hallucinatory retreat. It is important then that the analyst sees, together with her, the other side of reality, keeping the right distance and making sense of the hallucinatory transformation, and helps the patient differentiate herself and leave the delusional enchantment of her hallucinatory retreat.

Whereas delusion is a psychopathological construction aimed to transform psychic reality, the psychotic "dream" can become one of the available means to *communicate* what is going on. This kind of dreams, which represents the delusional pressure that colonizes the ego (this being prone to yield to it), helps the patient to perceive the danger and, in each case, to get rid of the seductive hold of psychosis.

In the therapy of these patients, it is important to grasp the attractive force and the power of the delusional imagination, by identifying its underlying anxieties or omnipotent wishes, with a view to *deconstructing* it. I use the term *deconstruct* because the word "interpretation" that we use to denote our therapeutic instrument seems unsuitable for tackling the clinical problems posed by the power of the delusion.

I think that analysand and analyst must be able to examine and to recognize gradually and in detail how the delusional experience is constructed and develops. It is important to carefully peruse the present emotional situation and the remote roots of the delusion, linking up the various scattered fragments that have appeared and continue to emerge during the analysis. This work must be done constantly, session by session, over a prolonged period.

From a technical point of view, my assumption is that delusional structures do not correspond to undigested beta-elements *waiting for transformation. There is no continuity between the unconscious thought, which helps perceive psychic reality (K), and delusional activity (−K).*

Whereas some authors (Caper, 1998) suggest a possible transition from delusional fantasizing to the world of intuition connected with the dream work, I consider that a radical incompatibility between delusional imagination and thinking activity (as well as dreaming) exists (De Masi, 2006). The delusional fantasies are non-transformable and indigestible elements, and cannot be "dreamed" in order to be transformed into thoughts. They are alien to and incompatible with psychic reality.

The psychotic patient is fascinated by this kind of perversity, by his power to destroy psychic reality and remove any differentiation between fantasying, delusion and reality.

Such an exercise, apparently pleasant and similar to a mental drug, sooner or later becomes persecutory, (self-)destructive and catastrophic because it produces a never-ending process that overwhelms the patient himself.

The spur to coerce the mind with an addictive quest for pleasure reaches a breaking point with no return. Then, psychotic anxiety emerges in its full power and goes to a psychotic break-down.[5]

It is essential for the patient in analysis to reach a point where he can *see* his psychotic construction, as it is the case with this patient. The dreams that psychotic patients bring to analysis are very illuminating because they describe, frequently with great accuracy, the psychotic functioning and the exciting and confusing power of the delusional nucleus while the patient is struggling to achieve mental health. In the course of the treatment we need to support those parts, which have stayed outside of the delusional system, to prevent them from being drawn into it and to help them *see*, by deconstructing the power of delusion. This is the reason why I stress the importance of orienting the analytic work to promote the patient's awareness of the meaning of his psychotic organisation, which tends to incorporate the self and destroy the sense of reality.

However, dismantling delusional proneness is a very long and complex process because of the obstinate and constant re-emergence of the pathological organisation that endlessly tends to carry on plotting.

The coming back of the delusion

As a rule, once the psychotic episode is over, the patient tends to preserve the precarious equilibrium attained, even if it involves substantial limitations. He learns to keep away from potentially destabilizing emotional experiences and senses that there is a limit beyond which he cannot push himself. To this end he maintains tight control

---

[5] My personal opinion is that the catastrophic anxiety grips the psychotic patient only when he loses self-sensorial pleasure or the grandiose experience created by him and he became unable to control the process of continuously transforming his perceptive apparatus which he had set in motion.

Before being overwhelmed by catastrophic experience of destruction of the world and by delusional persecution centred on Prof. Flechsig, President Schreber was caught in the sensual pleasure of being transformed in a woman during sexual intercourse. If we don't admit the fascinating and pleasurable feature of the psychotic experience in his beginning we cannot understand the attraction and the "passive" submission of the patient to it.

Often this fascinating feature of the delusional state is hidden by the patient's unwillingness to communicate it.

over relationships and affective cathexes that might trigger new psychotic processes.

When the patient smashes through his personal pillars of Hercules, catastrophe ensues: the relapse into psychosis is facilitated precisely by his having thrust himself forward while lacking a progress-sustaining structure. It is rather like adding a storey to a building constructed on inadequate foundations: the extra load causes the entire structure to collapse.

In order to underline how the delusional experience, even after many years of analytical work, can always recover its power I will briefly present a patient, 35 years old now in the eighth year of treatment, who was hospitalised for a paranoid episode which took place before the beginning of his analysis. The delusional disposition still emerges nowadays during critical periods when the patient is unable to face new emotive tasks.

In his analysis Carlo has improved significantly. Many mental spaces have opened up for him. He maintains a good dependence and communication with me. He has been able to have meaningful and stable relationships with his peers and lately he has formed an emotionally important relationship with a young woman. Recently, due to conflicts and arguments between them, he has decided to abandon her. During a session he says that he decided to separate from his girlfriend, although he declares that he is very fond of her. He feels perfectly serene. Listening to him, I am surprised that he doesn't feel any sorrow about his decision. In the next session Carlo tells me he has had a delusional attack the day before (for a long time the patient has regularly brought to analysis his delusions providing us an opportunity to work together on them). He reports feeling anxious, as if he had lost his bearings (he doesn't say that the anguish might derive from the loss of his girlfriend). On the verge of a panic attack, he phoned his mother to be cheered up but afterwards he felt persecuted, he was afraid of being poisoned ...

Listening to him I feel puzzled and I try to find a link between his decision to separate from his girlfriend and the resurgence of the delusional state. I hypothesize that he had obliterated his feelings and for this reason he felt deprived of his frame of reference and the grandiose and persecutory mechanisms had reappeared again. I tell him he had lost his bearings because had annihilated psychic reality together with a potential mourning for the loss of his girlfriend. He listens to me, he meditates for a while and says that it is true, he never thought about his girlfriend, he cancelled

her from his memory. I tell him that he erased his feelings because he felt
unable to face psychic pain. The loss of the girl created a suffering and he
had to cancel the pain and, what is more, the whole apparatus for perceiving
emotions. When he performs this operation, the "other reality" comes back
again. The patient listens to me silently and answers: "It's true that I can't
stand any psychic pain. I remember that, when I was a baby, I was always
very excited and I had to be in a splendid mood all the time. I think it was
to escape from all pains! My mother once told me that when I was nine
months old she abandoned me for three weeks. My parents wanted to go
on holiday and I was left in the charge of a woman whom I did not know at
all and who lived in another town. So I lost both my parents and my home.
My mother remembers that when she came back I was completely changed,
deeply depressed and without vitality.

I want to underline how in this patient, unable to stand an emotive conflict, the annihilation of psychic reality causes panic and
the resurgence of persecutory imagination. He gets trapped into
the delusional world because he destroys the very same apparatus that could save him, allowing a potential containment of the
negative emotions and offering a way to learn from his conflictual
experience.

The loss of this emotional apparatus seems connected to an early
trauma. The patient can remember the mother's account of the traumatic event of his childhood but he can neither relive it, nor think
about it or indeed learn from this experience. He can only understand
that he becomes manic or grandiose when he has to face pain but he
is still unable to feel and work through the mourning. I emphasize
that the patient entered into a psychotic state with a grandiose delusion followed by persecution when he suffered an emotive trauma
after being abandoned by a friend, with whom he had an idealised
adolescent relationship.

Therapeutic progress

A durable transformation of the psychotic structure might coincide,
not only with the release of the patient from the delusional lie, but
also with his acquisition of a true identity, i.e., of an emotive readiness to understand psychic reality and to face frustrations connected
with human relationships. These goals are strictly intertwined. Psychotic patients do not get a true structure to their personality. Their

evanescent identity breaks down when a psychotic crisis occurs and this often coincides with the breach of an idealized bond with a supportive object. During the analysis they try to establish the same balance they had before the psychotic crisis i.e., to restore the same false identity which makes them appear to be functioning properly. For this reason their attempt to conform themselves to external reality deceives people around them, even including the analyst.

We might evaluate therapeutic progress on the basis of their development of a true personal identity.

Since Abraham and Ferenczi, many theoretical developments have widened the clinical field of the psychotic illness and given new strength to the analytic therapy of such patients. The analytic literature offers the precious legacy of many analysts (to name only a few: Federn, Fromm-Reichmann, Searles, Pao, Rosenfeld, Benedetti, Segal, Aulagnier, Lacan, Volkan) who worked in this field with creative endeavour. Despite these unquestionable developments the psychoanalytic thinking is, in my opinion, still lacking an organic theoretical and clinical conception on the nature and dynamic of the psychotic process. The many explorations in this field have not yet managed to trace a useful and accurate map of knowledge.

In my clinical work I am continuously engaged in focussing on the problematic knots, which are essential to the outcome of the therapeutic process. I endeavour to outline some of the specific patterns of psychotic development and try to determine how the patient, since his childhood, starts building a prison from which it will be very hard to escape.

I hope that in the future, the cooperation of many psychoanalysts and meetings like the one so well organized in Belfast by Paul Williams and Lord Alderdice will help improve our knowledge of the mysterious ways through which one becomes psychotic and will offer new prospects in the treatment of this form of mental pathology.

References

Badaracco, G., & Mariotti, P. (2000). Affect and Psychosis (*Panel Report*) In *Int. J. Psychoanal.*, 81, pp. 149–152.

Caper, R. (1998). Psychopathology of Primitive Mental States. *Int. J. Psychoanal.* 79, pp. 539–551.

De Masi, F. (1997). Intimidation at the helm: Superego and allucinations in the analytic treatment of a psychosis".

De Masi, F. (2000a). The unconscious and psychosis. Some considerations on the psychoanalytic theory of psychosis". *Int. J. Psychoanal.*, 81, pp. 1–20.

De Masi, F. (2006). Vulnerabilità alla psicosi Cortina (*Vulnerability to psychosis. In press by Karnac*).

De Masi, F., & Capozzi, P. (2001). Meaning of Dreams of Psychotic State. *The Intern. Journ. of Psychoanal.* 82:939–52.

Freeman, T. (2001). Treating and studying schizophrenias in *Williams, P. (ed) A Language for Psychosis. Psychoanalysis of Psychotic States*. London: Whurr. pp. 54–69.

Williams, P. (2004). Incorporation of an invasive object. *Int. J. Psychoanal.* 85:1333–1348.

CHAPTER SEVEN

"First you were an eyebrow" and "How do I know that my thoughts are my thoughts?"

Bent Rosenbaum

This presentation will focus on some phenomenological and psychodynamic characteristics of psychotherapy with human beings who for shorter or longer periods of their life find themselves trapped or imprisoned in schizophrenic modes of existence. It is my claim that difficulties in symbolisation play a major role in the understanding of what is going on: in the mind of the person, in the mind of the therapist, and in the clinical researcher. Furthermore, from a developmental perspective entering the mode of "we-ness" and acquiring a "group mind" is difficult for the person with a mind in the schizophrenic mode marked by autism. The developmental perspective is coherent with the emphasis on difficulties in symbolization, and outlines for a relevant therapeutical approach in the state of psychosis will be presented.

"If you did like me, you would be mad"

As a young resident I took my first job in the largest Danish State Hospital, which at that time had two thousand beds and was divided in two sections for respectively men and women, except for the two units in which Maxwell Jones' ideas of "therapeutic society" was tried out. Through my previous interest in semiotics I had been studying thinking and thought forms, especially in the thought disorders of the psychotic states of mind. Every week I spend two or three evenings sitting together with the patients listening to their life stories, their thoughts and fantasies. I heard the most incredible and fascinating things and learned how the mind in a psychotic state viewed the world–not the least the relation between self, body and others. One evening I sat next to a woman, age 55, who had spent 35 years in the Hospital. She was sitting on her hands and I asked her for the reason for this behaviour. She said that she had to protect herself against the evil spirits that came from the depth of the earth trying to penetrate her anus. After a while I asked her whether I, too, had to protect myself in a similar way against the evil spirits. "Oh no", she said, "If you did like me you would be mad". After a pause I said that she must be special since the evil spirits had picked her as a victim and not me. She said that it all started with the war (2nd world war), and then she would not say more. I was left with a lot of tentative ideas connected to her behaviour, but without any confirmation on any of these ideas.

I stayed in the hospital for four years and learned the functioning of double book-keeping and dissociated minds, about the regression to and the use of another scene of thoughts with only a few links to the common sense world and secondary symbol-formation, about the simultaneous pain and safety feelings of being able to isolate oneself from others, and also that thoughts come in bits and pieces, and through many simultaneous trains which can never be detected fully.

In the following I shall discuss the phenomenology and psychodynamics of schizophrenic modes of existence. I shall begin with a vignette from a psychotherapy that taught me many things in addition to my experiences from my years at the psychiatric state hospital and other psychiatric hospital units. I shall touch upon the problems of symbolformation, i.e., some basic structural conditions underlying the increasing integration of apperception, emotions, thoughts and thinking. Furthermore I will discuss the concept of we-ness and group-identification and its importance in the development of psychotic modes of relating to the world. In the end I shall turn to some ideas about the supportive psychodynamic approach to therapy with people in psychotic states.

"First you were an eyebrow"

Approximately 2½ years into a psychoanalytic psychotherapy with a woman who came twice a week, we were talking about trust, mainly her ability to trust her women co-workers but also with the twist to the possible trust in me in the therapeutic space. After reflecting on her own words and mine she looked at me and said: "During the first year you were an eyebrow, then you became a doctor with a white coat and shortly after a doctor. But I am not sure that I will ever be able to experience you as a person".

I hesitated in my response because many thoughts that went through my head:

- What is an eyebrow able to perceive and say, and does it have the capacity for listening?
- What is the symbolic meaning of an eyebrow for this patient–if it has any?
- Why the sequence of the doctor in a coat and then one without a coat?

> Did I in spite of my assumed analytical listening attitude raise the feelings in her that she should be communicating with someone with a non-listening, authoritarian, paternalistic attitude?
>
> Or was the transformation from 'with coat' to 'without coat' an indication that she experienced me as moving from a super-ego position–punitive or controlling–towards a more caring object raising sensual feelings in her?
>
> Or, was her utterance it an indication of pain from her side, telling me that however much progress we would be able to make then I (and she) should anticipate a limit–either an existential limit which always would impede her more or less in being able to experience immediately and subjectively that she and I were persons, or a limit to her ability to feel that she and I were separate individuals with background in our own history and who would meet in respect of each other?
>
> Did she tell me that she could not imagine any way out of the claustrum in which she was chained and that any push toward this would be a possible all-absorbing catastrophe?

From my time as a resident at the State Hospital I acquired the idea that communication with minds in psychotic modes gains by starting at a level of a joint perceptual field–either imagined or real-, and thus I decided to explore the idea that an eyebrow could be an insufficient perceptual organ. I said that I felt that as an eyebrow I may have observed many things but I might not have been able to listen properly to her–and I wondered what she had permitted me to see and say from that perspective. She responded to my words by saying that my words made her think of an episode after she had moved from home when she visited her parents for a dinner. The main course at that dinner was roasted lamb culotte in which "the bone stood out as a penis without the foreskin". She had to leave the dinner immediately. She believed her mother understood her reaction since she (the mother) "was made of that stuff dreams were made of".

I did not respond immediately to her associations since I for a moment was stuck in the countertransferential split between on one side being able to empathize with her fear of being attacked by some penetrating stimuli, impressions or words–father's gaze or voice, memories from childhood or youth–against which she could not defend herself, and on the other side her depressive feelings in striving towards a state of integrating her different emotions and, by means of the therapy, finding objects which she could trust loving.

She told me that she wanted to find a man who did not scare her or was too demanding of her. She had not been lucky with previous relationships to men, one of them with whom she had two children. She could not look into a man's eyes without feeling filthy or invaded. The act of sexuality could be very frightening to her since she might experience her labia enlarge to the extent that they would fill out the whole room in which the act took place, and she would feel suffocated. Walking into a kiosk in order to buy a packet of cigarettes could lead to a feeling that the man who handed her the cigarettes also wanted to rape her judging from the way "his hand was moving". In several sessions I had experienced her in hallucinatory states–looking at people in the street and reading street-signs could become a nightmare. She could for instance see a man wearing a big black plastic bag and she would immediately believe that in this bag were her two children cut up into small pieces. She could look at a street sign and the words could be cut up into small fragments, which had, or did not have, an immediate, but not-integrated, symbolic meaning. When her children were babies it was hard for her to have them close to her body since she could feel that they literally crept under her skin, or ate her breast.

She thought that some of the difficulties with relationship to men had their origin in her father's ways of behaving when she was a baby. In one of her memories her father would lift her in the air when she was ½ year old and did not wear a nappy, and he would place her behind on his nose while blowing air on her genitals. I a later session she told me that one of his characteristics was his eyebrow.

She was brought up in a family whose members in the midst of the 19th century were of politicians and literary people.

Her father was a captain in the army and he wanted her to be boy-like. He punished her and wanted her to avoid sex while he at the same time said that had she not been his daughter he would have had sex with her. In her mind the patient had killed the father several times together with other persons whom she found intrusive and abusive. "I have an inner cemetery where I can allocate people to whom I dislike", she told me. Sometimes she could fear that the killing really had taken place (in outer reality) and not only inside her mind.

Her mother was an etheric, fairy-tale like woman, living in her own world, having creative talents for painting and storytelling. The patient could easily identify with mother's skills and at the same time she felt that the mother, but not herself, was living in a fairy-tale like world, distant from daily life activities.

My patient had never felt quite safe with her schoolmates. During childhood and adolescence she always communicated with "an inner friend, which was experienced more alive than the living persons in my surrounding". In a way she was morbidly capable of being alone, i.e., she was not capable of being alone in the mature way that Winnicott (1958) is speaking about when he says

> [Thus] the basis of the capacity to be alone is a paradox; it is the experience of being alone while someone else is present. (ibid, p. 417)

"Being alone" in the mature way is integrating otherness and at the same time feeling safe regardless where my thoughts and actions lead me to. In opposition hereto, my patient had always felt that even though others were present she would have to exclude them from her awareness, or she would feel that they were intruding into her thoughts and feelings. In primary school, she had had connections to schoolmates, but always felt different from them, both below and above their standard but never like them. She couldn't just feel ordinary and natural.

Psychoanalytic viewpoints have often excluded–wrongly I believe–phenomenology from its considerations (the opposite move has even more fiercely taken place, but that does not need to bother us here). From a phenomenological point of view[1] characteristics of my patient's experiences would include:

- Disturbed, automatic context-sensitive attunement to the world Loss of evidentiality (e.g., "Erlebnis der Einfachheit im Augenblick" (Jaspers, 1913)), and disturbed familiarity (e.g., "Erlebnis der Identität im Zeitverlauf" (ibid))
- Morbid awareness of inner fantasy life, and a lessened interest in outer reality and in anchoring ones subjectivity in the social life A strong tendency to equate immanence (that which is immediately experienced and reacted upon in thought and action) with transcendence (that which transcends the sphere of experience).

All these phenomena undermine in a fundamental way[2] the ability to think and experience in a common sense mode. When this common sense mode is undermined then everything and every situation

---

[1] These viewpoints rely on Karl Jasper's work (Jaspers, 1913) and are recently developed by Joseph Parnas (Parnas and Handest, 2003). Authors devoted to phenomenology usually find it problematic to link these with psychoanalytic informed concepts, although the viewpoints of Sandor Rado often are quoted by the phenomenological psychiatrists as a basis for the understanding of the concept of schizotypical disorder. The argument from the point of view of phenomenology is that phenomenology as a philosophy is more basic to the understanding of human being than psychoanalysis, which is seen as a psychology with reductionistic tendencies. Psychoanalysis takes the opposite view that phenomenology–"to let that which shows itself be seen from itself in the very way in which it shows itself from itself" (Heidegger, Being and Time, 7,53; 34)–is not able to explain the in-depth phenomena which characterizes the human mind.
[2] Fundamental in the sense that we are dealing with both pre-verbal and pre-reflective functioning.

may gain unconscious significance and is in danger of being reacted to with feelings of strangeness, mistrust and alienation from time, space and ones own body.

Theory of symbolisation

From the patient's often eloquent and articulated mode of speaking and thinking one might get the impression that the autobiographical account above, i.e., the narrations of the experienced situations and events, the associations and so forth seem both intelligible and coherent. But that was not the case in the patient's understanding of herself. From her point of view very little of what she said was *felt* natural or as commonsense. Sometimes she experienced her own story as a continuum but at other times her own feelings of her narration was rather fragmented and they were experienced as isolated thought-gestalts that only with great difficulty could be related to a whole picture of her life situation from which she could learn and outline perspective for her future life.

Bion conceived symbol-formation as a transformation from raw sense impressions (which he called beta-elements) through elements of thoughts and ideas (experiences which he called alpha-elements) into preconscious and conscious psychological work, such as dreaming, thinking, mourning, and learning from experience. Thus in Bion's conceptualisation, the patient would often confuse sense impressions, proprioception and thoughts, and sometimes–in moments of lack of reality testing capacity–she would evacuate the sense impressions and perceptions into the soma, or into hallucinations and hallucinatory acts. In these situations, parts of the patient's mind, or "the thinker who should think the thoughts", had broken down and as a result mostly unanchored thoughts were being communicated in the therapeutic space. It was then hard for her to distinguish *real knowledge*, in the sense of coming to know oneself through experience (Bion's concept of K), from its many substitutes (see Bell, 1995: 71). Instead of experiencing the reality of objects she would experience a kind of *negative reality*, a reality stripped of depth and immediate meaningfulness. At other times, perceptions and sensations were transformed into thoughts which sustained her in her work and even helped her being able to form assisting attitudes towards others–e.g., by means of protecting herself she carried out her professional functions to everybody's admiration except from her own.

Lacan's ideas of symbolformation rely on the distinction between the Real, the Imaginary, and the Symbolic order. In general, the relationships between these three orders account for the individual's capacity for thinking in a symbolic mode. A Lacanian view would describe the psychotic patient's ways of thinking as being confined to imaginary modes of using signs and signifiers. Instead of relating to and reflecting upon the words in the communications, and thus creating a "third-position-distance" to the possible and multiple meanings in the dialogue, the psychotic is hit or imprisoned by the words hen and others utter, or he is thinking magically about the ways they affect others, e.g., believing that others understand the words in exactly the same manner as he does himself. For the psychotic, the mind is in a state in which speech and thinking are in one way or another denied access to full symbolicity, or to the Symbolic order. Since access to the symbolic order is a prerequisite for the extended consciousness (Damasio, 1999)[3], the obstruction of this access means that the psychotic mind has difficulties with:

- The ability to create helpful artefacts
- The ability to consider the mind of the other in different perspectives
- The ability to sense the minds of the collective and to take into account the interests of the other as well as of the collective
- The ability to suffer with pain as opposed to just feel pain and react to it
- The ability to value life
- The ability to construct a sense of good and of evil distinct from pleasure and pain
- The ability to sense beauty as opposed to just feeling pleasure
- The ability to sense a discord of feelings and a discord of abstract ideas which is the source of the sense of truth

---

[3] It is interesting to see how the neuroscience description of the autobiographical self (Damasio, 1999, p. 230) goes hand in hand with the psychoanalytic description of the appearance of the Symbolic order.

FIRST YOU WERE AN EYEBROW   159

Normally, if normality has a place within psychoanalysis, the mind will make as much use of the above abilities as possible. It will strive for establishing an intersubjective relationship in the symbolic, with a mutual and stable exchange of subjectively based messages and informations between I and others. In doing so, the "I" accepts the other's not knowing as a given pre-condition for conveying the messages.

In psychotic states of mind, these I-You-, or I-Other-, relationships become vulnerable, and the vulnerability concerns the experience of unexpected, immediate phenomena in the intersubjective space. These phenomena are intruding into and disrupting emotional thinking and affective experience. Single words, perceptive stimuli and sensations are experienced as isolated, painful, intrusions rather than being integrated into an experience as a whole which may serve as guidelines for the person's thoughts and acts. These elements may be seen as effects derived from the 'Real', i.e., effects of that which cannot be symbolized and thus is experienced as anxiety, catastrophe, abyss-like without anchorage and without time, and on a purely perceptual level. A situation in the daily social life–going shopping, talking to persons, or standing close to somebody in a bus–could for my patient turn into an area with hidden bombs, and shells, which could explode and undermine her existence. A sentence, action or movement could trigger this catastrophe. In a narration of great interest to both of us, she could suddenly experience confusion and lack of capacity to trust her own experiencing, as if the whole system of internal connections was in danger of breaking down in her, or already had broken down.

The danger of breakdown and its influence on symbolisation also brings to mind Donald Meltzer's description of two kinds of pain, related to two kinds of internal object relations. The first kind of pain is the *confusional anxiety* in which the threat against the capacity to think is dominating. The other is the *persecutory anxiety* in which the threat against being psychically alive is dominating.

Both concepts of anxiety are related to Bion's concept of *attacks on linking* (Bion 1959). These attacks exhibit themselves in undermining the emotional thinking, leaving to the mind a mode of thinking that on its surface may appear logic but which beneath the surface is characterised by cruel, abortive and private thoughts and impressions.

These attacks make the work of the symbolic impossible and the symbolic modes of being is experienced troublesome and painful to the extent that a patient one day asked me with an almost desperate tone of voice: "How do I know that my thoughts are my thoughts, and how do I know that my I is my I".

Schizophrenia and developmental psychopathology

One of the important contributions of psychoanalysis to the under-standing of the human nature is its emphasis on developmental psychopathology (Fonagy, 2003). This term, developmental psycho-pathology, connotes dialectical relations between 'subject', 'time', 'psychopathology' and 'psychic structures'. This dialectics, in addi-tion to the special causal mechanism invented by Freud, called 'Nachträglichkeit', distinguish the developmental psychopathology model of psychoanalysis from any model of linear causality, and from simple risk factor and vulnerability models, and even from the widely used stress-vulnerability model.

Furthermore, there is a link between developmental psychopa-thology and symbolisation. This link has many aspects–biological, evolutionary, physiological, psychological and cultural.

Freud depicted several entrances to the understanding of the mechanisms and structure of the psychotic mind

1. Withdrawal of psychic investment (Versagung) followed by a denial/of inner reality (Verleugnung/Verwerfung/forclusion) and the establishment of another kind of reality (Freud, 1924)
2. Primary processes intruding into the secondary processes (Freud, 1900)
3. Regression in the psychic apparatus towards fragmented memories and perceptions being the preferred ground of experience (Freud, 1900)
4. Withdrawal of libido from thing-presentations and collapse of thing-presentation (Dingvorstellung) and word-presentation (Wortvorstellung) (Freud, 1915). Instead of integrating thing- and word-presentations (and thus forming an object presentation), the psychotic mind confuses the two–treating words and thoughts as if they were images and un-anchored emotions
5. Problems of autoerotic, narcissistic and homosexual structure (Freud, 1911)

I shall here dwell on the last one concerning the developmental line from auto-erotism through narcissism and homosexuality to hetero-sexuality[4]. I shall summarise a longer version, which I presented in Scandinavian psychoanalytic Review 2006.

The short version is that although problems in the domain of autoerotism and narcissism are often (or may be always) found in schizophrenia, the particular demands of the homosexual structure seem developmentally insurmountable for the person suffering from schizophrenia. The question is of course: what do we mean by using these concepts in the definition of the schizophrenic states? In my answer, I take the liberty to let the concepts of autoerotism, narcis-sism and homosexuality not only signify libidinal investment in the different kinds of objects, but in addition let these concepts signify fundamental identity structures for the embodied mind's orienta-tion in the world and in other minds. I thus hope in a simple way to shed new light on the developmental psychopathology in the case of some psychotic states of schizophrenia.

The structure of autoerotism signifies that the body on its surface immediately cognises and recognizes pleasure and unpleasure as coming either from inside or from outside. Autoerotism thus empha-sises the basic structure of the inside/outside, especially the ability to distinguish what is pleasurable and unpleasurable and whether these affects and emotions originate from perceptual (exterior) or sensory/emotional (interior) stimuli. In states of schizophrenia the distinction between inside and outside is often obliterated, and confusion arises as what stems from inside and what originate in the outside.

The structure of narcissism mainly concerns the mirroring of the self in the other of similar, opposite and divergent relations. In the nar-cissistic structure the subject envisions an object (another) outside of itself but that object resembles the subject in major aspects. The subject measures itself on projections of its own unconscious states and it is thus bound to states of mirroring. However, the mirroring

---

[4] Freud wrote: "Since our analyses show that paranoids endeavour to protect themselves against any such sexualization of the social instinctual cathexes, we are driven to suppose that the weak spot in their development is to be looked for somewhere between the stages of autoerotism, narcissism and homosexuality, and that their disposition to illness (which may perhaps be susceptible of more precise definition) must be located in that region. A similar disposition would have to be assigned to patients suffering from Kraepelin's dementia praecox or (as Bleuler named it) schizophrenia (Freud, 1911, p. 62).

is constituted by ideals (from the Other), which the subject assumes as his own ego (ideal-ego).

The structure of narcissism can thus be seen as the basis for the ability to establish an object outside the self, a dyadic object relation harbouring the distinction between self and other, even though self and other are established as related domains. In states of schizophrenia this basis may be undermined by a confusion of the two spheres, a lack of separation and an experience of transitivism.

The structure of homosexuality concerns the homoerotic relationship between the self/subject and the group of homogenous others (peers, other subjects). The libidinal tie in the homoerotic structure concerns not a dyadic relation (like in narcissism) but a link between the subject and the group of like-minded others[5]. The homoerotic identity structure concerns the being-in-the-world of homogeneity. It is a complex experience, constituting the feelings of being part of a group (group identity)

1. The experience of being in accordance (homologue) with the others, i.e., being ordinary, like-minded, one amongst many;
2. The experience of being a person with individual qualities, a subjectively marked individuality, i.e., being in some respect unique and thus different from the others in the group.

The homoerotic identity structure commences developmentally with the acquiring of the stable *sense of we-ness* (at around the age of three years, at a time when the child is mature enough to start the kindergarten experiences).

Acquiring *we-ness capacities* is a complex process in which the mirroring processes forming the self-understanding no longer take place in a visible mirror (employing the other as a mirror) but in

---

[5] Freud expresses the social group as the basic scenario for the Schreber's homoerotic feelings in the following statements:

··· the strikingly prominent features in the causation of paranoia, …, are *social humiliations and slights*. [...] the really operative factor in these *social injuries* lies in the part played in them by the homosexual components of emotion … [] …. delusions never fail to uncover these [emotional] relations [to his neighbours in society] and to trace back *the social feelings* to their roots in a directly sensual erotic wish (Freud, 1911b: 60) [italics are mine, BR]. In the end of the argument Freud distracts the argument about social origin of affects and falls back on his ideas of libidinal investment in the parents.

an invisible one (based in the group matrix). From a developmental perspective this step goes along with the embodiment of:

1. *narrativity*: I am a subject in so far I am telling stories about myself and is subjected "to be told" by other storytellers who include me in their stories;
2. *argumentativity*: I am a subject with identity in time and space in so far that I can argue my opinion so that others can understand what I am referring to and what the meaning and intentions are;
3. *Experiencing being both unique and ordinary*: being a subject means subjecting my experiences to categorisations and generalisations—and in that sense being a human being whose ideas and acts are equated and exchangeable with these of other human beings—and at the same time I am different from all the others in one respect or another, and thus unique.

Persons in psychotic states of schizophrenia have immense difficulties establishing the "group-as-a-whole"-functions of the mind. They will experience difficulties in identifying themselves as part of a group of like-minded, regardless whether these like-minded are other patients, other family-members, schoolmates, friends, work-colleagues, members of sport clubs, etc., They feel that they simultaneously belong and don't belong. Just like the ego may function as a boundary connecting subjective experiencing with the immediately experienced world, and a third may function as a connector linking the subject and the other, in the same way does the we-ness mode function as a connector linking the separate individuality with the societal whole.

Therapeutic approach

It is not so easy to learn from a psychotic mind even though the therapist may have "learning-from-the-patient" as an underlying philosophy of his/her techniques. The patient is the one who informs the therapist, who can do no more than listen with as much empathy as his countertransference allows him to and through this (open-minded, respectful, no-better-knowing, neutrally exploring) listening process motivate the patient to feel safe in this "teaching position" from where the informations (on situations, experiences, perceptions, etc.,) to both therapist and patient can emerge.

Learning from the patient also demands something more that is difficult for the psychotherapist namely to sense and not be frightened about the complexities of the psychotic states and their, in many cases, slow pace of developmental change. The changes that take place in psychosis psychotherapy may be subtle and minimal so that the therapist hardly senses them and looses track of them in the course of treatment. If the therapist can manage being sometimes a few steps ahead of the patient, at other times a few steps behind, and again at other times side by side with the patient, then it is a very gratifying learning experience for both.

Finally, the patient's mistrust in the dyad is an area, or may be *the area*, in which the psychoanalytically informed psychotherapist plays a major role. In the dyad, the therapist may help the patient to perceive, apperceive, feel and think the myriads of processes this dyad encompasses. But the long-term perspective in the development is the integration of the patient's thinking in the "we-ness"-modes. Only by achieving this may the therapy help the patient to gain a firm foothold in the symbolic order of language. This certainly challenges the therapist's ways of intervening.

In the following I shall dwell on some practical and technical steps or moments in which possible curative movements of the psychotic states may take place. They are psychoanalytically informed in the sense that they fully acknowledge: the fundamental work of the Unconscious; the transference-countertransference processes; the libidinal investment in internal and external object relations that may be distorted, destructive or integrated; the pre-conscious as a transforming mediator between the radically unconscious and the communicating consciousness. One might always dispute whether the therapy offered is really psychoanalysis or not, but mostly such disputes are futile. All the modifications of the psychoanalytic methods mentioned in the American psychoanalytic literature of the 1950'es (Eissler, 1953), are relevant in the clarifying and interpreting modes of listening. In its nature the analyst's intervention will be supporting and enhancing the thinking processes of the patient.

In the Danish National Schizophrenia project (Rosenbaum et al. 2005) we outlined some principle for the psychodynamic psychotherapy (Rosenbaum and Thorgaard, 1998; Thorgaard and Rosenbaum, 2006). They included among other elements the following:

A focus on the non-psychotic aspects of being simultaneously with a focus on the psychotic ones

This principle acknowledges two modes of functioning—one mode which is thinking in spite of the grief it is to harbour the evolving process of psychosis, and another mode which undermines the common sense of thinking, and renounces ordinary ways of mourning the losses and feeling the pleasures, and finally taking initiatives for change. When working with the psychotic patient, the therapists should keep these two modes of functioning in mind, and they should be able to empathise with the difficult complexities of: symbiosis and separation; distrust and loss of trust; identity and relational confusion; control and loss of control; care- and self-care-failing (Thorgaard and Rosenbaum, 2006).

At the same time the therapist and patient should together develop creative areas which can be used for thinking, counteract some of the regression, and which as a therapeutic alliance will show itself stable enough to resist more and more of the attacks on conscious reasoning which appear as part of the psychotic personality. It is recommended that the therapist, together with the patient, already from the initial assessment sessions explores the patient's talents, interests, creative fantasies, and interpersonal capacities. In successful therapies, the therapist may make use of viable metaphors from this exploration to enlighten what is going on in periods, or moment, dominated totally by the psychosis.

Entering the patient's universe through his or her talents, interests and creative fantasies also enables patient and therapist to link to the existence of the we-ness mode that often is frightening and incomprehensible for the patient. The advantage of using these creative areas of experience is that the explorations of the dangers and difficulties of experiencing the "ordinary-unique"-dialectics of the we-ness mode might be easier for the patient to overcome when the work is done in areas where he or she may be able to feel pleasure and experience positive self-esteem.

Making use of the necessary modifications of the technique

Without falling into traps of deadening and moralistic, norm-seeking countertransference, the therapist should be able to make use of e.g.,:

- **Clarifications**: "Tell me more about that", or "Tell me more about what you saw and heard, and what you feel about it". Often the therapist may ask for clarifications that concerns perceptions (hearing, seeing, tasting, sensing, moving) rather than emotions; psychotic patients may many times have difficulties in acknowledging and describing emotions, and may either be bewildered or feeling intruded by the request concerning these;
- **showing explicit empathy with the patient's painful state of mind**: "it sounds like unbearable memories/experiences that you are carrying with you", "It must be hard", or just an empathic "Yes" affirming the patient's emotional state. Sometimes the affirmation lies in the sound of the therapist's voice or in the facial expressions;
- **Indirect proposals:** "What would happen if you …", "Considering the situation, could you think of any alternative thoughts about what happened?"
- **exemplifications from life experience:** "Having been in a similar situation, I thought by myself …", "Sometimes that kind of human behaviour is unavoidable", "pleasure and fear may sometimes go hand in hand, especially when one experiences entering unknown land", etc., The use of metaphors is frequent when the therapist expresses his life experiences. The metaphors should be seriously thought through by the therapist either before or after using them. And metaphors that may help entering the we-ness modes are of importance to have in mind;
- **responding to questions after having examined their possible meanings:** "You asked me a question and I will respond to it, but first you and I will investigate the meaning of the question from your perspective, and the possible responses you may have to it".

A new orientation of the mind in its process of overcoming and defending against the losses it has experienced

Living through a psychosis is not only a painful experience in itself, but it also implies internal and external losses: losses of ideas, values, plans of life, cohesion with friends, peers in school, university or work, family members, etc., It is important to empathise with these losses, face their reality, and at the same help the patient to start retelling his life in another way. Since the psychosis retrospectively disturbs ones whole identity and alters the image of what that identity was even before the manifestations of the first psychotic episode, then the possibility of telling other narratives must include even those narratives embedded in ones self-understanding in the pre-psychotic experiences. Constructing ones narratives of the self in a new way can be used as a creative counter-move against self-destruction.

The shared responsibility for the work to be done

The concept of shared responsibility is an ethical dimension that belongs to the symbolic order, and it is too abstract to be immediately understood by the psychotic mind. Searles called the first phase of therapy the "out of contact phase" (Searles 1965), and Ogden called it "Stage of non-experience" (Ogden 1980), and with these characteristics they both described relationships in which shared responsibility lied very much on the shoulders of the therapist. The share of the patient seems primarily to come to the sessions, stay in the room and have a minimal awareness of two separate persons being in the room. Sometimes the elements of exchange relate to what is perceptually concrete and evident, and easy to describe for the patient. At other times attitudes, feelings, behaviour and fantasy can be drawn into the communication. An important principle in the beginning of the therapy is that the shared responsibility is demonstrated as a non-polarised relationship between the therapist's and the patient's viewpoints. Later when the patient's becomes more interested in the therapist's point of view, it will be important to listen to and emphasise new angles of the therapeutic material. Then a genuine analytic relationship may rise in which the patient searches answers to questions in him-/herself, by listening to himself in the presence of the analyst's intervening comments.

Shared space and shared responsibility must ultimately be demonstrated in what kind of thoughts that can be exchanged. If the patient participates in group psychotherapy, which is highly recommendable, many different points of views and angles of perspectives expressed by the others in the group must be considered by the patient. From learning-from-experience by responding responsibly to others the patient may gain access to a more stable life in the we-ness mode.

And finally

Many other technical and methodological advices can be pointed at, and will be in the supervision process that is always necessary when one is doing work with persons in psychotic states of mind.

References

Bell, D.L. (1995). Knowledge and its pretenders. In Ellwood, J. (ed). Psychosis: Understanding and treatment. London: Jessica Kingsley pp. 70–82.

Bion, W.R. (1959). Attacks on Linking. *International Journal of Psycho-Analysis,* 40:308–315.

Damasio, A. (1999). *The feeling of what happens: Body, emotion and the making of consciousness.* London: William Heinemann.

Eissler, K.R. (1953). Notes Upon the Emotionality of a Schizophrenic Patient and its Relation to Problems of Technique. Psychoanalytic Study of the Child, 8:199–251.

Freud, S. (1900). *Interpretation of Dreams.* Standard Edition 4 & 5. London: Hogarth Press.

Freud, S. (1911/1958). *"Psycho-Analytic Notes on an Autobiographical Account of a Case of Paranoia (Dementia Paranoides)".* Standard Edition 12. London: Hogarth Press.

Freud, S. (1915e). *The Unconscious. Standard Edition 14.* London: Hogarth Press.

Freud, S. (1924b). *Neurosis and psychosis. Standard Edition 19.* London: Hogarth Press.

Freud, S. (1924e). *The Loss of Reality in Neurosis and Psychosis.* Standard Edition 19. London: Hogarth Press.

Freud, S. (1940a). *An outline of psycho-analysis. Standard Edition 13.* London: Hogarth Press.

Jasper, K. (1913). *Allgemeine Psychopathologie*. Berlin: Springer Verlag.

Ogden, T. H. (1980). On the Nature of Schizophrenic Conflict. *International Journal of Psycho-Analysis*, 61:513–533.

Parnas, J., Handest P (2003). Phenomenology of anomalous self-experience in early Schizophrenia. *Comprehensive Psychiatry*, vol. 44/2:121–134.

Rosenbaum, B. (2005). Psychosis and the structure of homosexuality: Understanding the pathogenesis of schizophrenic states of mind. *Scandinavian Psychoanalytic Review*, 28:82–89.

Rosenbaum, B., Valbak, K., Harder, S., Knudsen, P. et al. (2005). The Danish National Schizophrenia Project: Prospecive, comparative, longitudinal treatment study of first-episode psychosis. *British Journal of Psychiatry*, 186:394–399.

Rosenbaum, B. & Thorgaard, L. (1988). Early and continuing intervention in schizophrenia. Short version of The Danish National Schizophrenia Project manual for psychodynamic individual psychotherapy with schizophrenics. Unpublished.

Searles, H.F. (1965). Phases of patient-therapist interaction in the psychotherapy of chronic schizophrenia. In *Collected papers on schizophrenia and related subjects* (pp. 521–559). New York: International Universities Press.

Thorgaard, L. & Rosenbaum, B. (2006). Schizophrenia: Pathogenesis and therapy. In Johannessen, J.O. et al. (eds). *Evolving Psychosis*. London: Routledge.

CHAPTER EIGHT

Pre-suicide states of mind

Donald Campbell

Freud on suicide

- During a suicide attempt the body is perceived as a separate object—to be killed

In his paper *'Mourning and melancholia'* (Freud, 1917) Freud observed that in melancholia after a loss or a 'real slight or disappointment' coming from a person for whom there are strong ambivalent feelings, the hate originally felt towards the person may be redirected towards the self. He writes:

"It is this sadism alone that solves the riddle of the tendency to suicide, which makes melancholia so interesting—and so dangerous. The analysis of melancholia now shows that the ego can kill itself only if ... it can treat itself as an object—if it is able to direct against itself the hostility which relates to an object and which represents the ego's original reaction to objects in the external world" (Freud, 1917, p. 252).

In the suicidal individuals I have analysed it is the body that is treated as a separate object and concretely identified with the lost loved and hated person. My understanding of suicidal patients is influenced by Freud's observations and begins with the view that in these patients a split in the ego has resulted in a critical and punitive super-ego perceiving the body as a separate, bad or dangerous object.

Whatever else is said about suicide, it functions as a solution born of despair and desperation. An individual enters a pre-suicide state whenever the normal self-preservative instinct is overcome and their body becomes expendable. In some cases, the patient's rejection of his or her body comes silently, or may appear only indirectly in the material, but once this has occurred a suicide attempt may be made at any time.

The nature and function of the suicide fantasy

- The suicide fantasy involves splitting, projection and denial
- In the suicide fantasy a dangerous mother identified with the body
- The aim of the suicide fantasy is to kill the body so that an essential part of the self can survive in another dimension
- In the suicide fantasy the surviving self is free to fuse with an omnipotently gratifying, desexualised mother

A pre-suicide state of mind is influenced, in varying degrees, by a suicide fantasy, based on the self's relation to its body and its primary objects. The fantasy may or may not become conscious, but at the time of execution it has distorted reality and has the power of a delusional conviction. The suicide fantasy is the motive force. A person's promise or conscious resolve to not kill him or herself, or even a strong feeling that suicide is no longer an option, does not put them beyond the risk of another attempt on their life. The suicide fantasy illuminates the conflicts, which the suicidal act aims to resolve, and the wishes that self-murder gratifies. As long as the suicide fantasy is not understood and worked through, the individual is in danger of resorting to suicide as a means of dealing with conflict, pain and anxiety. For many despairing individuals, suicide is the secretly held trump card, which insures that they will triumph over adversity.

I found that suicidal patients' fantasies about death and their affects and thoughts during the build up to a suicide attempt confirmed Freud's (1917) observation. When these patients reached the point at which they intended to kill themselves, they experienced their body as a separate object. While each patient expected his or her body to die, they also imagined another part of them would continue to live in a conscious body-less state, otherwise unaffected by the death of their body. Although killing the body was an aim, it was also a means to an end. The end was the pleasurable survival of a self that will survive in another dimension. This survival was dependent upon the destruction of the body (Maltsberger and Buie, 1980).

One half of the dyadic relationship embodied in the suicide fantasy is the body experienced as a separate object. This raises two critical questions for the professional: What is the nature of the object that is now identified with the body? Why is that object expendable?

Self-preservative aggression and sadistic aggression

- Self-preservative aggression aims to eliminate or negate a threatening object
- Sadistic aggression aims to control a threatening object

Developmentally speaking, the ego's first line of defence is self-preservative aggression. The aim of self-preservative aggression is to negate the threat. However, when the object perceived as threatening the child's survival is the same object upon which it depends for its survival—his mother—the exercise of self-preservative aggression poses a dilemma for the child. How can the infant survive the unmitigated and unmediated terror of the other? How is the child to survive if it cannot afford to get rid of mother? How can it survive the consequences of its omnipotent violence? Children fashion an ingenious solution by libidinizing their aggression towards the mother. In this way the child changes the aim of its aggression from eliminating mother to controlling her in a libidinally gratifying way. Self-preservative aggression is, thereby, converted into sadism.

In a self-preservative attack where the aim is to negate a threat (Glasser, 1979) the impact upon the object is irrelevant beyond this. However, in a sadistic attack where the aim is to control the object by inflicting pain and suffering, the relationship to the object must be preserved, not eliminated. By radically altering the relationship to the threatening object to insure that both self and object survive, sadism offers the child a second line of defence.

As with every relationship, the two partners gradually establish the rules by which they can control one another. However, when something occurs which alters the balance of the relationship, it may enter the crucial, pre-suicide phase. The potentially suicidal patient sees the event as a betrayal of a fragile trust, which has held the two in equilibrium, and is perceived, as a direct attack on their psychological integrity. When psychological defences are breached, the body is also felt to be at extreme risk. The at-risk individual mobilises his aggression in a psychic self-defence. His aggression may be aimed at his own body or another's.

Body barrier

The term *body barrier* describes the *resistance* that exists in everybody to translating a conscious fantasy of violence into physical action. The suicidal individual has withdrawn from others in favour of the cathexes of his own body, so that the primitive anxieties of annihilation are experienced in relation to his body, which has become identified with the engulfing or abandoning object. Violent individuals attack an external object in order to break out of an engulfing state, with the self more or less intact. A suicidal individual leaves the external object intact and assaults an internal object, represented by the body, identified with the abandoning or engulfing mother who is perceived as someone who would kill by suffocation or starvation. The body must be killed if the self is to survive. In intrapsychic terms, this is homicide, justifiable homicide. Just as there is a split between the good self and the bad body, there is a split between the hated and engulfing or abandoning primal mother, now identified with the body, and the idealised one with which the self will fuse once the bad mother's body has been eliminated (Campbell and Hale, 1991).

Types of suicide fantasies and the pre-suicide state of mind

- The revenge fantasy
- The self-punishment fantasy
- The elimination fantasy
- The dicing with death fantasy
- The merging fantasy

Suicide fantasies, which elaborate the relationship between the 'surviving self' and the body, take at least five forms. The suicide fantasies of revenge, self-punishment, elimination and merging that I describe here, were elaborated by Maltsberger and Buie (1980). I have added a fifth—the dicing with death fantasy. Although one type of fantasy may dominate consciousness, suicide fantasies are interdependent and at an unconscious level not mutually exclusive. Within the patient, each fantasy is organised around a wish to gratify pre-genital impulses, which are predominantly sadomasochistic or oral-incorporative in nature.

First, a common suicidal fantasy is the *revenge fantasy*. The revenge fantasy centres on the impact that the suicide makes on others. Here, a conscious link to a real object is maintained more strongly than in other suicide fantasies. The destruction of something precious to another person is a devastating attack. A son or daughter who takes his or her own life robs the parents of their dearest possession, knowing that no other injury could possibly be so painful to them (Menninger, 1933). The often conscious thought in the revenge fantasy is *'They will be sorry'*. The implicit message is that the parents have raised a child who hates himself because they did not love him enough. The threat of suicide to blackmail others may accompany the revenge fantasy.

This suicide fantasy has a markedly sadistic orientation, with the surviving self' often enjoying the role of the invisible observer of others' suffering, especially due to their feelings of guilt and remorse because of the suicide. There is a sense of retaliation, revenge and irrevocable, everlasting triumph.

A second fantasy is that of *self-punishment*, which is dominated by guilt, frequently associated with masturbation, which aims to gratify, in fantasy, incestuous wishes, and an erotisation of pain and death. Here, the surviving self is gratified by its sadistic treatment of its own body rather than that of others, as occurs in a revenge fantasy. Masochistic impulses are satisfied as well, in the self's identification with the helpless, passive, submissive body.

Case study: Self-punishment fantasy and erotisation in a completed suicide

This sadomasochistic dynamic is evident in the complexity of those sexually deviant practices that maintain a delicate balance between masochistic pleasures in self-torture and the risk of death, as in the dicing- with-death phenomenon, which I will describe later, and is illustrated by the suicide of a man who had broken off treatment two years prior to his death.

He was found hanged above a fallen chair and dressed only in a raincoat surrounded by burning candles. From the patient's earlier accounts of his elaborate ritual, it was clear that the 'surviving self' in his suicide fantasy was secretly identified with Joan of Arc, a woman who victoriously led men in battle and was martyred and reincarnated in a new dimension as a saint.

Based on my understanding of this ex-patient's unconscious wishes from his previous therapy, I would speculate that underlying the risk-taking, sadomasochistic dynamic was an infantile wish to get inside a woman; he was naked inside the raincoat, thereby sharing her death. The sacrifice of his male body was the means to that end. The candles represented her execution pyre, the noose introduced excitement because of the real risk of death. This tragic and extreme case illustrates the interplay between sadomasochistic and oral incorporative impulses and the coexistence of one or more fantasies during a pre-suicidal state.

This interplay of fantasies is particularly remarkable during the turbulent, fluctuating time of adolescence. Adolescents who are dominated by pre-genital needs and have had difficulty in separating from their parents may blame their sexual bodies for the incestuous guilt they feel over intrusive wishes. These adolescents believe that punishment of their body by killing it is the only way to relieve them of their guilt.

In the third fantasy, the *elimination fantasy*, the body is experienced as a destroyer. In some cases, it threatens to destroy sanity, while in other cases the body threatens to kill the self. The mechanism is similar to that seen in paranoid cases, with its reliance upon splitting aspects of the self and projecting them into others, But for the suicidal patient with an elimination fantasy, a split-off body is the object upon which is projected murderous impulses in such a way that the 'me' self then feels that it's 'not me' body is occupied by an assassin (Maltsburger and Buie, 1980).

What distinguishes this suicide fantasy from others is that the surviving self is motivated less by malicious intent, as in the revenge and punishment fantasies, than by primitive self-preservative instincts. The body is not an object of sadistic attack by the self, nor is the self-preoccupied with revenge upon others. The body must simply be gotten rid of.

The internal dynamics are similar to those of the individual who feels ensnared in the Core Complex to the extent that he believes his life is at risk and reacts with self-preservative violence. In the psychotic life and death struggle contained in the elimination fantasy, the only thing that matters to the *surviving self* is the elimination of the *killer* body to avoid total annihilation. In this fantasy, suicide is conceived of as killing the *assassin body* before it kills the *me* self. The elimination fantasy views suicide is an act of self-defence.

Case study: An elimination psychosis

A 19-year-old boy was tortured by unacceptable perverse fantasies during a pre-suicide state. In a session, as the tension created by suicidal thoughts reached the breaking point, he shouted, 'I have got these thoughts. (He tapped the top of his head,) Up here. I can't get rid of them. They are driving me mad. I just want to get a gun, put it right here (he pushed his index finger into the top of his head), and blast it out. POW!'

I believe that the elimination fantasy is the predominant fantasy when suicide occurs in the context of what, in descriptive psychiatric terms, would be regarded as a paranoid psychotic (or schizophrenic) state.

A fourth fantasy is the *dicing-with-death fantasy*. The patient who is compelled to dice with death actively puts his body, or a symbolic representative of it, at risk in order to both attract and attack the primary object. This may take obvious forms, such as driving whilst drunk. It may be structured and socially sanctioned in activities such as parachuting and mountaineering or motor racing, or involve various kinds of delinquency and sexual deviancy. Whatever the risk-taking activity, it should alert the clinician to the fact that the patient may enter a pre-suicide state, and careful attention should be given to the fantasies that are being gratified. Obviously, many risk-takers do not lose touch with reality and do not exceed the limits of their bodies, their equipment or their environment. Nevertheless, because they maintain a delicate balance between failure and triumph, changes in their internal state can alter that balance with fatal results.

Case study: The reckless driver

A patient who had numerous car accidents assumed that others should look out for him. He saw no need to drive within speed limits. He was, in Freud's terms, 'the exception'; that is, someone who had unjustly suffered enough as a child and felt he had a right to a fantasised mother he had never had–an omnipotent mother represented by fate and other drivers who would anticipate his behaviour and protect him from any danger. By putting himself at risk, he hoped to arouse anxiety in others, especially his analyst, and provoke them to rescue him and make him safe and secure. But this attitude towards his body, a body that he did not value enough to protect, represented identification with his neglectful mother, as well as his condemnation of her. There is a strong sadomasochistic dynamic in both passive submission to fate, on the one hand, and actively flaunting the risk-taking, on the other.

The fifth suicide fantasy underpinning all of the other fantasies is a *merging fantasy*. Patients who harbour a merging suicidal fantasy imagine death as a return to nature, becoming one with the universe, achieving a state of nothingness, a passport into a new world, a blissful dreamless eternal sleep; or as a permanent sense of peace. The patients believe that in death the self will survive in a state akin to that of the sleeping infant. The dominant wish is to be fused 'with the image of the Madonna of infancy. By becoming one with her, the suicidal patient hopes to taste again the omnipotent, timeless, mindless peace of his baby origins, far from the wearisome hostile inner presence of his miserable adulthood' (Maltsburger and Buie 1980).

However, as seen in the core complex, the wish to fuse with an omnipotent mother is accompanied by an anxiety about the consequences of fulfilling that wish, the annihilation of the self. In the psychotic state typical of those dominated by suicidal fantasies, splitting of the self from the body leaves these patients believing that the body is actually an impediment to the fulfilling of the merging fantasy. The body is identified with the engulfing or abandoning mother and is then eliminated. Once the body is eliminated the 'surviving self' is free to fuse with the split-off, idealised, desexualised, omnipotently gratifying mother represented by states of oceanic bliss, dreamless eternal sleep, a permanent sense of peace, becoming one with the universe, or achieving a state of nothingness (Maltsberger and Buie, 1980).

The father in the pre-suicide state of mind

- The good enough pre-oedipal father sets limits on his child's fantasised timeless relationship with mother and represents the world outside the exclusivity of the mother/child relationship, e.g., the realities of time and place
- Prior to a suicide attempt father's failure to stake a claim on his child, which left the child with no alternative to the pathological mother/child relationship, is revived in the transference

The clinician should not expect the suicidal patient to be entirely conscious of their suicide fantasies, or to report conscious aspects of their fantasies during therapy. The transference and counter-transference may be the most reliable indicator of the form and content of the patient's suicide fantasies. These suicide fantasies, whatever form they take, represent internalised early pathological relationships between mother and child and father, and will inevitably be played out in the transference and counter-transference. In the time I have available I will focus on only one, but important, transference dynamic—the pre-oedipal father. In my experience, the pre-oedipal father's role was often obscured by the patient's relationship with the mother, which dominated the suicide fantasy, and by the father's absence or ineffectiveness. However, it was during the pre-suicide state that the internalised father's failure to intervene in the pathological mother/child relationship became most critical. I found that the therapist was repeatedly drawn into enacting the withdrawn or out of touch father that, in the patient's mind, sanctioned the suicide state (Campbell, 1995, 2006).

In normal development, both pre-oedipal parents represent to the child the world outside the exclusivity of the mother-infant relationship, e.g., the realities of time and place and objects. The "good-enough" pre-oedipal father is a friendly rival with both his child and his wife, in offering each of them a dyadic relationship that is parallel to and competes with the mother-child unit.

The attractive and attracting father stakes a claim on his child and, with mother's help, enables the child to move from the exclusivity of the infant-mother relationship into an inclusive position as part of a pre-oedipal triad.

Father's gender role identity and parental Oedipal impulses influence the idiosyncratic nature of the claim he makes on his child. For instance, his conscious and unconscious fantasies and anxieties about female sexuality will affect the way he relates to his daughter from the beginning. She may be 'daddy's little girl'. Gender influenced relating will also play a part in the way a father helps his son dis-identify from mother (Greenson, 1968) and father's view of the way his wife relates to his male offspring. The father may even be conscious of not wanting his wife to 'feminise' his son. Whatever form this process of claiming his child takes, and there will always be infinite variations influenced by mixtures of projections and reality, the child will become aware that he or she occupies a place in father's mind that is separate and distinct from mother.

The child also becomes aware of a place for mother in father's mind and a place for father in mother's mind. Father reclaims his wife by seducing her back to him and rekindling her adult sexuality. The father who reclaims his wife and engages his child on his own terms protects them both from lingering overlong in a 'fusional' or symbiotic state and facilitates the separation and individuation process (Mahler and Gosliner, 1955).

The father's twofold response supports the child's right to an independent existence that is separate from mother while providing the toddler with a means of coping with its longing for her. Abelin (1978) postulates that around eighteen months this process results in an early triangulation in which the toddler identifies with the rival father's *wish* for mother in order to form a mental representation of a self that is separate and longing for mother. The good-enough father provides a model for identification as well as an alternative relationship to the child's regressive wishes to return to a 'fusional' state with mother with subsequent anxieties about engulfment.

I have found in the analysis of suicidal patients that it often becomes apparent that they perceived their fathers as either withdrawn or actively rejecting them, and as having failed to reclaim their wives. Each patient had felt abandoned to his or her anxiety about surviving as a differentiated self when left with a disturbed mother.

I was involved simultaneously in two transferences; firstly, a dyadic primitive sado-masochistic struggle with a smothering, 'murderous' mother, and, secondly, as the abandoning father in a more triangular situation. The danger is in recognising only one transference at the expense of the other, despite the patient's unconscious invitation to do so.

Working with a pre-suicide state of mind

- There is a danger of a collusive counter-transference
- There is a risk of a sado-masochistic interaction
- There will be consequences of the patient's narcissistic regression

The patient's pressure to involve the therapist in the suicide scenario is the primary factor in the creation of a collusive counter-transference response to the patient's pre-suicide state of mind. This counter-transference takes the form of unconscious, and sometimes conscious, wishes to negate the patient. For instance, there is a heightened danger during a pre-suicide state of enacting the transference of a father who fails to stake a claim on its child, and abandons it to a disturbed mother. Straker (1958) pointed out: "A decisive factor in the successful suicide attempt appears to be the implied consent or unconscious collusion between the patient and the person most involved in the psychic struggle." The unconscious collusion is buried in the analyst's counter-transference.

The patient consciously and unconsciously attempts to provoke the analyst to behave in such a way as to confirm the patient's illusory (transference) image of the analyst (Sandler, 1976) as an active participant in a sado-masochistic interaction. When this is enacted the analyst has unwittingly been manoeuvred into the role of the executioner. This gives the patient justification for retaliation via a suicide attempt.

The sadomasochistic dynamic may also manifest itself in the subtle, superficially benign form of the patient's feeling of being at peace, which contributes to increased self-assurance and confidence (Laufer and Laufer 1984). Depressive affects, anxieties and conflicts are no longer communicated. This narcissistic withdrawal cuts the therapist off from moods and behaviour, which would normally elicit an empathic response of alarm or worry and may result in the sudden loss of subjective emotional concern (Tahka, 1978) for the patient.

In a narcissistic regression, which dominated my patients during the pre-suicide state, there is the prospect of imminently fulfilling a merging suicide fantasy. As far as these patients were concerned, they were already at peace because they had crossed a rational barrier of self-preservation, identified the assassin/mother with their body, and had no doubts about killing it.

The professional, burdened with anxieties about his or her patient's life or exhausted by the patient's relentless attack on hope or angry about being blackmailed (often before a holiday break from treatment), may be tempted to retaliate by giving up on his or her patient, or try to put the patient out of his or her mind, or use the patient's sense of peace to justify relaxing his or her therapeutic vigilance. This is a frequent problem for therapists and represents a familiar counter-transference to the patient's pre-suicide state of mind. You may feel like surrendering or retreating from the battle, but it is a battle worth fighting nevertheless.

References

Abelin, E. (1978). "The role of the father in the pre-oedipal years". *J. Amer. Psychoanal. Assn.* 26:143–161.

Campbell, D. (1995). "The role of the father in a pre-suicide state". *Int. J. Psycho-Anal.* 76:315–323.

Campbell, D. (2006). "A pre-suicide state in an adolescent female". *J Assoc Child Psychotherapy* 32:3 pp. 260–272.

Campbell, D. & Hale, R. (1991). "Suicidal Acts" in *Textbook of Psychotherapy in Psychiatric Practice*, ed. J. Holmes, London: Churchill Livingstone, pp. 287–306.

Freud, S. (1917 [1915]). *Mourning and melancholia, Standard Edition*. 14: 237–260. London, Hogarth Press.

Glasser, M. (1979). "Some aspects in the role of aggression in the perversions", *Sexual Deviations*, 2nd Edition, ed. I Rosen, Oxford U. Press, pp. 278–305.

Laufer & Laufer (1984). *Adolescence and Developmental Breakdown*, New Haven and London; Yale University Press.

Mahler, M.S. & Gosliner, B.J. (1955). "On symbiotic child psychosis, genetic dynamic and restitutive aspects". *Psychoanal. Study Child*. 10: 195–212.

Maltsberger, J.G. & Buie, D.H. (1980). "The devices of suicide". *Int. R. Psycho-Anal.* 7:61–72.

Menninger, K.A. (1933). "Psychoanalytic aspects of suicide". *Int. J. Psycho-Anal.* 14:376–390.

Sandler, J. (1976). "Counter-transference and role-responsiveness". *Int. R. Psycho-Anal.* 3:43–78.

Stekel, W. ([1910] 1967). "Symposium on Suicide" in *On Suicide*, ed. P. Friedman, New York: International Universities Press, pp. 33–141.

Straker, M. (1958). "Clinical observations of suicide". *Canad. Med. Assoc. J.* 79:473–479.

Tahka, V.A. (1978). "On some narcissistic aspect of self-destructive behaviour and their influence on its predictability", Psychopathology of Direct and Indirect Self Destruction. *Psyciatra Fennica,* Supplementum 59–62.

CHAPTER NINE

Individual and large-group identities: Does working with borderline patients teach us anything about international negotiations?

Vamık D. Volkan

Many years ago, I had a peculiar experience with one of my patients who had a severe borderline personality organization. During the third year of his analysis, Joseph began coming to his sessions 25 minutes late. Without offering an excuse for being late, or mentioning the subject at all, four times a week he simply came to my office, lay on the couch with a smile on his face, and began talking. I sensed that this unexpected behaviour pattern reflected his developing "hot" split transference towards me. To avoid interfering prematurely with this development, I waited for several weeks before I told him that he was losing half of his sessions each time he came to see me. I inquired if he was curious about this development, for I certainly was. Joseph appeared very surprised—he seemed genuinely convinced that he was attending his full sessions.

I stayed calm and continued to encourage him to be curious about our discrepancy regarding what time he came to my office. Slowly I came to understand what was occurring and learned that Joseph was, in a way, telling the truth about coming to our sessions on time. He did in fact arrive at the scheduled time, but instead of entering my office, he would go into the bathroom next door where he spent

25 minutes holding an inner conversation with me during which he felt like an angry monster and likewise perceived me as a horrible person. He then would get off the toilet, come to my office, lay on the couch, and behave in an extremely friendly way and perceive me as friendly as well.

Through his "dual" sessions, Joseph directly and fully brought the splitting of his self- and object images into the transference relationship with me. Elsewhere I describe this case and how the patient split his hour with me into "bad" and "good" sessions (Volkan, 1976). Although this aspect of the case was interesting, a different aspect is also relevant to this chapter: the fact that I thought of him as the "Penguin Man." This name, which I kept to myself, simply seemed to describe him, since he was stocky and waddled slightly when he walked.

Sometime later, I realized that I had given animal names to other long-term patients. Besides Penguin Man, there were Giraffe Lady, Cat person, and Dogman. I discovered that each of these patients lacked integrated identities; they had psychotic or severe borderline personality organizations—I never gave an animal name to a person with a neurotic personality organization. They were simply Mary or Jack—whatever name they were born with, or one I substituted for confidentiality when writing or talking about them.

My giving animal names to individuals with unintegrated personality organizations had a great deal to do with my countertransference towards them. I am a "replacement child" (Poznanski, 1972; Cain and Cain, 1964; Volkan and Ast, 1997) the idealized mental representation of an uncle who died unexpectedly before my birth and under mysterious circumstances was deposited into my self-representation by my mother and grandmother. I was named after him, and in turn he was named after my great-great grandfather who had been an important Ottoman administrator on the island of Cyprus. This grandfather lost his fame and fortune in one day when a British governor and his entourage arrived on the island after the Ottomans rented Cyprus to the British and turned over the island's administration to them. I believe that as a child I assimilated the combined idealized images of my uncle and my elite Ottoman ancestor into my self-representation. Nevertheless, at times this assimilation was shaky and I felt forced to live up to these idealized images. This induced a tension between the idealized and not so idealized aspects within my internal world. In a prejudicial way I associated my patients who had unintegrated self-representations with animals. By doing so, I separated them from me so they would not remind me of the tension within my own self-representation due to my integration difficulty and the influence of the idealized images that had been deposited in me.

When we are involved in analytic work, the analyst partly regresses, as Stanley Olinick said, "In the service of the other." (1980, p. 7) We on one hand maintain an observing and working ego, while on the other we regress in order to understand our patients' inner worlds at their own level. In the service of my patients with unintegrated self-representations, I was trying, unconsciously at first, to assist with their struggles to find out who they were. They had identity problems and I gave them animal identities. I also created "teddy bears," living transitional objects (Winnicott, 1953) with which, in the shadows of the analytic process in my office, we would play in order to help the patients develop integrated self-representations.

Clinicians often use the term "identity" when describing patients who fragment or divide self- and object images into "good" (libidinally loaded) and "bad" (aggressively loaded) categories. The terms "good" and "bad" themselves have prejudicial connotations. However, these terms often appear in contemporary psychoanalytic literature when we refer to the concept of identity, something which is relatively new in psychoanalysis. Erik Erikson (1956), one psychoanalyst who focused on an individual's identity and in a sense made it a psychoanalytic term, first used the term "ego identity," and then dropped the word ego and used simply "identity." He described a person's identity as "both a persistent sameness within oneself ... [and] a persistent sharing of some kind of essential character with others" (p. 57). Since this chapter also focuses on large groups, "large-group identity" needs to be defined as well. Large-group identity refers to the subjective experience of thousands or millions of people who are linked by a persistent sense of sameness while sharing characteristics with others in foreign groups.

This volume primarily examines various aspects of individuals with severe identity disturbances. Most of these individuals possess split self- and object images and are considered to have borderline personality organizations. In order to link this chapter with the main theme of this volume, I will explore whether individual psychoanalysis of patients with borderline personality organization teaches us anything about psychoanalytically informed international negotiations. I will compare working on the splitting mechanism in individual patients with attempting to narrow the psychological gap between fractured communities or enemy groups. Some political leaders have made references to the necessity of examining such psychological gaps. For example, when Egyptian President Anwar el-Sadat spoke to the Israeli Knesset in 1977, he referred to the significance of a psychological wall (gap) between the two countries in the continuation of the Arab-Israeli conflict.

In today's world, there are many "conflict resolution" practitioners who are involved in unofficial efforts to reduce tensions between opposing large groups, but they very seldom apply psychoanalytic understanding of individuals and large groups in their work. There are exceptions. In 1993, John Alderdice in a lecture entitled, *Ulster on the Couch,* proposed the creation of what he called, a "political consulting room" where both the surface elements as well as emotional and unconscious issues could be addressed in order to improve the chance of success in the Northern Ireland peace process. Mitch Elliott, a former president of the Irish Psycho-Analytical Association, and his colleagues describe how a psychoanalytically informed process paralleling Alderdice's suggestions was designed and employed in the 1990s and what it accomplished (Elliot, 2005; Elliot, Bishop, and Stokes, 2004). Maurice Apprey (2005) compared the method described by Elliott and his colleagues with the psychoanalytically informed method developed at the University of Virginia's Center for the Study of Mind and Human Interaction (CSMHI) (closed since 2005). Apprey stated that the first one stopped at a diagnostic level and Elliott and his colleagues hoped that policy makers would benefit from its findings. CSMHI went beyond making an assessment of conflict by adding a facilitating team that conducted years-long dialogues between the representatives of antagonistic large groups, transformed their grievances and narrowed the psychological gap between them.

Because CSMHI's method is discussed in full detail elsewhere (Volkan, 1999a, 2006a), I only present a brief summary here. Nicknamed the "Tree Model" to reflect that the slow growth and branching of a tree are analogous to the way this method unfolds, it has three basic phases: assessment, dialogue, and institutionalization. During the first phase, which includes in-depth interviews with a wide range of members of the large groups involved, the interdisciplinary facilitating team of psychoanalysts, historians, political scientists, and others begins to understand the main aspects of the relationship between the two large groups and the surrounding situation to be addressed. Next, influential representatives of enemy large groups are brought together for a series of unofficial negotiations over several years under the guidance of psychoanalytically informed facilitators. This facilitating team borrows technical principles from psychoanalysis as it applies to individuals. The team does not provide advice. Resistances against changing opposing large groups' "pathological" ways of protecting their large-group identities are brought to the surface, articulated, and fantasized threats to large-group identity are interpreted so that realistic communication can take place. By increasing understanding of the conscious and unconscious dynamics at work on both sides, new ways of interacting become possible. In order for the gained insights to have an impact on social and political policy, as well as on the populace at large, the final phase requires the collaborative development of concrete actions, programs, and institutions. By developing programs and institutions that implement and encourage such new ways of interacting, what is experienced at first by a few during the psycho political dialogues can be spread and made available to many more. With appropriate modifications, this approach can be applied to a wide variety of situations to help alleviate tensions, prevent violent conflict, heal traumatized societies, and promote peaceful coexistence.

In cases like Joseph's, the aim of analysis is to help the patient to mend his or her split self- and object images in order to establish an integrated self-representation and corresponding integrated object representations. This produces anxiety and other troublesome emotions, which I will name later and which can be tamed through analytic work. Does what clinicians learn in the clinical setting about mending an individual's internal splitting provide information about difficulties in psycho political dialogues, such as those that occur during the second phase of the Tree Model? This chapter attempts to answer this question.

Individual identity

Sigmund Freud seldom referred to "identity," and when he did, it was in a colloquial or unsophisticated sense. One well-known reference to identity is found in a speech written by Freud (1926a) for B'nai B'rith. In it, Freud connected his individual identity with his large-group identity and wondered why he was bound to Jewry since, as a non-believer, he had never been instilled with its ethnonational pride or religious faith. There is a consensus that the concept "identity" refers to a subjective experience. It can be differentiated from related concepts such as "character" and "personality." The latter terms describe the impressions others perceive of the individual's emotional expressions, modes of speech, typical actions, and habitual ways of thinking and behaving. Traditionally, character is a person's ego-syntonic, habitual mode of reconciling intrapsychic conflicts. Some authors believe that personality is an umbrella term that covers both character and "temperament." Temperament refers to constitutionally determined affectomotor and cognitive tendencies (Moore and Fine, 1990). If we observe someone to be habitually clean, orderly, greedy, and to use excessive intellectualization, show excessive ambivalence and controlled emotional expressions, we say that this person has an obsessional character. If we observe someone who is overtly suspicious and cautious, and whose physical appearance suggests that she is constantly scanning the environment for possible danger, we say that this person has a paranoid personality.

Unlike character and personality, which are observed and perceived by others, identity refers to an individual's inner working model—this person, not the outsider, senses and experiences it. Some authors (Kernberg, 1976, 1984; Volkan 1976, 1995) use the term "personality organization" and differentiate it from the simple word "personality." Personality organization refers to the analyst's theoretical explanation of the inner construction and affective experience of a patient's self-representation and the nature of this individual's internalized object relations. Personality organization parallels the concept of identity, which is sensed by the individual himself.

In everyday life, adult individuals can typically refer to numerous aspects of their identity related to social or professional status—one may simultaneously perceive oneself as a mother or father, a physician or carpenter, or someone who enjoys specific sports or recreational activities. These facets superficially seem to fit Erikson's (1956) definition but do not truly reflect a person's internal sense of sustained sameness. If a person's social or career identity is threatened, the individual may or may not experience anxiety. Anxiety is more likely to occur if the threat is connected, mostly unconsciously, to danger signals originally described by Freud (1926b): losing a loved one (a mothering person) or that person's love, a body part (castration), or self-esteem. In some cases, the anxiety is severe enough for the individual to seek treatment, but it is otherwise unlikely that changing jobs or membership in a sports club, for example, would cause severe psychological problems that change the structure of a person's internal world.

On the other hand, let us consider an adult who acutely decompensates and goes into psychosis. Such an individual's unique identity is fragmenting and may have an inner sense of terror and a star exploding into a million pieces (Pao, 1979; Glass, 1989; Volkan, 1995). The experience of this person helps to define what I mean by "core identity"—one that individuals are terrified of losing—and differentiates it from other social or profession-related identities. Not to have a cohesive core identity is intolerable unless the individual utilizes primitive defences to hide it, such as fragmenting, splitting, introjective-projective relatedness, dissociation and denial. At times, when one cannot protect oneself and faces the loss of one's core identity, it feels like a psychological death. When Erikson (1956) referred to the aspect of identity that involves a persistent sense of inner sameness he, I believe, was specifying core identity.

In "normal" development, when children become able to possess an integrated self-representation, they also begin to have a subjective experience of a persistent sameness within themselves. They have now formed the foundation of a core identity. During childhood the self-representation and the corresponding core identity will be enlarged and modified with various types of identifications. Some identifications connect the child's core identity to the parents' cultural and group heritage. Think of a man—let us say he an Englishman—who is an amateur photographer. If he decides to stop practicing photography and take up carpentry, he may call himself a carpenter instead of a photographer, but he cannot stop being an Englishman and become French. His Englishness is part of his large-group identity, which is interconnected with his core individual identity, his subjective experience of his self-representation. Not all identifications are healthy, however. Clinical work has demonstrated maladaptive childhood identifications.

Identifications and identity are related but they are not interchangeable concepts. As Erikson (1956) stated, identity starts when a process of identification ends. I modify this by saying that a cohesive core identity starts when identifications are assimilated within a differentiated and integrated self-representation. Peter Blos (1979) described in detail how an individual's character crystallizes during the adolescent passage. During the adolescent passage there is a psychobiological regression and the youngster loosens up her investments in the images of important others of her childhood and modifies and even disregards her identifications with them. Furthermore, she adds additional identifications, this time from her peer group or far beyond her restricted family or neighbourhood environment. Through these there is an overhauling of her persistent sense of inner sameness. I suggest that the formation of core identity also finalizes during this period (Volkan, 1988).

Once a person's core identity crystallizes, it can be defined by looking at it from different angles. Salman Akhtar (1992, 1999) looked at the individual's core identity from different angles. He stated that the sustained feeling of inner sameness is accompanied by a temporal continuity in the self-experience: the past, the present, and the future are integrated into a smooth continuum of remembered, felt, and expected existence for the individual. The individual core identity is connected with a realistic body image and a sense of inner solidarity and is associated with the capacity for solitude and clarity of one's gender. Akhtar also connected the individual's core identity with large-group identity, such as a national, ethnic or religious identity.

Akhtar's last characteristic of an individual's identity refers to a link between one's personal core identity and large-group identity. His description of this characteristic implies that the link occurs at the oedipal level when a child's superego is crystallized. The child then identifies with his parents' prohibitions and ideals, and by extension, his large-group's prohibitions and ideals. To support this view, Akhtar refers to Chasseguet-Smirgel's (1984) remark that successful resolution of the Oedipus complex adds to the child's entrance into the father's universe. I contend that the foundation of the core large-group identity is created during the pre-oedipal period; oedipal influences, however important, are added later.

Large-group identity

In the psychological literature the term "large group" sometimes refers to 30 to 150 members who meet in order to deal with a given psychological issue (Kernberg, 2003a, b), but I am *not* referring to such gatherings. My focus is on ethnic, national, religious or political ideological groups composed of thousands or millions of people. In such large groups most of the individuals will never meet during their lifetimes. In fact, they will not even know of the existence of many others belonging to the same entity. Yet, they will share a sense of belonging, usually a language, sentiments, nursery rhymes, songs, dances, and representations of history. They share what John Mack (1979) called, "cultural amplifiers," which are concrete or abstract symbols and signs that are only associated with a particular large group and which are usually accepted as "superior" and as a source of pride. The sharing of the large group's national, ethnic or religious elements begins in childhood. This applies also to those who are members of a political ideological group whose parents and the people in the childhood environment are believers in the ideology. To become a follower of a political ideology as an adult involves other psychological motivations.

Depending on the focus of a large group's identity, the child's investment is in ethnicity (I am an Arab), religion (I am a Catholic), nationality (I am a German), political ideology (I am a communist), or a combination of these. A psychoanalytic examination of how a large group's identity evolves goes beyond the phenomenology of large-group identity concepts. A child born in Hyderabad, India, for example, would focus on religious/cultural issues as she develops a large-group identity, since adults there define their dominant large-group identities according to religious affiliation (Muslim or Hindu) (Kakar, 1996). A child born in Cyprus would absorb a dominant large-group identity defined by ethnic/national/political sentiments, because what is currently critical in this part of the world is whether one is Greek, Turkish or politically simply "Cypriot" (there is no Cypriot nation), with less emphasis placed on whether one is Greek Orthodox Christian or Sunni Muslim (Volkan, 1979).

Questions of investment in ethnicity versus religion, or nationality versus race, or one ideology versus another are not as essential to understanding large-group identity as are the psychodynamic processes of linking individual identity to large-group identity.

Belonging to a large group, after going through the adolescence passage, endures throughout a lifetime. Sometimes belongingness can be a shadow identity, as we sometimes see in persons after voluntary or forced migrations (Volkan, 1993a, Akhtar, 1999). Nevertheless, such belongingness never disappears. Only through some long-lasting drastic historical event may a group evolve a new large-group identity. For example, certain southern Slavs became Bosniaks while under the rule of the Ottoman Empire, which lasted for centuries.

Through early identifications with mother, father, teacher and important persons in their environment small children begin to "learn" that they are members of a specific large group and what cultural amplifiers are theirs. Some children have parents who belong to two different ethnic or religious groups. If an international conflict erupts between these two large groups, these youngsters may, even as adults, have severe psychological problems. In South Ossetia, for example, after the initial wars between Georgians and South Ossetians following the collapse of the Soviet Union and before the 2008 summer tragedies there, I met persons with "mixed" lineage who had become confused and psychologically disturbed due to their situation (Volkan, 2006a).

There is another childhood process that more clearly creates the precursors of children's notions of large-group enemies and allies and separates their large-group identity from the "others'" large-group identity. This process also illustrates how people, without being aware of it, need to have large-group enemies and allies, to one degree or another, throughout their lifetime. Belonging to the same large-group identity allows thousands or millions of people to share the same large-group enemy and ally representations. This childhood experience can be understood with a concept that I call "suitable targets of externalization" (Volkan, 1988).

The object relations theory of psychoanalysis (Kernberg, 1975, 1976) and observations of children, tells us that when children become able to tolerate ambivalence they integrate their previously fragmented or split self- and object images. However, such integrations are not totally complete. Some self- and object images remain unintegrated and the child finds ways to deal with them in order to avoid facing and feeling object relations tension. One psychological method a child uses to deal with this problem is to externalize his or her unintegrated self- and object images onto other persons, or animate or inanimate objects. The child later may re-internalize such images. The people in the child's environment also help the child to find *permanent* reservoirs in which to keep the externalized unintegrated "bad" and "good" self- and object images. Since externalizations into such reservoirs are approved by the individuals important to the child, what is externalized will not boomerang, will not be re-internalized by the child. Such reservoirs are the suitable targets of externalization that become the precursors of large-group enemy and ally representations (Volkan, 1988). A child is, to use Erikson's (1966) term, a "generalist" as far as nationality, ethnicity, religion or political ideology are concerned. Once the child utilizes suitable targets of externalization, he or she ceases to be a generalist.

To illustrate this idea, let us consider Cyprus, where Greeks and Turks lived side by side for centuries until the island was de facto divided into two political entities in 1974. Greek farmers there often raise pigs. Turkish children, like Greek children, invariably are drawn to farm animals, but imagine a Turkish child wanting to touch and love a piglet. The mothers or other important individuals in the Turkish child's environment would strongly discourage their children from playing with the piglet. For Moslem Turks, the pig is "dirty." As a cultural amplifier for the Greeks, it does not belong to the Turks' large group. Now the Turkish child has found a permanent reservoir for depositing unwanted, aggressively contaminated and unintegrated "bad" self- and object images. Since Moslem Turks do not eat pork, in a concrete sense what is externalized into the image of the pig will not be re-internalized. When the child unconsciously finds a suitable target for unintegrated "bad" self- and object images, the precursor of the "other" becomes established in the child's mind at an experimental level. The Turkish child at this point does not know what Greekness means. Sophisticated thoughts, perceptions and emotions, and images of history about the "other" evolve much later without the individual's awareness that the first symbol of the enemy was in the service of helping him or her avoid feeling object relations tension. Since almost all Turkish children in

Cyprus will use the same target, they will share the same precursor of the "other" who may become the "enemy" if real world problems become complicated.

Children also are given suitable targets as reservoirs for their "good" unintegrated self- and object relations. For example, a Finnish child uses the sauna as such a reservoir. Only when Finnish children grow up will they have sophisticated thoughts and feelings about Finishness. Most shared reservoirs remain constant for a long time, while certain historical events may shift the group's investment in them. In Scotland, Highland dress dates from the 13th century, but it was an event in the 18th century that transformed the tartan kilt into a shared reservoir of Scottishness. When England defeated Bonnie Prince Charles at Culloden in 1746, the English banned the wearing of the kilt in Scotland under the Act of Proscription. The act was repealed thirty-six years later, and the kilt was adopted as Scottish military dress. When George IV made a state visit to Scotland in 1882, his visit strengthened Scottish investment in the kilt, which served to enhance Scottish unity in the face of a visit from the figurehead of powerful England. Many Scottish families even have their own tartan design, which they sometimes use in their personal clothing. Efforts to suppress the wearing of the kilt have been unsuccessful; the dress continues to serve as an ethnic reservoir signifying Scottishness.

It is interesting that when there is an international conflict or a war-like situation, members of a large group who feel victimized regress and create adult versions of suitable targets of externalization. In childhood, reservoirs are chosen because they have been culturally invested in by parents and other adults who direct the children to choose them. Adults who regress under a shared trauma, however, choose reservoirs that symbolically relate to their threatening environment. For example, when Gaza fell under the Israeli occupation, Palestinians began to carry small stones painted with the Palestinian flag's colours in their pockets. When facing humiliating external situations, they would reach into their pockets and touch the stones. Having the stones created a network of "we-ness" that supported the large-group identity of Palestinians living in Gaza at that time and separated their large-group identity from the Israelis' large-group identity.

Below I will describe what clinicians learn when a patient with an unintegrated personality organization in analysis attempts to develop a cohesive identity. Then I will illustrate how such a clinical experience illuminates what happens when "neutral" facilitators guide the representatives of opposing large groups to shrink the psychological gap between them.

Mending splitting in individuals

In 1963, Donald Winnicott played with diagrams, using a circle to represent a person. He wrote, "Inside the circle is collected all the interplay of forces and objects that constitute the inner reality of the individual at this moment of time" (p. 75). In 1969, Winnicott added that an individual who is mature enough to be represented as a circle is one who is capable of containing conflicts that arise from within and without, and that it is necessary to divide this circle by putting a line down its centre, because "there must always be war or potential war along the line in the centre, on either side of the line there become organized groupings of benign and persecutory elements" (pp. 222–223). He continued to state that only idealists "often speak as if there were such a thing as an individual with no line down the middle in the diagram of the person, where there is nothing but benign forces for use for good purposes" (p. 223). According to Winnicott, "the individual" is a relatively modern concept. Until a few hundred years ago, he said, outside of a few exceptional "total individuals" (p. 222) everyone was unintegrated. When he wrote his papers on this topic he thought that even then the world was mainly composed of individuals who could not achieve integration and be a total unit.

Winnicott's references to unintegrated individuals reflect knowledge gained through examination of the internal worlds of patients with borderline personality organization that point to a split between libidinally invested self- and object representations and aggressively invested self- and object representations. A closer look at how one's self- and object representations evolve and become integrated and cohesive in childhood (Kernberg, 1970, 1975, 1976, Volkan, 1976, 1995), however, suggests a need to modify Winnicott's diagram of the unintegrated individual. It would be less confusing to consider a circle with a line through its centre as representing a mature individual who has achieved tolerance for ambivalence to one degree or another. Since opposite halves of the circle touch each other, metapsychologically speaking, such an individual has moved to a higher level (neurotic) personality organization from the previous level, that of a borderline personality organization. Perhaps a diagram representing a truly unintegrated person (as I drew— Volkan, 1981a) would have not a line, but a definable gap between the two halves of the circle.

The key issue during psychoanalysis of an individual with borderline personality organization is to help the person eventually reach a "crucial juncture" (Klein, 1946; Kernberg, 1976, 1984; Volkan, 1987, 1993; Volkan and Fowler, 2009). The term "crucial juncture" was first used by Melanie Klein in 1946. She wrote: "The synthesis between the loved and hated aspects of the complete object gives rise to the feelings of mourning and guilt which imply vital advances in the infant's emotional and intellectual life. This is also a crucial juncture for the choice of neurosis or psychosis" (p. 100). It is the failure to reach natural "crucial junctures" in childhood that cause the adult to be stuck in a personality organization in which splitting predominates as the key defence; the developmental "normal" splitting thus, in such individuals, becomes a defensive, pathological splitting and such patients come to treatment with this pathology. Therefore, a natural developmental occurrence in childhood will be observed in adults with borderline personality organization when they reach crucial juncture experiences during analysis.

Such patients will need many crucial juncture experiences before the integration of their self- and object representations become crystallized. Then, the ability to have ambivalence replaces their relating to their self- and object images in a split fashion. Such a patient becomes a circle with a line through its centre, replacing two separate components of a circle divided with a gap. The analyst absorbs, tames and deals with the patient's intense emotions prior to and during the patient's transformation from a split identity to an integrated one. These emotions usually include murderous rage that is originally directed to caretakers with disturbed mothering functions, envy due to a sense that one has developmental arrests while others moved on to higher levels of functioning, and remorse for badly treating objects contaminated with devaluation when "bad" images were externalized into them.

Furthermore, anxiety of losing "good" aspects when they are ready to be integrated with the "bad" ones and guilt and mourning over losing the former unintegrated self- and object images requires closer examination. When a patient with borderline personality organization arrives at crucial juncture experiences during psycho-analytic treatment, initially he or she fears that mixing "black" and "white" will not produce "grey" (Volkan, 1976, 1987, 1995). The individual's "bad" self- and object images are invested with exaggerated aggression and the patient becomes anxious due to an unconscious perception that during a crucial juncture experience his or her "good" parts will be absorbed with aggression too. Or, the patient senses that the mending will "kill" his or her "good" self- and object images. Once when my patient Joseph was ready to have a crucial juncture experience during a session, he suddenly got up from the couch and "attacked" me. I protected myself and in a few minutes he went back to lying on my couch. When he and I investigated this incident we understood that his physically touching me was neces-sary for him to be sure that he, representing his "good" self- and object images, would not die when (Volkan, 1976). He never touched me again. By being aware of the source of the patient's anxiety, the analyst helps the patient through emphatic explanations, interpreta-tions, and by indirectly offering himself or herself as a model who can take a chance on integration.

Otto Kernberg (1970) also discussed guilt and mourning dur-ing crucial juncture experiences in individuals. He states that "the deep admiration and love for the ideal mother" and "the hatred for the distorted dangerous mother" meet in the transference and the patient experiences guilt and depression "because he has mistreated the analyst and all the significant persons in his life, and he may feel that he has actually destroyed those whom he could have loved and who might have loved him" (p. 81). Kernberg also emphasized the possibility of suicidal ideation at such times. Although I am aware that the evolution of guilt feelings and depression is part of the pro-gression in the treatment of individuals with unintegrated personal-ity organization, mourning itself, without much guilt feeling, is a new experience for these patients, and its appearance signals a posi-tive outcome (Searles, 1986).

For practical purposes, we can divide the intensive approaches to the individual psychoanalytic treatment of patients whose defensive responses are centred on splitting, into two styles (Volkan, 1987). The first approach maintains the already regressed patient at a level where he or she is able to function without further regression, with the idea that further regression may usher in a psychotic condition. The strategy behind this method is to focus on providing new ego experiences for the patient, with clarifications, confrontation and interpretations, kept within the therapeutic setting and calculated to promote integration of opposing self- and object images. I feel that while this approach may be therapeutic, it does not provide for major structural change in the core of the pathological psychic organization. Because of this, when such patients begin to have crucial juncture experiences, they may feel intense guilt, depression, or even have suicidal ideation and may even escape from treatment.

The second approach in the individual psychoanalytic treatment is based on the premise that severely regressed or undeveloped patients should experience further (therapeutic) regression, even though such patients would most likely exhibit temporary, but therapeutically controlled, transference psychosis. After such regressive experiences, these patients would begin to relax their defensive use of splitting, and replace it with developmental splitting. Bear in mind, that all children experience developmental splitting due to their lack of integrative function. Eventually, children are able to reach naturally expected crucial junctures as part of their psychic growth when, for example, they have enough identification with their mothers' integrative functions and when they are capable of taming their aggression. When the child's integrative function is taxed and disturbed due to constitutional, internal, or environmental factors, splitting becomes permanent and is utilized defensively, as I indicated earlier.

Once an adult patient with an unintegrated personality organization is back on the track of developmental splitting following a therapeutic regression, "upward-evolving transference" (Boyer 1983; Volkan, 1987, 1995) develops and takes the patient to a point where opposing self- and object representations, together with their accompanying affects, will meet. Patients with borderline personality organization are constantly involved in internalization-externalization of self- and object images and introjection-projection of various affects and thoughts. In analysis, such relatedness to the analyst determines common transference and countertransference developments (Volkan, 1981a, 1987). Within the realm of patient-analyst interactions, the patient identifies with various functions of the analyst, including identification involving the integrative function, which supports the patient's progressive development. The patient's arrival at a crucial juncture is the result of collective accumulation within his psyche of all necessary identifications and his developing ability to tame his aggression. The patient who undergoes the second type of treatment is "prepared" during the initial years of his treatment, to reach and pass through the crucial juncture without much guilt and certainly without much depression or suicidal thoughts. Once the patient comes to the crucial juncture, he is ready to experience mourning over surrendering his old unintegrated self-representation and corresponding unintegrated object images (Volkan 1976, 1981b, 1987, 1993; Volkan and Fowler, 2009).

Joseph came to analysis as an adult with primitive defences against shame and humiliation, murderous rage, and a need to be understood and accepted as a human being—and not as a Penguin Man—by fellow human beings. Joseph's Christian mother from a small conservative town in the USA was encouraged by her family to marry a much older uneducated Jewish man who, as a new immigrant to the United States, first travelled from one state to another collecting scrap metal to sell. He became very rich in this business and married a young and beautiful woman who was not in love with him. Joseph's parents had come from two different cultures and religions and there was no emotional bond to bring them together. She had dreamed of becoming a great pianist, but had to give up this ambition when she married. Joseph's childhood environment, in a sense, was split into opposing elements and he, as a child, did not have help developing his "normal" integrative ego functions. His mother constantly gave him enemas throughout his childhood to make him "clean" and did not "teach" him how to integrate "good" and "bad" self- and object images. As an adult he had a borderline personality organization.

In analysis, a person like Joseph begins to give up his primitive defences against and primitive adaptation to his internal conflicts. The analyst becomes a "hot" transference figure, and the patient experiences the analyst as important figures from his childhood, a person on whom the patient depended and for whom he feels rage. Such developments are part of analytic treatment, and if it is to work properly, a "therapeutic space" has to be formed and maintained in the analyst's office. Let us visualize such a space with an imagined effigy representing the analyst sitting in the middle of it. The patient sends verbal missiles to mutilate and kill the effigy and the analyst tolerates this. The next day, the analyst-effigy is placed in the thera-peutic space again, showing the patient that his childhood rage did not commit a murder. A mental game is played in this space until the patient learns how to "kill" a symbol and not a real person, how to relinquish devastating guilt feelings, how to tame other intense emotions, and how to separate fantasy from reality. The patient also learns to establish a firm continuity of time, but with an ability to restore feelings, thinking, and perceptions to their proper places: the past, the present, or the future. In other words, the burdens of the past can be left behind, and a hope for a better future can be maintained. There should be no damaging intrusions into this space. For example, the patient does not really hit the analyst. (Joseph's "attacking" me and touching me was an unusual event and it occurred only once during his entire analysis.) The patient attacks only the analyst's effigy. The analyst does not have real sex with the patient who wishes to be loved, but the analyst, by protecting the therapeutic space, shows the patient that he or she is "loved."

Shrinking the gap between enemies

In peaceful times people usually turn their attention toward them-selves, their families, relatives, clans, neighbours, professional and social organizations, schools, sports clubs and local or national politics. But when a large group is humiliated or threatened by "others" who identify with another large group, the attacked popu-lation abandons its routine preoccupations and becomes obsessed with repairing, protecting and maintaining their large-group iden-tity. It is analogous to individuals who are not constantly aware of their breathing, but if they find themselves in a smoke-filled room or develop pneumonia, they notice every breath they take. Similarly, when a large group is under stress and the large-group identity is injured or threatened, the people who belong to it, such as those who come to negotiation tables and face enemy representatives, become keenly aware of their "we-ness" and quickly and definitively separate their large-group identity from the identity of the "other," the "enemy" large group.

During the last 30 years I have been present when influential representatives of Arabs and Israelis, Americans and Soviets, Russians and Estonians, Serbians and Croats, Georgians and South Ossetians, Turks and Greeks, and Turks and Armenians came together for unofficial dialogues that were carried out over a number of years in an attempt to achieve understanding and hopefully find "entry points" for strategies and actions for peaceful co-existence I also visited many refugee camps and met political leaders of many countries or large groups such as Mikhail Gorbachev, Jimmy Carter, Rauf Denktaş, Arnolf Rüütel, Yasset, Olesegun Obasanjo, and Abdullah Gül.

Last year I have begun a new project with Lord John Alderdice, the former leader of Northern Ireland's cross-community Alliance Party and former Speaker of the Northern Ireland Assembly who is also a psychiatrist and psychoanalyst. We are bringing representatives from Arab Emirates, Austria, India, Iran, Israel, Jordan, Russia, Turkey, United Kingdom and United States together to try to understand the post-September 11, 2001 world, in particular the Islamic-Western world split. In this, as in other projects I have been involved with (Volkan, 1988, 1997, 2004, 2006a), participants, as spokespersons for their large-group identities, become preoccupied with large-group identity issues. In places where refugees or internally displaced persons are living, these victims also constantly refer to their large-group identities. This is also true, I have noticed, of political leaders at the time of an international conflict. By listening to dialogues involving enemy representatives, dislocated persons, and political leaders I have learned much about large-group identity, large-group psychology in general and what occurs when attempts are made to shrink the psychological gap between the enemy representatives.

Returning to Winnicott (1963, 1969), he conceptualized the sociological world as millions of people superimposed upon each other. His belief that most individuals are unintegrated led him to examine political divisions. He suggested that much of what we call civilization may become impossible at the boundaries between large groups. He compared Berlin, which was still divided at that time, to his diagram of a circle with a line through its centre that represents the unintegrated individual.

Winnicott noted that some political divisions, such as the border between England and Wales, can be looked upon in terms of geography and mountains. But, the Berlin Wall was man-made and ugly and could hold no association to the word "beauty" in light of our knowledge that in the 1960s there would have been war without the wall. However, Winnicott acknowledged a positive aspect of the Berlin Wall. He suggested that a dividing line between opposing forces, "at its worst postpones conflict and at its best holds opposing forces away from each other for long periods of time so that people may play and pursue the arts of peace. The arts of peace belong to the temporary success of a dividing line between opposing forces; the lull between times when the wall has ceased to segregate good and bad" (Winnicott, 1969, p. 224). When there is anxiety and regression within large groups in conflict, a simple line between them is not enough to protect the antagonists' identities. They must defend against any possibility of interpenetration.

Large-group psychology primarily deals with a shared need to repair, protect and maintain large-group identity. Thousands or millions of people, without being aware it, are assigned these tasks and respond to ethnic, religious, ideological and international relations accordingly. If a foreign large group deliberately shames, humiliates, and destroys the lives of a number of individuals in the name of their large-group identity in, let us say, the northern part of a country, others belonging to the same large-group identity in the south will also feel their pain and rage. Large-group identity connects people in emotional ways wherever they live. Influences and consequences of traumas that are caused by "others" belonging to another large-group identity do not remain regional (Volkan, 1988, 2006a). The "split" in Israel during the 2nd Lebanon War, when the North suffered while the rest of the country continued its daily routine in an environment in which the stock markets were doing fine, appears to contradict the idea that pain and rage are shared by all who belong to the same large-group identity. This "split" in Israel was possible because underneath it all, Israelis everywhere shared chronic threats to their large-group identity.

When a large group's identity is humiliated or threatened, people belonging to that identity psychologically find it easy to humiliate, victimize and kill individuals belonging to the enemy group in the name of identity without blinking an eye. They use aggression in order to repair, protect and maintain their large-group identity. If people who belong to the victimized group feel helpless, they will in this case tolerate forced or voluntary shared masochism, again in order to hold on to their large-group identity. This abstract concept, the "large-group" identity, becomes the central force that influences international relations.

In their daily lives, members of a large group mostly unconsciously follow two unalterable and intertwined principles (Volkan, 1988, 1997, 1999a, 2006a), principles they may become aware of if the "other" humiliates and threatens them in the name of large-group identity. I call the first principle the "maintenance of non-sameness." One large group must not be the same as, or even closely similar to, a neighbouring large group that is perceived as an enemy. Although antagonistic large groups usually have major differences in religion, language and historical or mythological backgrounds, "minor differences" between antagonists can become major problems that lead to deadly consequences. Much earlier Freud (1921, 1930) noted minor differences among small and large groups, but did not study their deadly consequences in international relations. When large groups regress, any signal of similarity is perceived, often unconsciously, as unacceptable; minor differences therefore become elevated to great importance to protect non-sameness. Cypriot Greek farmers used to dress like Cypriot Turkish farmers in black shirts and loose black trousers. The Greek would put a blue or black sash around his waist and the Turk would wear a red one. Under increased hostilities the difference in sash colour became a matter of life or death (Volkan, 1979). Donald Horowitz (1985) reported that in 1958 Sinhalese mobs methodically victimized only men bearing earring holes in their ears and wearing shirts over their vertis. In the absence of differentiating skin colour or other dissimilar characteristics, these features identified people as enemy Tamils. Thomas Butler (1993) wrote about how in the former Yugoslavia differences in the pronunciation of certain words by Croats and Serbs increased in significance when antagonism between the two groups increased. When "minor differences" between antagonists become major problems that lead to deadly consequences, we recognize the existence of the "maintenance of non-sameness" principle.

Another unalterable principle in large-group relationships, intertwined with the first one reflects the need to maintain a psychological border, gap, or tangible space between large groups in conflict. Although the demarcation and maintenance of physical borders has always, especially in modern times, been vital to international and large-group relationships, closer examination indicates that it is far more critical to have an effective psychological border than a simple physical one. In 1986, when tensions between Israelis and Jordanians were high, I visited the Allenby Bridge over the Jordan River that separates the two countries. Trucks that went over the bridge looked like the factory had forgotten to finish them: doors and hoods were missing, and even the upholstery had been removed to allow fewer places to hide contraband items. Israeli customs officers would spend hours taking vehicles apart and putting them back together to assure that nothing was smuggled in from Jordan. In another precaution, the Israelis routinely swept a dirt road that ran parallel to the border in order to detect the footprints of people trying to cross it. It should be noted that the border was amply supplied with sophisticated electronic surveillance devices, minefields and the natural barrier of the Jordan River. Even if there was some justification for the extra precaution, it is most likely that the idea of a psychological border was intertwined with the physical border at this location, resulting in rituals that created a psychological gap between the two countries that went beyond realistic military activities.

After September 11, 2001 every traveller who is paying attention to large-group psychology, must be aware of how legal or traditional physical borders also symbolize the large-group identity that provides a huge umbrella protecting the people belonging to it. In Europe immigrants from the Middle East, Africa and Eastern European countries inflame the affected large groups' border psychology. When clear physical demarcations are perceived as ambiguous or indistinct, psychological borders are weakened as well, and shared anxiety can develop.

These two principles—maintaining non-sameness and psychological borders—influence international relationships, especially at negotiation tables. I have observed that one of the dangerous times during which diplomatic negotiations quickly may collapse is when the opposing parties, usually with the help of a third "neutral" party, come close to making a major agreement. This "coming close," for both parties, unconsciously threatens the two principles mentioned above. Anxiety about injury to large-group identity increases and this may lead to the collapse of negotiations, paradoxically after hard work and after coming very close to making an agreement.

Psychoanalysts analyzing individuals like Joseph know about the appearance of anxiety and other troublesome feelings when a person with borderline organization comes to a crucial juncture experience. If psychoanalysts are participants in a conflict resolution team dealing with large groups they, emotionally and intellectually, will be more prepared to respond to similar emotions when they surface at a time the opposing groups make efforts for a rapprochement. Knowing about the two principles described above will help the psychoanalytically informed "neutral" third party in negotiations to introduce strategies that will inform the opposing parties in the following way: "Making an agreement and signing a document does not mean that you will lose the border separating your large-group identity from the identity of your enemy's large group or that you will face the possibility of becoming the same as your enemy. When a mutual formal agreement on a difficult issue is reached, both sides will still keep their own identities."

Just as individuals with a borderline personality organization imagine losing "good" self- and object images, enemy negotiators that attempt to shrink the psychological gap between "good" and "bad" large-group identities when coming together for negotiations for a peaceful co-existence face a similar phenomenon. Negotiators become anxious about contaminating their large-group identity with the one that is invested, in their mind and often in reality, with terrible aggression. The possibility that their "good" large-group identity will become "bad" if an agreement is reached is a psychologically threatening event. The facilitating team that includes psychoanalysts should be aware of this. Furthermore, anxiety over closing the gap between the enemy representatives due to "mixing" large-group identities is complicated due to the fact that even before negotiations take place, large groups in the conflict, outside of their awareness, become alike.

While it is very threatening for a large group to lose its psychological border and contaminate its own large-group identity with the one belonging to the enemy, in situations where conflict between two large groups becomes hot, deadly or chronic, paradoxically, enemies become alike to a certain degree. This process, on a conscious level is denied vehemently. At the foundation of this paradox lies the fact that large-group enemies are both real and fantasized (Stein, 1990). They are real if they are humiliating, shooting and killing people in the other large group in the name of identity. They are also fantasized because they are reservoirs of the first large group's externalized unwanted parts, a result of a shared process that began in childhood when suitable reservoirs of externalization were established, and as a result of large-group regression in which adult members do the same thing children would do: create suitable targets of externalization.

In hot, deadly or chronic international conflicts, suitable reservoirs do not remain permanent, effective and distant reservoirs "out there." The externalizations and projections a large group puts in these reservoirs overflow and come back to contaminate itself. Thus, psychologically speaking, both large groups, to a certain degree, become the same. Al Qaeda divided the world into two categories. After September 11, the United States did the same. "You are either on my side or else," became a political doctrine. Ideas such as the "clash of civilizations" or in this case "clash of religions," directly or indirectly was supported within both large groups. Dissenters exist, of course, but they do not change the essential shared sentiments within the large group unless they recruit a huge number of followers who become a political force.

When speaking of enemies becoming alike, I refer to shared psychological movements, not to the actual methods used by each group involved in wars or war-like situations. One may kill through terrorism and the other may kill in "legal" and so-called "civilized" ways. Many factors, such as historical circumstances, reactivation of past victimizations, the existing political system, military power, technology, economy, and most importantly, the degree of large-group regression and the personality organization of the political leader can make a large group dehumanize the "other" and exercise terrible cruelty in both "barbaric" and "civilized" ways.

Elsewhere (Volkan, 2004, 2009) I describe how a political leader's personality organization plays a crucial role in inflaming or taming the process of one large group becoming like the enemy group. If the leader is able to explain to the followers where the reality of the enemy ends and where the fantasy about the enemy begins, this tames the process of becoming like the enemy. If the leader does not provide good reality testing that includes an understanding of the enemy large group's "psychic reality" and does not make some attempt to respond to it in humane non-destructive ways, dangers become magnified and regression is maintained.

Members of one group in conflict may attempt to define their large-group identity through externalizing unwanted parts of themselves onto the enemy, projecting their unwanted thoughts, affects, perceptions, and wishes just as patients with primitive personality organizations typically do. For example, it is not we who are troublemakers, but they. Often externalizations and projections into the opposing large group reflect a clear "us" and "them" dichotomy of rigid positions: we are "good," they are "bad." Such mechanisms can also involve a more complex relationship between representatives of the two opposing groups in a pattern similar to the mechanism of projective identification (Klein, 1946) that psychoanalysts see in individual patients, and typically in patients with borderline personality organization. While having a dialogue, representatives of one large group may externalize self- and object images and project onto the other their own wishes for how the opposing side should think, feel, or behave. The first team then identifies with the other that houses their externalizations and projections—this other is perceived as actually acting in accordance with the expectations of the former. In effect, one team becomes the "spokesperson" for the other team, and since this process takes place unconsciously, the first team actually believes their remarks about the enemy. However, the resulting "relationship" is not real since it is based on the processes of only one party. The psychoanalytically informed facilitating team interprets or interferes with the development of projective identification, since once it develops, the reality of perceptions is compromised.

During negotiations the facilitators should find non-controversial methods to examine openly the concept of a large group becoming like its enemy in order to conceptualize and realize opportunities for different responses, above and beyond destructive ones. The facilitators, instead of suggesting or "forcing" the enemy negotiators to ignore the threats to their large-group identities, should try to shrink the gap between the enemy groups, but *not* to remove it.

After some empathic communication begins, the opposing teams often experience a rapprochement. But, this closeness is then followed by a sudden withdrawal from one another and then again by closeness. This pattern repeats numerous times. I liken this to the playing of an accordion—squeezing together and then pulling apart (Volkan, 1988, 2006a). Initial distancing is a defensive manoeuvre to keep aggressive attitudes and feelings in check, since, if the opponents were to come together, they might harm one another—at least in fantasy—or in turn become targets of retaliation. When the negotiators of opposing large groups are confined together in one room sharing conscious efforts for peace, sometimes they must deny their aggressive feelings as they draw together in a kind of illusory union. When this becomes oppressive, it feels dangerous, and distancing occurs again. The most realistic discussions take place after the facilitating team has allowed the accordion to play for a while, until the squeezing and distancing become less extreme.

Practitioners of international "conflict resolution" may in fact do harm if they force the removal of identity differences between opposing large groups as swiftly as possible or focus on seeking "apologies" and encouraging "forgiveness" too hastily when dealing with coexistence. Concepts such as "apology" and "forgiveness" are only descriptive, and they should not, before adaptive solutions can be found, mask a need for shared psychological processes that respect the principles of large-group interactions and for resolutions of shared resistances (Volkan, 2006b). Even after the unification of Germany, where the aim was not to develop a co-existence between East and West Germans, but to evolve an absorption between them, the political and social strategies built to accomplish this were only successful through step-by-step adaptation. Forgiveness and apology can take place after shared feelings of remorse, guilt, and depression evolve in a shared mourning process.

I will now examine how we can apply what a psychoanalyst learns from observing and handling the mending process of a borderline patient accompanied by guilt, depression or mourning to bringing together enemy large groups. Large groups are made of individuals; therefore, large-group processes reflect individual psychology. But a large group is not a living organism that has one brain. Therefore, once members of a large group start utilizing the same mental mechanism, it establishes a life of its own and appears as a societal, and often a political, process. In this chapter I already referred a few times to "regression" of large groups. I borrow the word "regression" from individual psychology since I have not yet found a good term that describes a large group's "going back" to the earlier levels of its psychic development in defence of the shared anxiety caused by threats to large-group identity. First of all, it is difficult to imagine that large groups have their own psychic developments. The closest thing to the concept of a large group having a psychic development is the large group's usually mythologized history and the story of how the large group was "born." In fact, when large groups regress, they reactivate certain, sometimes centuries-old, shared historical mental representations, which I named "chosen glories" and "chosen traumas" (Volkan, 1999a, 2004, 2006a). They are linked to large-groups' difficulty in mourning, shared guilt feelings and depression and they become activated when representatives of enemy large groups become involved in negotiations.

Large groups celebrate independence days or have ritualistic recollections of events and heroes whose mental representations include a shared feeling of success and triumph among large-group members. Such events and heroic persons attached to them are heavily mythologized over time. These mental representations become large-group amplifiers called chosen glories. Chosen glories are passed on to succeeding generations in parent/teacher-child interactions and through participation in ritualistic ceremonies recalling past successful events. Chosen glories link children of a large group with each other and with their large group, and the children experience increased self-esteem by being associated with such glories. It is not difficult to understand why parents and other important adults pass the mental representation of chosen glories to their children; this is a pleasurable activity. Past victories in battle and great accomplishments of a religious or political ideological nature frequently appear as chosen glories. In stressful situations political leaders reactivate the mental representation of chosen glories and heroes associated with them to bolster their large-group identity. A leader's reference to chosen glories excites followers simply by stimulating an already existing shared large-group amplifier. During the first Gulf War Saddam Hussein made many references to Sultan Saladin's victories over the Crusaders even though Saladin was not an Arab, but a Kurd.

While no complicated psychological processes are involved when chosen glories increase collective self-esteem, the role of chosen traumas, in supporting large-group identity and its cohesiveness, is more complex. It is for this reason that a chosen trauma is a much stronger large-group amplifier than a chosen glory. A chosen trauma is the shared mental representation of an event in a large group's history in which the group suffered catastrophic loss, humiliation, and helplessness at the hands of its enemies. When members of a victim group are unable to mourn such losses, tame their depressive feelings and reverse their humiliation and helplessness, they pass on to their offspring the images of their injured selves and the psychological tasks that need to be completed, such as reversing humiliation and helplessness and completing the work of mourning. This process is known as the "transgenerational transmission of trauma." (For a review of the concept of transgenerational transmission and adults "depositing" their traumatized self- and object images into the developing self-representations of children, see: Volkan, Ast, and Greer, 2001.) All such images and tasks contain references to the same historical event, and as decades pass, the mental representation of this event links all the individuals in the large group. Thus, the mental representation of the event emerges as a most significant large-group identity marker, a large-group amplifier. Chosen traumas should be differentiated from shared traumas, like the Holocaust, which is still very "hot," or acute traumas like those that are happening at the present time in Iraq and the Republic of Georgia for various large groups. The reactivation of chosen traumas can be used by the political leadership to promote new massive large-group movements, some of them deadly and malignant. In one prime example of this, I have documented the story of how Slobodan Milošević allowed and supported the reappearance of the Serbian chosen trauma—the mental representation of the June 28, 1389 Battle of Kosovo (Volkan, 1997).

The reactivation of chosen traumas fuels "entitlement ideologies." Entitlement ideologies are also connected with the large group's difficulty mourning losses, people, land, or prestige at the hands of an enemy in the name of large-group identity. Mourning is an obligatory human psychobiological response to a meaningful loss. When a loved one dies, the mourner has to go through predictable and definable phases. The individual mourning processes can be "infected" due to various causes (Volkan, 1981b, Volkan and Zintl, 1993) just as "infected" large-group mourning for losses caused by the actions of another large group will appear on societal/political levels. For example, a political ideology of "irredentism"—a shared sense of entitlement to recover what has been lost—may slowly emerge that reflects a complication in large-group mourning and an attempt both to deny losses and to recover them. What Greeks call the "Megali Idea" ("Great Idea") is such a political ideology. Political ideologies of this kind may last for centuries and may disappear and reappear when historical circumstances change thereby influencing international relations. Diplomatic efforts then become very difficult to handle, because the reactivation of a chosen trauma with its accompanying entitlement ideology and associated affects, fantasies, wishes and defences causes "time collapse." This magnifies the image of the current enemies and current conflicts (Volkan and Itzkowitz, 1994).

When enemy representatives come together for a series of dialogues the facilitators will notice that eventually chosen glories, chosen traumas with their associated feeling states, entitlement ideologies and time collapse will contaminate negotiations. The representatives will compete and try to illustrate whose chosen trauma—usually associated with glories—is worse than the other's. The facilitator cannot order the negotiators to forget the past and focus on the present. Affects and ideas do not disappear because someone tells someone else to forget them. In a psychoanalytically informed negotiation process, the facilitators use strategies for absorbing feelings linked to reactivated chosen traumas and define how chosen traumas and glories are most significant markers of large-group identities. They become models for identification for emphatic understanding of the "other's" difficulty in mourning. This leads to the appearance of "normal" mourning among the representatives of opposing groups for their losses—people, land, prestige—during the current conflict, the separation of past realistic and fantasized grievances from the current issues, and more realistic negotiations.

Diplomacy and psychoanalytic insights

International relations primarily refer to interactions between political leaders such as presidents, ministers of foreign affairs or diplomats belonging to different nation states as they negotiate and decide upon, draft and sign, agreements between each other involving diplomatic, legal, economic, or even sports matters. The negotiating parties will be perceived as allies or enemies according to existing "formal" agreements. Their relationships will also conform, if controversies do not develop, to "international rules and regulations" accepted by organizations such as the United Nations or the European Union. In today's changing world, however, the term "international relations" includes much more. When there are wars or war-like situations or alliances between ethnic, religious or political ideological groups within one nation state or in different nation states, which are not accepted as legitimate entities, often legal international bodies are involved in their diplomatic negotiations. In today's world there are world-wide terrorist groups whose activities, at least in the public mind, are categorized as an aspect of international relations.

The modern version of the concept of "globalization" has expanded what people in the street think about what international relations means. Globalization has become the buzzword in political as well as academic circles that, especially with the help of modern communication technologies, personifies a wish for prosperity and well-being of societies by standardizing economic and political elements and by bringing democratic freedom everywhere in the world. The tragedy of September 11, 2001 and the Western World's—especially the United States'—response to it, the wars in Iraq and Afghanistan, war-like conditions in Africa and elsewhere and—as I write this chapter—the September 2008 economic crisis in the Unites States that influenced the financial markets worldwide, make an idealized version of globalization an illusion. Globalization that includes prejudice, racism and an indifference to large-group differences (Kinnvall, 2004, Liu and Mills, 2006, Morton, 2005, Ratliff, 2004) never brings about the well-being of the affected societies.

We can also consider non-governmental organizations (NGOs), giant business corporations, the media and electronic communications as players in international relations. However one defines the concept of international relations and whatever one includes under this term, it always involves interactions between national, ethnic, religious or political ideological large groups composed of tens or hundreds of thousands or millions of persons. In the twenty-first century once more we are witnessing the amazing ability of the human mind

to create incredible technological achievements, while the aggressive
aspect of human nature remains the same and always complicates
international relations.

When I think of official diplomacy, I remember W. Nathaniel Howell, the United States ambassador in Kuwait when Saddam Hussein's forces invaded that country, and the Resident-Diplomat at
CSMHI. A tall man who played basketball in his youth, he com-
pares good official diplomatic negotiation to playing basketball.
The opposing teams rush from one side of the basketball court to
the other using rules and regulations and try to score points. In the
end, one team wins, but the other team also scores and achieves
some degree of self-esteem for being a good competitor. According
to Ambassador Howell (2000), being involved in a well-managed
and fair official diplomatic activity is as pleasurable as watching a
well-played basketball game.

   If an international conflict becomes "hot" or chronic, a large
group's psychological identity issues contaminate all the real-world
problems such as the economy or legal issues, as well as the official diplomatic efforts for resolving them. Expanding Ambassador
Howell's metaphor, let us imagine that someone spills a large amount
of olive oil on the basketball court. Now the game becomes chaotic.
The first thing required is to wipe off the oil spill and clean the floor.
In an international relationship the oil spill that makes a routine play
impossible primarily centres around large-group identity, its protection and maintenance. When large-group identity issues become
inflamed and problematic, conducting international relations only
through "typical" diplomatic efforts becomes very difficult and
sometimes impossible. Utilizing psychoanalytically informed large-
group psychology can be compared to cleaning up olive oil on a
basketball court.

   In order to understand this cleaning process, once more let us
return to the concept of "therapeutic space" the maintenance of
which, as described earlier, is required during the analysis of an
individual. The Tree Model aims to create a therapeutic space in
unofficial diplomacy. Diplomats attempt to create it in official diplomacy usually without the benefit of psychoanalytically informed
large-group psychology. There is no definite technique for creating
a therapeutic space in official diplomacy between warring enemy

large groups where they can "play" a serious and deadly game while always killing the effigies rather than one another. It would be, of course, very difficult and perhaps impossible to establish such a place if enemy groups constantly invaded it with real bullets, missiles, torture, and live bombs—like suicide bombers. As Shapiro and Carr (2006) state, attempts to understand large groups are daunting. They may be "a defence against the experience of despair about the world, a grandiose effort to manage the unmanageable" (p. 256). Furthermore, many obstacles have hindered collaboration between psychoanalysts and authorities dealing with international relations. Elsewhere I tried to examine in some detail these obstacles that come from both the diplomatic world and psychoanalysis itself (Volkan, 1999b, 2005).

In spite of the difficulties mentioned above I hope that psychoanalysts and psychoanalytically oriented clinicians will become involved in interdisciplinary initiatives, make efforts for large groups' psychological well-being and provide information to the diplomats about large-group psychology. In this chapter I suggested that the insights learned from individual psychology and psychoanalytic techniques for helping individuals with borderline personality organization to mend their opposing self- and object images should not be blindly applied to large-group psychology, which must be studied in its own right.

Summary

When the representatives of large-group enemies are brought together in unofficial or official diplomacy with a "neutral" facilitating team for finding peaceful co-existence, these representatives' ability to hold on to their respective large-group identities may be threatened. This, in turn, may create severe large-group identity problems, complicate negotiations, and create stubborn resistances against making peace. The aim therefore, is not to mend, but only to narrow the psychological gap between the enemy large-group identities and to strengthen opposing representatives' hold on their large-group identities so they can make more realistic agreements. Psychoanalysts and psychoanalytically oriented clinicians are best equipped to notice conscious and, more importantly, unconscious elements in large-group conflicts to which official diplomacy may not pay attention. Such efforts include the development of a large-group psychology in its own right so that the meaning and influence of the abstract concept, large-group identity, can be better understood and so that we will have a theoretical foundation to suggest psychoanalytically informed strategies for finding peaceful answers for international conflicts.

References

Akhtar, S. (1992). *Broken Structures: Severe Personality Disorders and Their Treatment*. Northvale, NJ: Jason Aronson.

Akhtar, S. (1999). Immigration and Identity: Turmoil, Treatment and Transformation. Northvale, NJ: Jason Aronson.

Alderdice, J. (1993). Ulster on the couch. Public lecture hosted by the Irish Psycho-Analytical Association.

Apprey, M. (2005). A formal grounded theory on the ethics of transfer in conflict-resolution. Mind and Human Interaction, 14:51–74.

Blos, P. (1979). *The Adolescent Passage: Developmental Issues*. New York: International Universities Press.

Boyer, L.B. (1983). *The Regressed Patient*. New York: Jason Aronson.

Butler, T. (1993). Yugoslavia mon amour. *Mind and Human Interaction*, 4:120–128.

Cain, A.C., and B.S. Cain (1964). On replacing a child. *Journal of American Academy of Child Psychiatry*, 3:443–456.

Chassequet-Smirgel, J. (1984). *The Ego Ideal*. New York: W.W. Norton.

Elliott, M. (2005). Charting the cultural habits of the Irish Republic's Protestant community: A psychoanalytic perspective. *Mind and Human Interaction*, 14:16–50.

Elliott, M., Bishop, K., and Stokes, P. (2004). Societal PTSD? Historic shock in Northern Ireland. *Psychotherapy and Politics International*, 2:1–16.

Erikson, E.H. (1956). The problem of ego identity. *Journal of the American Psychoanalytic Association*, 1:56–121.

Erikson, E.H. (1966). Ontogeny of ritualization. *In Psychoanalysis: A General Psychology*, eds. R.M. Lowenstein, L.M. Newman, M. Schur, and A.J. Solnit, pp. 601–621. New York: International Universities Press.

Freud, S. (1921). Group psychology and the analysis of the ego. *Standard Edition* 18: 63–143. London: Hogarth Press.

Freud, S. (1926a). Address to the society of B'nai B'rith. *Standard Edition* 20:271–274. London: Hogarth Press.

Freud, S. (1926b). Inhibitions, symptoms and anxiety. *Standard Edition* 20:77–175. London: Hogarth Press.

Freud, S. (1930). Civilization and its discontents. *Standard Edition,* 21: 59–145. London: Hogarth Press.

Horowitz, D.L. (1985). *Ethnic Groups in Conflict.* Berkeley: University of California Press.

Howell, W.N. (2000). Personal communication.

Glass, J. (1989). *Private Terror/Public Life: Psychosis and Politics of Community.* Ithaca, NY: Cornell University Press.

Kakar, S. (1996). *The Colors of Violence: Cultural Identities, Religion, and Conflict.* Chicago: University of Chicago Press.

Kernberg, O.F. (1970). Factors in the psychoanalytic treatment of narcissistic personalities. *Journal of the American Psychoanalytic Association,* 18:51–85.

Kernberg, O.F. (1975). *Borderline Conditions and Pathological Narcissism.* New York: Jason Aronson.

Kernberg, O.F. (1976). *Object Relations Theory and Clinical Psychoanalysis.* New York: Jason Aronson.

Kernberg, O.F. (1984). *Severe Personality Disorders.* New Haven: Yale University Press.

Kernberg, O.F. (2003a). Sanctioned social violence: A psychoanalytic view part 1. *International Journal of Psycho-Analysis,* 84:683–698.

Kernberg, O.F. (2003b). Sanctioned social violence: A psychoanalytic view part 2. *International Journal of Psycho-Analysis,* 84:953–968.

Kinnvall, C. (2004). Globalization and religious nationalism: Self, identity, and the search for ontological security. *Political Psychology,* 25:741–767.

Klein, M. (1946). Notes on some schizoid mechanism. *International Journal of Psycho-Analysis,* 27:99–110.

Liu, J.H. & Mills, D. (2006). Modern racism and neo-liberal globalization: The discourses of plausible deniability and their multiple functions. *Journal of Community and Applied Social Psychology,* 16:83–99.

Mack, J.E. (1979). Foreword. In *Cyprus: War and Adaptation* by V. D. Volkan, pp. ix–xxi. Charlottesville, VA: University Press of Virginia.

Moore, B.E., and Fine, B.D. (1990). *Psychoanalytic Terms and Concepts.* New Haven: American Psychoanalytic Association and Yale University Press.

Morton, T.L. (2005). Prejudice in an era of economic globalization and international interdependence. In *The Psychology of Prejudice and Discrimination: Disability, Religion, Physique, and Other Traits,* Vol. 4. ed. J.L. Chin, pp. 135–160. Westport, CT: Praeger.

Olinick, S.L. (1980). *The Psychotherapeutic Instrument.* New York: Jason Aronson.

Pao, P-N. (1979). *Schizophrenic Disorders: Theory and Treatment from a Psychodynamic Point of View.* New York: International Universities Press.

Poznanski, E.O. (1972). The "replacement child": A saga of unresolved parental grief. *Behavioral Pediatrics,* 81:1190–1193.

Ratliff, J.M. (2004). The persistence of national differences in a globalizing world: The Japanese struggle for competitiveness in advanced information technologies. *Journal of Socio-Economics,* 33:71–88.

Searles, H.F. (1986). *My Work with Borderline Patients.* New York: Jason Aronson.

Shapiro, E., and Carr, W. (2006). "Those people were some kind of solution": Can society in any sense be understood? *Organizational & Social Dynamics,* 6:241–257.

Stein, H.F. (1990). International and group milieu of ethnicity: Identifying generic group dynamic issues. *Canadian Review of Studies of Nationalism,* 17:107–130.

Volkan, V.D. (1976). *Primitive Internalized Object Relations: A Clinical Study of Schizophrenic, Borderline and Narcissistic Patients.* New York: International Universities Press.

Volkan, V.D. (1979). *Cyprus–War and Adaptation: A Psychoanalytic History of Two Ethnic Groups in Conflict.* Charlottesville: University Press of Virginia.

Volkan, V.D. (1981a). Transference and countertransference: An examination from the point of view of internalized object relations. In *Object and Self: A Developmental Approach (Essays in Honor of Edith Jacobson),* ed. by S.Tuttman, C. Kaye and M. Zimmerman, pp. 429–451. New York: International Universities Press.

Volkan, V.D. (1981b). *Linking Objects and Linking Phenomena: A Study of the Forms, Symptoms, Metapsychology and Therapy of Complicated Mourning.* New York: International Universities Press.

Volkan, V.D. (1987). *Six Steps in the Treatment of Borderline Personality Organization.* New York: Jason Aronson.

Volkan, V.D. (1988). *The Need to Have Enemies and Allies: From Clinical Practice to International Relationships*. Northvale, NJ: Jason Aronson.

Volkan, V.D. (1993a). Immigrants and refugees: A psychodynamic perspective. *Mind and Human Interaction*, 4:63–69.

Volkan, V.D. (1993b). The intrapsychic story of integration in a borderline patient. In *Master Clinicians on Treating the Regressed Patient*, ed. by L.B. Boyer and P. Giovacchini, pp. 279–299. Northvale, NJ: Jason Aronson.

Volkan, V.D. (1995). *The Infantile Psychotic Self: Understanding and Treating Schizophrenics and Other Difficult Patients*. Northvale, NJ: Jason Aronson.

Volkan, V.D. (1997). *Bloodlines: From Ethnic Pride to Ethnic Terrorism*. New York: Farrar, Straus and Giroux.

Volkan, V.D. (1999a). The Tree Model: A comprehensive psychopolitical approach to unofficial diplomacy and the reduction of ethnic tension. *Mind & Human Interaction*, 10:142–210.

Volkan, V.D. (1999b). Psychoanalysis and diplomacy Part III: Potentials for and obstacles against collaboration. *Journal of Applied Psychoanalytic Studies*, 1:305–318.

Volkan, V.D. (2004). *Blind Trust: Large Groups and Their Leaders in Times of Crises and Terror*. Charlottesville, VA: Pitchstone Publishing.

Volkan, V.D. (2005). Politics and international relations. In *Textbook of Psychoanalysis*, eds. E.S. Person, A.M. Cooper and G.O. Gabbard, pp. 525–533. Washington, DC: American Psychiatric Publishing.

Volkan, V.D. (2006a). *Killing in the Name of Identity: A Study of Bloody Conflicts*. Charlottesville, VA: Pitchstone Publishing.

Volkan, V.D. (2006b). What some monuments tell us about mourning and forgiveness? In *Taking Wrongs Seriously: Apologies and Reconciliation*, ed. E. Barkin and A. Karn, pp. 115–131. Stanford, CA: Stanford University Press.

Volkan, V.D. (2009) Some psychoanalytic views on leaders with narcissistic personality organization and their roles in large-group processes. In *Leadership in a Changing World: Dynamic Perspectives on Groups and Their Leaders*, eds. R.H. Klein, C.A. Rice and V.L. Schermer, pp. 67–89. New York: Lexington.

Volkan, V.D., and Ast, G. (1997). *Siblings in the Unconscious and Psychopathology*. Madison, CT: International Universities Press.

Volkan, V.D., Ast, G., and Greer, W. (2001). *Third Reich in the Unconscious: Transgenerational Transmission and its Consequences.* New York: Brunner-Routledge.

Volkan, V.D., and Fowler, C.J. (2009). *Searching for the Perfect Woman: The American Civil War and Race Relations in the Unconscious.* New York: Jason Aronson.

Volkan, V.D., and Itzkowitz, N. (1994). *Turks and Greeks: Neighbours in Conflict.* Cambridgeshire, England: Eothen Press.

Volkan, V.D., and Zintl, E. (1993). *Life After Loss: Lessons of Grief.* New York: Charles Scribner's Sons.

Winnicott, D.W. (1953). Transitional objects and transitional phenomena. *International Journal of Psycho-Analysis*, 34:89–97.

Winnicott, D.W. (1963). The value of depression. In *D.W. Winnicott: Home is Where We Start From*, ed. C. Winnicott, R. Shepherd and M. Davis. pp. 74–90. New York: W.W. Norton, 1986.

Winnicott, D.W. (1969). Berlin walls. In *D.W. Winnicott: Home is Where We Start From*, ed. C. Winnicott, R. Shepherd and M. Davis. pp. 221–227. New York: W.W. Norton. 1986.

PLENARY DISCUSSION

APlenary discussion took place in which all presenters were invited to address key questions raised in the conference. Paul Williams took questions from the audience, read them out to the presenters and invited them to reply.

PW: *I'll read three versions of this question. What can be done to promote or enable psychoanalytic input into the psychiatric treatment of psychosis? Most Psychiatrist teams and services do not engage in any kind of psychoanalytic thinking.*

Another version—Most of the resources for people with severe mental disorders go to mainstream psychiatric services. What words and concepts used in the last two days can best build bridges with mainstream psychiatric services, what are the psychoanalytic ideas that can help build bridges.

A slightly different question—The Scottish Government is currently investing a great deal of money in suicide prevention. How would the panel suggest that analytic insights could be used within the psychiatric system successfully to help this situation?

Any thoughts?

1) Franco De Masi: In the paper which I read this morning I tried to convey my thoughts on the nature and analytic treatment of psychosis; thoughts that have taken shape over the many years of my clinical practice. At the start of my career, when I worked in psychiatric institutions, I thought that treating psychosis by means of psychopharmacological therapy and therapeutic interviews was possible, but full of uncertainty. It would sometimes happen that I could not explain why a certain patient had recovered from a psychotic crisis, or I would be forced to accept that the same patient who had apparently been "cured" could suddenly be re-admitted due to an inexplicable relapse. A new attack could also take place after pharmacological therapy had been suspended, although the dosage was so small as to appear to have almost no effect on the patient. Yet the suspension of pharmacological treatment, which was evidently effective at warding off the attacks, prompted a new crisis. When I left the psychiatric service twenty-five years ago to devote myself entirely to the profession of psychoanalyst, it was a long time before I took on a patient who suffered from psychosis or who had had episodes of it in the past. Despite my experience at university and in hospitals, the study of psychoanalytic works and attendance at conferences, I felt rather helpless in the consulting room. I therefore decided with great caution to undertake the analytic treatment of a psychotic patient. I still believe that it is inadvisable to have more than one psychotic patient in treatment at a time. My present aim is to make a contribution to our understanding of the specific difficulties we encounter in the analytic treatment of psychosis. I hope that by showing the strong points and limitations of our therapeutic abilities, we may go some way to explaining the complex nature of the disease and provide new thoughts on this mysterious field of study. At the present I am continuously engaged in supervising and discussing many cases of psychotic patients with psychiatrists, psychotherapists and psychoanalysts of my country. I could only say that I am learning a lot and at the same time I am giving them some hope for a better outcome of the therapy of this kind of patients.

2) Caroline Garland: I had the experience of working at the Maudsley for about fifteen years and the thing that struck me was a stand-off between the psychotherapy unit and the rest of the psychiatric hospital and I agree entirely with what the previous two speakers have said but I also think that if we could address the mutual content and hostility and actually develop an attitude of mutual respect we might do rather better. After all, not all psychoanalysts have psychiatric knowledge and not all psychiatrists have psychoanalytic knowledge and it seems to me that that might be when we are talking about building bridges at conferences such as this and perhaps others might help.

3) Don Campbell: I spent thirty years working in the NHS Portman Clinic where we see two types of patients on an outpatient basis, patients who are delinquent or violent and those who are suffering from a perversion. When I arrived there thirty years ago it was a rather isolated unit that was struggling for survival. The prevailing impression was that mainstream psychiatry and forensic psychiatrists were not interested in psychoanalytic thinking about our patient population. Then Margaret Thatcher closed down what were the asylums in the UK and in their place instituted what was euphemistically called care in the community. Some of you may remember this. Many psychiatrists, and I am speaking more about those in the forensic field, were interviewing patients with a view to assessing their dangerousness and the suitability of their discharge into the community. They became very interested in what makes problematic patients tick, why they do disturbing violent or bizarre things. Over the last ten years there has been a growing relationship between forensic psychiatrists and psychoanalysts working at the Portman Clinic. For instance, the Portman Clinic has been requested to consult with the staffs of secure and medium secure units up and down the country, and is training people who are working in these units. The Portman Clinic professionals are not offering psychoanalysis as a treatment modality, which is only appropriate to a narrow percentage of this population, but we are bringing our interest in how the patient thinks, works and manages their lives. By beginning with not having all the answers, but being interested in understanding severely disturbed patients, a bridge can be created between psychoanalytically oriented professionals and psychiatrists.

4) Franco De Masi: I am repeating good advice but I still say that it takes some kind of work from the one who has a stand in psychoanalytic thinking when you are working in a psychiatric hospital. You have first of all to believe in yourself, but not to believe that you are better or that you have a better knowledge or better opinion but you have to believe in yourself so you don't feel denigrated, expelled, subjected to the others, even though it is in the room so you have to kind of have an attitude that you understand that the other has a different attitude but you still have the ground to stand on. And you also have to have some kind of stubbornness, you have to go on day after day being there, listening to what the other thinks and make your contributions. I think it is kind of troublesome, you have to work for it really, but I think it is worth working for and if we have the attitude that we know better and we don't participate in the others thinking then I think we are out of the play: and just a reference to Glen's book on Psychodynamic Psychiatry, the others are in doubt with elements of Glen's book and say well you can get some ideas there also besides the ideas that you already have. So believing in yourself is very important.

5) Stephen Sonnenberg: I want to just add a dimension to what has already been said and it has to do with the love of teaching and learning how to teach. I think that all psychoanalysts really have to be dedicated to teaching about what we do and to teaching in a non-authoritarian way and in a way that isn't embedded in jargon, in a way that really recognises that people really want to learn about what we do and I am going to give you two very quick examples. I live in a city of about one million in the United States; it's an emerging city, an intellectual centre, a government centre but it's also a relatively small city and I have in response to a need established a centre for people, mental health professionals, psychiatrists, psychologists, social workers and other counsellors to learn about psychoanalysis. I meet with these people thirty times a year and the typical response I get from somebody who recently graduated from a typical American psychiatric programme where she learned no psychotherapy and a lot of pharmacology is—"I don't know what I'm doing here. I never thought I would be here, but this very important to me and I am learning so much". The other thing I would just mention is that the American Psychoanalytic Association has undertaken a new initiative and that is to provide education about psychoanalysis to the non mental health community per se; that is, education outside of psychotherapy training and outside of psychoanalytic training and actually the target audience begins with pre-kindergarten and ends at the nursing college and we developed a series of committees that are targeted to teach about psychoanalysis for example in the university for undergraduates, for graduate students and I think the end result of that is going to be reflected in what we might refer to as consumer demand because the more people we teach about psychoanalysis and the more people who know about it those people are going to demand to be heard quite concretely, they will not put up with medical care with health care in which they are not heard and once they demand to be heard then psychoanalysis finds its central place in teaching other health care providers how to listen, how to hear and how to respond.

PW: *The next question is a more clinical question, please could we have some discussion on how the conceptualisations of psychosis discussed today apply to psychotic phenomena in borderline patients? For example do these need different forms of understanding in treatment and what do we make of people with major psychotic illnesses who initially present with a borderline picture?*

1) Otto Kernberg: First of all, we have to carry out a good diagnostic evaluation of patients before treating them. Unfortunately, in psychoanalytic tradition very often you have one or two initial interviews, and then you see whether the patient fits on the couch or not: in other words, there is not really a careful analysis, not only of symptoms, but of the characterological structure. It is not too difficult with a good knowledge of diagnostic psychiatric criteria to make the diagnosis not only of borderline personality disorder, but borderline personality organisation—in other words, the structure that characterises severe personality disorders, and then to determine the evaluation of each of the symptoms they present. From that viewpoint, there are very few cases, which initially raise the question, is this a patient with a borderline structure or is it an atypical psychosis? We have developed in our institute a method of "structural interviewing:" I don't have time to talk about this now, that permits a rather sharp differential diagnosis in patients where that is not clear. That is my first point.

Then, in the course of the treatment, these patients may develop micro psychotic episodes. The transference focused psychotherapy has particular techniques to deal with such micro psychotic episodes. I can't go into detail, but just by way of demonstration, first of all, we maintain strictly the frame of the treatment in order to protect the patient, the relatives and, the therapist. Within that context, in the psychotherapeutic situation, we explore what usually emerges as a transference psychosis. The micro psychotic episodes, usually in the middle of such treatment starts with the therapist. This is "bad" in the sense that one has all the problems in the sessions, but it is also "good" because we can diagnose and help the patient avoid the expanse of psychotic functioning beyond the sessions. The methods that we have developed for that particular circumstance is that of "incompatible realities." The patient has the conviction, for example, that the therapist has been spreading rumours about him to other people; he is convinced of it. We first check is he really convinced? And, if that is so, we acknowledge that conviction by the patient and then we tell him, "I acknowledge that you are convinced of that; I will not try to convince you of any different things, so you should be aware that I respect your conviction. Now, are you able to hear my conviction? If the patient is not able to listen, we have to wait; but if the patient is able to listen, we may tell him, I am convinced that that is totally absurd. I am convinced that that is crazy. Now, there are two of us in this room, we have no witness. It could be that I'm crazy and that you are right, or that you are crazy and I am right, but what is clear is that we are living in an incompatible reality". Many patients at that point try to soften this, as if I were not fully aware of what I am doing. I tell the patient "I'm totally convinced that I am 100% aware of what I am doing, as you are 100% convinced that I am spreading rumours about you. We are in the situation of incompatible realities, but we can agree on one thing: that there is madness in this room. If we can agree that there is madness in this room, the only problem is to locate it either in you or me. We can study the nature of this "madness," what is the content about, and thus we transform this into a primitive fantasy that represents the psychotic nucleus of that patient. We can analyse the implications, who is doing what to whom—self and object, who is doing what and for what reason. As we explore that in depth, what gradually emerges is a concrete, often historical issue in the patient's life. It's an extremely effective technique. I am giving you only this one example, there are other such situations, but a good understanding of psychoanalytic technique, modified in our approach to borderline patients permits the resolution of those psychotic elements. There are other cases where such a psychotic development spills over into external reality and I can't go into all the details except to express my conviction that this can be dealt with psychotherapeutically with remarkable speed, once you are aware of and are able to manage these technical approaches.

I would like to add something more general regarding the earlier question, about how we can influence the psychotic field. I think that one thing we have not stressed enough is that we have to learn and integrate the input of knowledge from psychiatry. It is not only that we teach psychiatrists what we do, but we have to really be able to engage other fields with their own words, with their understandings. Only then we will be trusted. That doesn't take away anything from what has been said; it is just an addition.

2) Glen Gabbard: I think that the issue of psychosis in borderlines is complicated by the fact that things are much more messy than the DSM IV or the standard diagnostic manuals indicate whereas the psychotic episodes in borderline personality disorder are supposed to be mini psychotic episodes, I can tell you from years of working with borderline patients there is a sub group that are always a little bit south of the border and they have a subtle thought disorder that goes on chronically, not just situationally, they may have acutely psychotic episodes of which the distortion of reality is more striking but often there is a background disturbance in reality testing, it is not schizophrenia, it is not schizoaffective, it is not bipolar but one has to be tuned into the fact that many of these patients have thinking that is very loose. Similarly there is another category that doesn't fit anything, it is an affectively labile person who doesn't meet the criteria for bipolar, who doesn't meet the criteria for schizophrenia is more psychotic than what we would think about for a borderline patient and often you have this group of patients that are very disturbed where you have to borrow techniques both working with borderline patients and working with psychotic patients and they find some kind of amalgam that works for the individual. Back to the question about what do we have to contribute to psychiatry, what we have to contribute is that we value the unique, the idiosyncratic, the complex about people. We don't simply put a label on them and say this is what this is and this is something we can always bring to our colleagues.

3) Franco De Masi: I think you can accept a patient without saying that he can or will develop a psychotic episode. In my book related to psychosis I write on two patients, one borderline patient who developed a psychotic crisis because I was not able to understand a very important question and he developed a transference psychosis. Another woman whom I saw as a depressed woman developed an erotic delusion and erotic attachment to me. It is not so uncommon to not see at first interview that treating the patient psychoanalytically can produce a psychosis during the treatment.

PW: *This is another clinical question and it is about the aetiology of borderline personality disorder. Very similar failures and impingement by the mother in relation to the infant have been cited as generating both BPD and psychotic functioning. Can more be said by the panel about exactly what factors they think lead to borderline personality disorder or to psychosis, or do we not know?*

1) Peter Fonagy: Very similar factors lead to lots of different things so for example smoking causes a range of problems, a lot of pleasure I'm not trying to deny that but in addition to that you can get heart disease, cancer all kinds of things, so a risk factor mustn't be confused with a cause. In particular when we are talking about early mother infant relationship we are talking about something that sets up a vulnerability in a person and the evidence is consistent with what psychoanalysts have been suggesting over the last fifty or so years, that the first year or eighteen months of life is formative in a number of ways, notably in the way the brain gets itself organised. But it doesn't mean that everybody who has impingements in that time will be vulnerable. Genetic factors have an enormous amount to do with this so for example now we know,—many of you may not know this—there is a gene, a serotonin transporter gene, 5HDT that exists in two alleles forms, short alleles and the long alleles. Sitting here 30% or 25% of you, depending on the ratio, would have the short form. Most of you will have the long allele. It turns out that people with the short allele are vulnerable to environmental impingement so if you had the short allele then you are more likely to be depressed in the following six years after adverse life events. If you have the long allele it doesn't matter how many life events happen to you, you will be absolutely fine. You are like me! It turns out—and this is really the important thing—is that in infancy if you have, as we have also known, sensitive care giving you are more likely to be securely attached but it turns out that if you have the short allele of this gene you are environmentally vulnerable and it matters a great deal how sensitive your care-giver is. If you had the long allele it doesn't matter at all, you can be neglected, and you're fine! It gives you a resilience, a robustness that is genetic. So what I am getting at here is that these risks, events or risk factors interact with each other, constitution interacts with early environment which then creates in turn a vulnerability to later impingements which in turn then might create a vulnerability for later provoking factors. Developmental psychopathology is actually quite complicated. Psychosis it turns out is probably a vulnerability. I think it is created in the very first years of life. The evidence is coming together on that. With borderline states I don't think it's that simple. I think it needs a whole host of other things. Why am I saying that? It turns out that the prevalence of borderline personality disorder is very different depending on what country you live in. So in the United States— lots of psychiatrists, lots of borderline personality disorder. Norway lots of psychiatrists, very little borderline personality disorder, so it's probably not psychiatrists that cause borderline personality disorder! But there are differences in the cultures between those two countries and there have been those who suggested that the powerful correlation between the strengths of religious organisations that are valued by the community relates to some depth of underlying social networking or structure, which correlates very highly with the prevalence of borderline personality disorder. If people feel an absence of Venus if I can borrow the term that we had heard in a couple of presentations I think that probably is a major risk factor for BPD. Given all kinds of historical influences, so I wouldn't want to over-emphasise its importance–its part always of a much larger developmental picture.

2) Vamik Volkan: I have not spoken about clinical matters. What we heard here is fascinating but there are also certain things that we cannot measure as far as I am concerned. For example how can you measure a mother's unconscious fantasy that the child she gave birth to should be dead. There are aspects of psychoanalysis that makes psychoanalysis such a rich thing. Beside the thing that we can measure and focus on in actual practice when we have a patient we ask the question, what are we treating and the story comes out, the story gets hot and needs to be worked through. Basically what you find out if somebody going to develop borderline personality disorder is that there is something besides the measurable things, something in the environment that interferes with the normal developmental splitting. Such things as, for example, if you are a replacement child you are unconsciously given two identities; you are a girl and you are also a replacement child for a male dead child and you then have problem in integrating this. One problem in America is that there are intensive one to one relationships and quick individuation pushes in children, which makes more borderline people. In multiple mothering, as in the Middle East, if one mother is a good extension of the other mother then we have no problem but if multiple mothers are not, they don't fit each other then they interfere with the child's personality organisation. So there are many, many stories that enrich our way of looking at borderline personality organisation. The other thing that I briefly want to mention is that there are so many such patients and so I much appreciate the mentalization technique or what you call transference technique but we should also not forget that there are more typical psychological techniques for dealing with these problems. In America there are two kinds of borderline treatment, one is most of what we heard here, the other one is that you allow them to regress, the patient comes and you knows they are going to regress through a psychotic transferences and then move up. My beef if I can call it that is that when we write about borderline treatment we should write from the beginning to the end, we have to provide detailed case reports on the whole process which I think is then very useful for teaching in order to show the complexity of it.

PW: *Nine analysts on the panel only one female analyst, Why?*

Answer from one panel member: I think the answer to that is clear— it is Paul's fault!

PW: *I can only tell you that it is the reverse of meetings in the British Psychoanalytic Society where there are nine female analysts to one male!*

PW: *A question for Prof. Fonagy—wait a second (another voice from the audience)—isn't it true that one woman really is smarter than nine men! (applause)*

This question is for Prof Fonagy but it is also open to others. Peter, you said and wrote in the past that the most appropriate treatment for borderline patients was psychoanalysis. In your presentation psychoanalysis seemed to have no role but only MBT as the panacea for borderline conditions. Can you clarify whether in what role you see for psychoanalysis in the treatment of borderlines?

1) Peter Fonagy: Thank you for that! It is indeed true that I did write and I still believe that psychoanalysis has a place in the treatment of severe disturbance by psychoanalysis. I now mean that intensive psychoanalytically oriented therapy has a place in the treatment of borderline personality disorder. I want to add two qualifications: the first is that unmodified psychoanalysis I think is possibly unhelpful and quite likely to be harmful for the individual with borderline personality disorder because if the individual who has no privileged access to their own internal state cannot read off their mental state, there is nobody really judging what they are being told and whether it is correct or not. Quite often this literally creates a psychotic, certainly very regressed state, and suicidality. I think I would need to see the empirical evidence for thus way of doing things before I believed it. The second issue is that it has to be modified and a modified psychoanalysis par excellence is mentalization based treatment. It is a treatment that focuses on exploring the patient's mental state associated with the analyst's mental state. However it does require a firm basis so I would see the role of psychoanalysis and the role of more complex explorations of the patient's mind to be a second phase in, if you like, a two phase treatment–so you have to establish a relatively robust capacity in the patient to mentalize and usually this would be associated with a dramatic reduction in suicidality, a reduction in self harm, a reduction is hospitalisation and also most of the time improvement in adjustment in a number of other areas, employment and so on. And then that person I think can benefit from further more classical, traditional or holds unbarred or at least less barred treatment.

PW: *This is a question about art psychotherapy on behalf of a large number of art therapists attending this conference from Great Britain/ Northern Ireland and beyond. I have been asked to tell you how wonderful this conference has been. We feel that active engagement in the arts therapies has a valuable contribution to make to these client populations in terms of primary process understanding mentalization, symbolising and containment. The conference has opened up some complex principles in a non reductive way, we would welcome any views of the panel on the role of the arts therapies in the treatment of severe disturbance.*

1) Stephen Sonnenberg: I just have a real quick anecdote. A highly skilled very brilliant mental health professional who I have just completed analysing just two weeks ago after twelve year analysis, a person who was an addict in recovery, took up an art form during the last couple of years of his analysis, I am not going to say what that form is. I am not going to give any more information about the person but I can tell you that the person has become an accomplished artist and that experience has been very therapeutic for him.

2) Bent Rosenbaum: For me the question comes a few months too early because there is a Danish PhD thesis, which will be evaluated during September and October on these matters. What I have experienced myself from different parts of psychiatry—I have always been interested in the art form. I think it cannot be underestimated. I think it is underestimated but it shouldn't be really. To engage patients in music, dance, theatre, painting not the least, I have my wife sitting in the back who has been in the treatment centre for severely psychotic, she had a workshop with paintings. In the beginning nobody went into the room. She was just sitting there and painted herself, then came one patient, and another patient and then there were twenty patients. They made exhibitions. When she stopped six years after I have never seen so many touching letters from patients thanking her for just being in that room, demanding nothing but putting up some kind of possibilities for them to do something with the skills they have. I think it is underestimated and if I had the? I would have both music and painting and theatre also.

3) Otto Kernberg: Art forms can also be very diagnostic—you have a real typical borderline patient and goes through occupational therapy and makes painting and you look at it, my god there is splitting, they make a rug there is a line in the middle, so the patient gets better even his/her art form changes, they start integrating, so those of you who work with borderline patients please go and look at their paintings. You will be surprised to find out how much the internal world gets reflected in their art form.

4) Paul Williams: I would like to support those comments in my own work in the Centre for Psychotherapy, the clinic we have here in Northern Ireland. We are doing work with very severely disturbed patients who undertake art therapy and music therapy and it's remarkable how the inner worlds of these patients emerge quite quickly. I'm not an art therapist or a music therapist but I sit and talk with these therapists. I talk about psychoanalysis, they talk about music and we try to come together in creating a sense of meaning around these communications and often the patients move on to individual work or group work.

PW: *This is a question directed principally to Bent Rosenbaum, I am working with a client who had a diagnosis of paranoid schizophrenia had intrusive persecutory delusions, hears voices, the delusions he believes are real, people really are poisoning his food whereas the voices he started to accept are a creation of his own mind. As a result he has been able to make some connections in the way he feels when the voices persecute him to how he felt persecuted in various situations when he was a child. Despite a gradual increase in his understanding of the aetiology of these voices they remain unremitting. He can ignore them more but they are still present just as much. Have any techniques or understanding you have used actually alleviated auditory hallucinations, not necessarily with the simultaneous medication changes.*

Bent Rosenbaum: We know that there are different techniques to try to alleviate the voices. I think this patient has come quite far actually getting the patient to acknowledge the hallucinations, getting the patient to acknowledge the idea that these hallucinations or the meaning of them, they are coming from somewhere. I would also like the patient to understand that the past is not something behind him but in front of him, something that he will meet. It is not only they are coming from somewhere but the past is something that you meet and then limit your ability to think about the future. But the specific techniques, its true that psychoanalysis as such doesn't come up with specific technique for symptoms but why shouldn't you be able to explore within the clarification concept these voices, how do they sound like, are they different, what are they aiming at, who are the persons who have the voices, how are they dressed, what do they look like. So in the perceptual field explore with the patient these kind of voices in order for him to give them, I mean he has got them already in his mind, but try to neutralise the anonymity of the voices. Because the anonymous voices are difficult to cope with. If you get persons, if you get ideas, if you get meaning, that's one of the techniques to do it. I don't guarantee anything, nobody can do that, but that is really a way forwards. And then comes the idea whether the voices are really going to tell you and me. I mean the voices say something but what are they really going to tell me, can they tell other stories. You have to look at this from the outside perspective. I think also the delusions in this man go together with the voices, so as long as you go into the voices you might also get to the delusions in the same round. I think you have to find your techniques if you are going to deal with symptoms within the psychoanalytic framework but there are ways to do it.

PW: *In Brazil children as young as 8 are paid in crack cocaine so become addicted and then live a life of poverty. Crack cocaine dealers are targeting mental health units in the United Kingdom in similar ways. How can we compete as a therapist for the drug that gives a high that we can never possibly offer patients particularly when their life for example if they are diagnosed with a schizophrenic illness hold so much daily distress. This is directed principally at Steve.*

PLENARY DISCUSSION   237

Stephen Sonnenberg: That's obviously a very complicated question. I have seen the Favelas in Brazil and I have worked with chronic mentally ill patients. It's very clear that addiction must be appreciated within a bio-psycho-social framework and that its societal framework, its societal context is very important. Now I think it is important to remember that the notion of the bio-psycho-social, and Glen Gabbard has written a wonderful paper on that, pointing out how it's a slippery slope to think that way, but nevertheless it has some utility and that is a psychoanalytic notion. So I think that as psychoanalysts approaching this problem we should be very comfortable with the idea that drug addiction does take place within a social framework and it can only be addressed within that framework. If we are dealing with the kinds of patients whom I was talking about yesterday there can still be a great deal that might necessarily be done within a social framework which is why for example I advocate communication outside the analysis, I mean families that enable addiction need to be dealt with just as the kinds of problems in this question. Now I don't want to avoid the question, it's a very daunting question and it is a very serious problem. I think that we have to keep in mind that a brain/mind slowed to develop agency, power, capacities for reflection, capacities for human intimacy, opportunities to grow through interactions, through education, I think we have to keep in mind that that is a better alternative to drug addiction whether we are dealing with a child in a Brazilian Favela or a chronic mentally ill patient and I really believe that's true. If you come at the problem from that perspective I think recognising that we do have something to offer is extremely important. Now in order to offer what we potentially can we also have to be socially active, we have to remember that for example interdiction of the drug trade is a law enforcement problem and we do need to make sure that we are heard by our governments and that they do deal with criminals who are selling drugs to chronic mentally ill patients and to kids in slums. We have to recognise that our social context, that our societies leave much to be desired and so as psychoanalysts we should be very active advocates for creating a better society, a better world and you heard of course from two analysts today who are very committed to doing that and to doing a great deal of that in the realm of international relations and I think we all have to do it within our countries and our communities.

PW: *I can see some tiredness coming over one or two faces. Would you like me to continue with the questions or should we draw it to a close in a little while.*

1) Caroline Garland: If I might interrupt the powerful but remorseless male logic of question/answer, I would like to go back to the statement that came from the art therapists. It is not just 'art therapy' that is therapeutic, it's art. If you look at great works of art you are put back in touch with your good internal objects: great works can make you feel better about life even when they are about terrible events. One of the things that has interested me very much recently has been a series of etchings by Goya called Los Caprichos. Goya had a near fatal illness when he was in his late 40's and as a result of this he became stone deaf, he could no longer hear a voice, could hear nothing—and as you know this is closely associated with an increase in paranoid ideation. Yet Goya as a great artist could take some of the absolutely horrific fantasies and images and demons that he then felt himself to be locked up with, transform them and put them down on paper in a way that speaks to us universally. There is nobody who looks at those works who doesn't know what he is talking about; we feel better for having our monsters pinned down on paper. So I would like to advocate therapy-via-great-art as well as art therapy.

2) Don Campbell: I just wanted to go back to a question that we didn't get a chance to address. Perhaps other panellists would like to chip in. It is a question about the application of psychoanalytic ideas, particularly within the area of suicide prevention. Earlier Peter Fonagy reminded us that identifying risk factors is not necessarily identifying a cause, but it does flag up vulnerability. There are many demographic studies of attempted suicides, suicides by age range, socioeconomic factors, family structures, and so forth, all of which will flag up at risk individuals. I think any approach to the prevention of suicide needs to take those risk factors into account. I also think that it needs to follow, from a very early age, children who could be identified as at risk. That doesn't mean that they are *necessarily* going to end up attacking their body or the body of another. In fact, psychoanalysts are not very good at predictability; they are much better at looking backwards in retrospect and learning from that perspective. However, taking a developmental approach to these vulnerable children, and following them as they grow up could enable social services and schools to know when a child becomes struck in their development, or when there is a slow down in development. Some of the most at risk children are those who get lost sitting in the back of the classroom. They don't act out, but are quietly depressed and breaking down alone and isolated, while they are largely ignored because they do not create a nuisance. Now these kids may be at risk of suicide or assaults on others in adolescence. Of course adolescence is the time that is absolutely critical because the child's body takes the centre of its psychic stage. Vulnerable children whose breakdowns went undetected before adolescence are often ill equipped mentally to deal with the conflicts and anxieties about their bodies and the development of their sexuality and their gender identity that are triggered by puberty. Adolescent development is, by definition, going to be disruptive and anxiety provoking for the adolescent and the adults around them. In fact, it is appropriate to be concerned about those adolescents who appear to be untroubled by what they are going through. Psychoanalysts can help other professionals identify children and adolescent who are at risk of killing themselves or others.

3) Otto Kernberg: I appreciate you coming back to the subject of suicide prevention. I thought it might be of interest to mention the criteria for risk and the triage for treatment that we have developed at our outpatient clinic for personality disorder. We get suicidal patients either from the crisis line in our local area or patients whose rapid triage has to be made by the person on call. We have a general outline, and I don't want to say that it is rigid, but I have to summarise it a little: It has been very helpful and over a number of years we really have been able to prevent most cases of suicide in those who came to our attention. The criteria are relatively simple. If a patient is acutely suicidal, we try to assess whether he is depressed or not depressed. If the patient is depressed, whether it's a major depression, or a dysthymic reaction or a characterological depression or a neurotic depression—whatever you want to call it. Of course there are cases that are uncertain. In general, patients with major depression and suicidal tendencies we hospitalise immediately. It is just too high a risk. If it is a characterological depression, we consider the possibility of treating these patients psychotherapeutically in the outpatient setting with the combination of anti-depressant medication and this is assessed from case to case. The basic criterion is, is the patient able to establish an object relationship quickly? Can he tolerate an intensive psychotherapy that can "hold" him while the outpatient treatment proceeds? That depends on the type of character pathology: it's better for the dependent, histrionic, and depressive personality, worse for the schizoid, schizotypal, paranoid,—how strong is the impulsivity of this patient? Is there a history of antisocial behaviour, drugs or alcohol abuse or dependency, and, of course, the general risk factors that have already been alluded to in terms of age, social environment, support etc? A combination of criteria give a sense as to whether it is safe to treat the patient on an outpatient basis, or whether he or she should go into the hospital. If the patient has carried out a suicidal attempt and is really not depressed, then we have a typically characterological suicidality, what we call "suicide as a way of life," and here we really have the severe personality disorders—a few of them are depressive-masochistic personalities. Their indication is clearly for psychotherapeutic or psychoanalytic treatment. These are cases for psychoanalysis. Most others are at a borderline level, particularly those with narcissistic personality structure, infantile, histrionic and borderline personality disorder and a few bi-polars. For bi-polar patients, mood stabilisers are very important. For those where characterological pathology predominates, we try to decide whether they would benefit from psychoanalytic psychotherapy—particularly transference focus psychotherapy, or from supportive psychotherapy based on psychoanalytic principles, or dialectic behaviour therapy—if there is a specific, circumscribed, suicidal or para-suicidal syndrome. So we use specialized psychotherapies in these areas. That's our practical approach, and it requires a good collaboration between the members of the team. We have managed it so that cognitive behaviour therapists and psychoanalysts don't see each other as enemies! But in our "research atmosphere," we try to learn what are the indications and contra-indications.

4) Glen Gabbard: I know we have to end but I think that this has been an extraordinary conference and we owe a debt of gratitude to

John and Cathal and the College and especially to Paul Williams and I suggest we give them a round of applause.

Dr. Cassidy

The honour falls to me to make a few remarks. I am Cathal Cassidy, Chairman of the Royal College of Psychiatrist in Northern Ireland and I am the one who was persecuting you to get you in on time during the course of the two days. I would like to thank some people. I would like to thank our inspiring speakers. I hope you were inspired by the content of their talks and inspired also by hearing it from them in person. I would like to thank our efficient chairs, who ran things so well during the course of the two days. It is important that we thank the sponsors of the conference including those who supported it financially. It is very important that I thank Nora McNairney who is a very important lady in this conference. She is manager of the Royal College of Psychiatrists Northern Ireland office. Nora has done an incredible job of organising 440 delegates in this conference over two days.

I think we have to thank two people for vision and leadership for this conference: Professor Paul Williams and Lord Alderdice.

INDEX

243